D1616740

&#10086; Irony and Ethics in Narrative

# Irony and Ethics in Narrative

*From Schlegel to Lacan*

Gary J. Handwerk

*Yale University Press*
*New Haven and London*

Published with assistance from the Kingsley Trust
Association Publication Fund established by
the Scroll and Key Society of Yale College.

Designed by Sally Harris
and set in Palatino type by
American–Stratford Graphic Services, Inc.,
Brattleboro, Vermont.
Printed in the United States of America by
BookCrafters, Inc., Chelsea, Michigan.

Library of Congress Cataloging in Publication Data

Handwerk, Gary J., 1954–
  Irony and ethics in narrative.

  Includes index.
  1. Irony in literature.   I. Title.
PN56.I65H27   1985      809'.91      85-40462
ISBN 0-300-03421-0 (alk. paper)

The paper in this book meets the guidelines for
permanence and durability of the Committee on
Production Guidelines for Book Longevity
of the Council on Library Resources.

10  9  8  7  6  5  4  3  2  1

Versions of chapters 3 and 4 have been
previously published as journal articles
and are reprinted here with the kind per-
mission of the journal editors: chapter 3
appeared as "Linguistic Blindness and
Ironic Vision in *The Egoist*" (*Nineteenth-Cen-
tury Fiction*, volume 39, September 1984), ©
1984 by The Regents of the University of
California; chapter 4 appeared as "Irony as
Intersubjectivity: Lacan on Psychoanalysis
and Literature" (*Comparative Criticism*, volume 7, 1985), © 1985 by Cambridge University Press.

# Contents

# Preface

My attraction to the topic of irony springs from a long-standing interest in the great ironist of the Western tradition, Plato's Socrates. This Socrates is characterized above all by his insistence that philosophical discourse must focus on human matters, on ethics, so that any treatment of Socratic irony that fails to link it to this ethical center seems to me to be unjust to the Platonic legacy. While studying various Platonic texts, I came to feel a dissatisfaction with those treatments of irony that see it as a detachable rhetorical overlay or a transitional historical moment. Contemporary literary criticism would generally grant that there is indeed more than this to irony, but would not yield any wide consensus about the philosophical premises attendant upon an ironic sensibility, or even about where irony begins and ends.

Irony is defiantly elusive, all too easily coming to mean everything to everybody (a tendency to which this book may itself not be altogether immune). Yet rather than compartmentalizing irony, my intention has been to follow a particular thread of ironic discourse in the Romantic and post-Romantic periods, while at the same time seeking to define those elements that are characteristic of many diverse kinds of literary irony. The best starting point for such an inquiry is in the works of Friedrich Schlegel, whose complex understanding of irony has much still to teach us. There I located the thread that I chose to follow—in the conviction that irony possessed from the first for Schlegel an ethical facet at least as significant as its aesthetic one. Just as even the most basic verbal irony is interactive—one cannot be ironic with oneself—so was the literary irony so central for Schlegel profoundly concerned with the capacity of discourse to generate and regenerate reflective community.

The kinds of irony that I have linked to Schlegel, then, are united by

what I call their "intersubjective" character, that is, by the ironist's awareness of how dependent the signifying process is on the constant reloca-
tions of meaning within verbal interactions. All discourse is typified by
what Schlegel called the "hovering" (*schwebende*) quality of signification; an
ironic discourse differs essentially in the greater or more constant awareness on the part of the interlocutors of how inextricable their identities are
from that discourse. Irony is, I believe, finally a question of the human
subject, of how and where that subject emerges into language. My use of
the term *subject* throughout this text derives largely from Lacan's ironic
juggling of that term. His choice of *subject* is a deliberate rejection of the
spiritual overtones of *psyche* or the existential overtones of *self.* Even more
significantly, the term is intended to hover between its most contrary significations, for *subject* refers both to the mind, the traditional philosophical
subject, and to the discourse itself, the subject matter that has a much
more alien, objective status. Lacan's *subject* is also the subject of a sentence,
for the subject is always embedded in language, as well as the subject vas-
sal, far from controlling that language within which it finds itself. Lacan
uses *subject* to evoke and enact the de-personalization of the psyche to
which he is committed and to break down the subject-object dichotomy as
determinative of the structure of human relationships.

More precisely, then, irony is a form of discourse that insists upon
the provisional and fragmentary nature of the individual subject and thus
forces us to recognize our dependence upon some mode of intersubjectivity that exceeds the furthest extension of any individual subject. Yet
irony is more than an expression of the subject's incapacity, for it simultaneously acts to bypass the limits of that individual subjectivity by inciting
pursuit of the verbal consensus on which a coherent and self-conscious
community must rest—while never underestimating the hermeneutic
obstacles to such consensus. The same dynamics at work in the Lacanian
subject or the Beckettian narrator can be traced back through hermeneutically self-conscious novelists such as Meredith to the initial Romantic
posing of this problem—what, or where, is the subject?

The final irony of this procedure is that my own subject may seem to
some to disappear and the discussion to diverge from what they would
comfortably term irony. My only apology is that irony needs to be seen,
and was so seen by theorists from Schlegel to Lacan, as a manifestation of
a more basic concern with defining the nature of the human subject.

All translations in the text that follows are mine, although I have consulted and drawn valuable assistance from the translations of Schlegel by Ernst Behler and Roman Struc, and by Peter Firchow, and also from Alan Sheridan's translations of Lacan.

My debts in this project are far beyond measure. First, to Albert Cook, Robert Scholes, and Roger Henkle, each of whom had a significant impact on how the topic came to be shaped. What merits this book possesses are due in large part to what I learned from them about the techniques and purposes of literary criticism. The sobering influence of winter walks homeward with Peter Baker, Sarah Webster Goodwin, Steve Goodwin, and Jay Baker is, I hope, evident at many points in the text, as is the impact of my long-pursued ironic dialogue with Rogers Smith.

I would also like to thank the Fulbright Foundation for the fellowship that allowed me to devote the proper attention to Schlegel and Novalis at the project's inception, and Professor Jochen Hörisch, who kept the initial research from going too far astray.

But my deepest thanks go to my parents, from whom I learned a firm respect for basic virtues, and to Nancy, who taught me more about irony than we both may know.

Seattle, Washington
December 1984

# Introduction

## The Status of Irony

It would doubtless be pleasing to Kierkegaard that contemporary literary criticism appears to have mastered that troublesome moment when irony was elevated to the role of a universal and defining literary attribute. Yet although Cleanth Brooks went further in the 1940s than one might wish to go today in incorporating all literature within the field of irony, the idea that there is something fundamentally ironic about the most complex uses of language remains a provocative one. As Brooks noted, the sort of contextual loading we perform in reading literary texts does indeed create competing significations, even if one would now hesitate to term all these ambiguities "ironic" ones.[1]

More recent critics have clarified this difference, while tending to elaborate more restricted claims for the role of irony. The identifying trait of irony is that there be an *incompatibility* between competing meanings, between a proffered and an implied alternative.[2] Acknowledging the diversity of variants of irony, critics since Brooks have moved toward classification of ironies or else toward analysis of one particular kind of irony.

Yet irony still reveals its propensity to mean everything to everybody. Various treatments of irony seem even incompatible with one another because they stress different facets of a complex intellectual operation. There is clearly an enormous distance between German Romantic irony and Beckettian irony, or between Booth's normative irony and de Man's epistemological irony. One finally wonders if these writers and critics are indeed dealing with the same intellectual phenomenon.

A truly comprehensive history of irony that could answer such a question has yet to be written.[3] Such a work would have to account for as

well as recount the shifts in the meaning of this term. Only thus could
one explain the tendency of irony to slide from a restrictive to an all-
encompassing meaning. As such an aim is beyond my capacity here, so
too is the expectation of doing justice to all the recent work on irony. Instead I have chosen the more modest task of examining one particular
strain of Romantic and post-Romantic irony, one largely neglected by critics, though it seems not least essential to the total ironic operation. As an
introductory gesture, I intend to define that irony briefly, to locate it with
respect to its sources and certain central critical positions on irony, and
thus to justify what remains a personal history of irony.

## Ethical Irony

I shall begin by pinning down and provisionally labeling that species
of irony with which my text will be most concerned. What I shall term
*ethical irony* focuses on how verbal incompatibilities set up and provoke a
deeper interrogation of self-consciousness. For ethical irony, an incompatibility in discourse suspends the question of identity by frustrating any immediate coherence of the subject.[4] Such suspension, of course, requires
that there be a certain undecidability between alternatives rather than an
easy either-or choice. This is fostered in that the implied alternative is un-
stated and the degree of assent to the proffered alternative remains un-
clear; judgment hovers between the two.

Ethical irony begins with the recognition that this state necessitates
an expansion of the frame of reference, given that well-balanced alternatives can remain undecidable at the level of the text or utterance. Most
characteristic of ethical irony, however, is the insistence that such expansion of context can only effectively occur through the interrogation of another subject. Whether intentional or unintentional, the limitation on
awareness that generated a verbal incompatibility is embedded in the discourse of the individual. This discourse, however, is part of the system of
language with which that individual subject tries to define itself,* and

---

* In general I have used *it* and *itself* as the pronominal referents both for *subject* and for
*individual*. This choice is dictated by fidelity to the Lacanian critique of the subject, where
such usage is becoming standard. Besides the connotations of a de-personalized subject that
this usage is intended to foster, it has the further advantage of allowing me to evoke a subjectivity that is not restrictively marked by gender-encoded pronouns such as *her* and *him*.
See the preface, above, for a fuller explanation of the issues at stake in such a choice.

which is a priori social.[5] Hence the subject requires another subject, requires the entrance into dialogue, if it is to chart its own meaning.

The ironic subject is thus defined in and by the process of interrogation, an idea whose embodiment stretches back to the Socratic elenchus. If in addition the other as interlocutor is necessary to pursue self-definition, then identity itself needs to be seen as fundamentally shifted from the individual subject to some mode of intersubjectivity. The goal of ethical irony is to show that incompatibilities at the level of language, if pursued as far as they lead, can be seen to arise from the attempt to establish coherence at the level of the isolated subject. From an ironic perspective, the individual is constitutively unfinished and incoherent.[6]

This is of course only a single aspect of irony, but one that I would argue is implicit in many occurrences of irony, for irony is by nature a progressive intellectual phenomenon. Even the simplest ironies establish linkages between the most discrete areas of mental activity. Establishing the possibility of such connections is more significant than the particular linkage created, since irony refuses to privilege any one level of analysis or any one juxtaposition. Recognition of incompatibility demands judgment, but the difficulty of definitive assessment forces further probing into the basis of judgment, hence into the structure of identity.[7] Ethical irony thus implies a holistic view of identity, a possible reintegration beyond incompatibles.

In the most general sense, then, irony is a linguistic act used to define the place and movements of the subject. This book attempts to trace such an irony from the Romantic period through exemplary nineteenth- and twentieth-century texts. In so doing, I hope to demonstrate how all irony can force us to examine identity in the broadest terms. By focusing on the ethical moment of this passage through incompatibilities, I intend to show how self-revelation necessarily passes through another and remains open-ended because it is dependent on that other subject.

The ultimate force of ethical irony is thus to undermine the integrity of the subject it seemed to imply existed. It attacks the notion of the subject as equivalent to a conscious intentionality or a personal self-consciousness. To be in language is instead to be located in and by the social domain. Ethical irony relocates identity in the language through which we pose the question of identity. This is language seen not in its referential or expressive aspect but instead in its communicative one, as a process of understanding. The presence of the subject is displaced in ironic communication to a place between individual subjects and to a time outside the mere present. By demonstrating how self-knowledge rests upon knowing others, ethical irony insists on the fundamental interdependence of subjects. The ironic basis of knowledge is *consensus;* even the apparently routine yeses of the Socratic interlocutor may not be so pointless as they are frequently assumed to be. Ethical irony appeals to a future consensus, rather than passively enacting an existing one.

This outlet into consensus is the way in which ethical irony, in positing and enacting the limits on the individual subject, simultaneously acts to bypass them.[8] It seeks a dialogic response to the provisional suspension of the question as to the identity of the subject, thus forcing the isolated subject beyond its internal inconsistencies. Engaging a dialogue allows the subject to relocate itself in the here and now of discourse and to see how that discourse insistently recalls the history that lies outside it. In sum, ethical irony takes the incompatibility characteristic of all irony as an impetus toward the searching out of consensus.

## Romantic Irony

My tracing of ethical irony begins with Friedrich Schlegel and the German Romantics.[9] This type of irony emerges from the linking of irony and the problem of the subject in German Idealism. A full discussion of this question is hardly possible here, although it is taken up in somewhat more detail in my consideration of Schlegel in chapter 1. Yet one needs to stress the philosophical foundation for what is too frequently seen in reductively aesthetic terms, as though Schlegel and Novalis left broader philosophical concerns behind when they took up poetic questions. Such a perspective is misleading, for it opens up Romantic irony to charges of aesthetic solipsism.[10]

For Schlegel, irony was a response to the perceived incongruity of the Fichtean *Ich.* He recognized an irreducible tension between the finite ego and an Absolute it can perceive or intuit and sought some mediation between these to resolve their fragmenting inconsistency with each other. How, for instance, can the transcendental ego both ground the subject and need to be recovered or found by that reflective subject? How can the empirical subject be said to conceive or create that of which it is only a part?

Schlegel adopted the conception of the *Ich* as a process (a *Herausgehen* and *Rückkehr*), while questioning how such a process can produce a radically different sort of subjectivity.

The rigor of his fragmentary theorizing was quickly lost, however, amid the unsympathetic polemics of his critics. Hegel, with Kierkegaard in his wake, attributed to the Romantics the simplistic equivalence of individual subject and transcendental ego, which they had been at pains to reject. "The Fichtean principle that subjectivity, the ego, has constitutive validity . . . was seized upon by Schlegel and Tieck and with this they proceeded to operate in the world. But this involved a double predicament: first, it was to confound the empirical and finite ego with the eternal ego; and secondly, it was to confuse metaphysical actuality with historical actuality."[11] Romantic irony was thus allied to an untrammeled subjective willfulness, a taking of the self at its most immediate and naive level as absolute. This purported Romantic subject would obviously be cut off from both historical actuality and objective reality.

Despite the resurgence of interest in irony and in its Romantic incarnation, most critics have continued to operate from the Hegelian schema wherein irony is an aesthetic expression of the individual subject. The Romantic achievement is seen as a shift of irony from a rhetorical device in the text to a characterization of its process of creation, hence of the artist's mind itself.[12] Its recent restoration to prominence (and extension to the English literary tradition) is based upon a revaluation of the reformative power of irony and the parallel privileging of demystification over inspiration in the artistic process.[13] In this light, irony is inevitably construed as a reflection and further elaboration of a heightened self-consciousness, confidently aware of its existential predicament. This enlightened subject can proceed without stumbling to conscious self-correction, serenely superior to even its own errors on its Olympian (or Goethean) heights. Irony permits the self-transcendence of an isolated individual, provided it has the good faith to recognize its own empirical lapses.

Such a perspective is not wholly incorrect, for Schlegel did indeed first elaborate Romantic irony on the pattern of the artisan of *Wilhelm Meister*. Yet it is decidedly incomplete, because Schlegel went further to establish the workings of an ethical and intersubjective mode of irony. He sought to analyze the dynamics of the transition between the subject and the other subjects that compose community, rather than ignoring or blurring the complexities of this transition as so many of his critics have done.

The index of this in his own work is the shift signaled as early as 1800–1801 by the replacement in his philosophical vocabulary of *irony* by a word with a more communal resonance, *conscience*. This development forms the focus of my initial chapter on Schlegel and Romantic irony.

## Normative Irony

The equation of the ironist and the detached aesthetic subject holds even for Wayne Booth, despite his sensitivity to the intersubjective basis and ethical force of irony as a rhetorical device.[14] His characterization of irony as an "intricate intellectual dance" (Booth, p. 31) captures many elements of the ironic interchange. Yet there is never any question who is leading and who follows in this rhetorical two-step. His ironist remains stably elevated in his self-perception, however unstable his world may become. Regrettably, the dance metaphor finds itself increasingly pushed aside by the more mechanical metaphor of irony as reconstruction. In this smoothly operating model, the integrity of the ironist and of the reader and their mutual permeability are never seriously put in doubt. "[Irony's] complexities are, after all, shared; the whole thing cannot work at all unless both parties to the exchange have confidence that they are moving together in identical patterns" (Booth, p. 13). Yet when hermeneutic patterns become identical, irony necessarily ceases to be, as it was for Schlegel, a heuristic device.[15]

This congruity of ironist and audience means that the presence of irony can never long be in doubt. Rather than delineating an irony that suspends alternatives and requires analysis in terms of degrees of commitment, Booth prefers to consider an irony that operates in terms of an "on-off switch" (Booth, p. 81). Those incompatibilities that do arise are easily resolvable into determinate meanings, even at the borders of the most unstable and infinite irony.

Booth's analysis prematurely resolves incompatibilities at the level of coherence of the individual subject in the form of a conscious intentionality.[16] His irony enacts and relies upon accepted human values within a clearly defined context; it is essentially normative. The subject itself is constituted by the accretion of particular values and character traits, the sum of its intentions, which combine in a "set of beliefs" that Booth can accept as coherent.[17]

Given this concept of the subject, Booth's analysis coincides in some ways with Kierkegaardian perspective in which irony is justified only as a "moment."[18] The resolution of any particular irony leaves behind no significant cognitive content; ironies characteristically deal with only low-level incompatibilities. What remains is simply the satisfaction of solving a puzzle and achieving a deceptively easy congruity with another person.[19] Irony is privileged as a quantitatively superior mode of communication, owing to the density and economy that allow much to be said briefly. It adds, however, nothing essential to the process of self-consciousness. Instead, normative irony directs our attention to what we already know; it reaffirms accepted verities. Its result, even as infinite unstable irony, is to establish (or perhaps only make evident) "amiable communities" of interpretation (Booth, p. 28).[20] Booth's normative irony thus falls far short of Kierkegaard's recognition that irony, once engaged, tends to become infinite. It is an intellectual, not simply a rhetorical moment for Kierkegaard, fundamentally altering the world by its momentary presence, making the very supports of that world tremble. Booth concedes this possibility in a footnote devoted to Kierkegaard, admitting that "it is not irony but the desire to understand irony that brings such a chain [of interpretations] to a stop" (Booth, p. 59). Yet he insists on turning off the ironic current, containing it within neatly "concentric circles of interpretation" (Booth, p. 92).

Once this possibility has been admitted, however, any stopping point must seem idiosyncratic, imposed by the interpreter with some measure of arbitrariness. One senses this in his elaborate expansion of the statement, "Think it'll rain" (Booth, p. 12), and even in his subtle and persuasive reading of Swift's "Modest Proposal" (Booth, pp. 106–120). Swift's essay not only makes the satiric points extracted by Booth but could easily be said to go further, to mock not only Irish collaborators of English exploitation but also anyone who would find any easy answers to a situation whose complexity defies naive optimism of any kind. Further ironic turns would be little harder to construe, dependent largely on the scope of the frame of reference desired by the interpreter.

Kierkegaard defines the ironic moment precisely by the way it always pushes further in what he refers to as an endless process of abstraction. "The [ironic] method properly consists in simplifying the multitudinous combinations of life by reducing them to an always more and more abstract abbreviation" (Kierkegaard, p. 70). What surface incompatibilities reveal to Kierkegaard's ironic eye is the eternal inadequacy of phenomena to the ideas. His Socrates attacks not just this particularity and incongruity but particularity in general. "Irony in the eminent sense directs itself not against this or that particular existence, but against the whole given actuality of a certain time and situation" (Kierkegaard, p. 271). One need not always accept the invitation to continue ironic interpretation, but it is always there.

The cognitive force of irony for Kierkegaard is to shift attention to the as yet dimly perceived universals (ideas), whose existence is never in doubt for the young philosopher. Its negative aspects are justified because it elevates the subject from a naive, sensual egoism to the level of abstraction where idiosyncratic beliefs vanish. What Booth elides by resisting this Kierkegaardian insight is the dialectical power of irony, its progressive force.

As Kierkegaard makes clear, irony establishes the principle of the interdependence and connection of all human truth; it is synthetic. It demonstrates how verbal incompatibilities inevitably result from attention to the fragmentation and inconsistencies of consciousness. "That life is full of contradictions seems to escape the notice of immediate consciousness, and it confidently and trustingly clings to its inheritance from the past like a sacred relic; reflection, by contrast, discovers this fact at once" (Kierkegaard, p. 227). This awareness alone is not yet ironic, but becomes so when supplemented by a recognition of "the eternal moment wherein it must render an account of the whole" (Kierkegaard, p. 228), a whole necessarily prey to ironic incompatibilities. Socratic irony marks an advance over the Sophists in its essentially systemic character. It not only juxtaposes beliefs within a given and stable context but constantly juxtaposes competing contexts, none of which is dominant. For the system irony envisages is emergent, and irony is dynamic in its capacity to change any context.

Yet for Kierkegaard, irony (as embodied in Socrates) does this in the name of "the being-for-itself subject" (Kierkegaard, p. 286). He inveighs repeatedly against the ironic incitement to subjectivity, the heightened and potentially self-indulgent self-awareness that irony fosters. The negation of any particular context convinces the ironist that freedom from *any* actual context is possible. "But for the ironist this context . . . has no validity. . . . he not only poetically produces himself but his environment as well" (Kierkegaard, pp. 299-300). This detachment and negation of history and culture is essentially anticivic, so that the Athenian state can be seen as justified in its condemnation of Socrates, having recognized the absolute incongruity between their values. Socratic irony can finally be justified only by its momentary character. As a response to Sophistic egoism it has its necessary role, but its reappearance in a Romantic guise is unhesitatingly condemned by Kierkegaard.

For the German Romantics, however, irony was not essentially self-centered. Schlegel knew that the moment of stupefaction born of irony unsettles the certainties that make up any naive sense of identity. The ironist thus feels a personal stake in the resolution of incompatibilities, while doubting his ability to resolve them alone. This uncertainty that begets hermeneutic interaction with others is the tale that I examine in chapter 2 through analyses of four Romantic narratives. They explore the nature of the ironically limited subject with devices such as roles and role-exchange; the interactions they set out define the problem of vision and its potential for communalization. These narratives use ironic structures to call into doubt the integrity and boundaries of the subject.

It is actually Kierkegaard who remains locked into an individualist model of discourse. His ironic individual, negating all particulars, is unable to negate its own immediate existence without a leap into religious ecstasy (Kierkegaard, p. 275). Irony must therefore be condemned because it falls short of attaining a fully unique and individual personality; it rests content with subjectivity. "[Irony] has the movement of turning back into itself which is characteristic of personality, of seeking back into itself, terminating in itself. . . . But this reserve is the reflex of personality into itself that is clearly abstract and void of content. The ironical personality is therefore merely the outline of a personality" (Kierkegaard, p. 242). The infinitude of irony maintains it on a single level and keeps it from returning to the particular.

Kierkegaard, guarding against unrestrained subjectivity, resorts nonetheless to a notion of the subject that sustains its self-certainty and self-transparency. From egoistic dreaming, the subject must pass on to "the true happiness wherein the subject no longer dreams but possesses himself in infinite clarity, is absolutely transparent to himself" (Kierkegaard, p. 313). This perfectly self-enclosed individual attains a point beyond irony and change, a moment of closure that is distinctly Hegelian and illustrates the distance between Kierkegaard's and Schlegel's concepts of irony. For the former, the assurance that Being exists beyond any individual paradoxically allows any individual, alone, to come into contact with it. Kierkegaard himself puts the difference best: "But the true actuality becomes what it is, whereas the actuality of romanticism merely becomes" (Kierkegaard, p. 332). Like Schlegel's and unlike Booth's model, this ironic pursuit of identity is progressive. But only for Kierkegaard is the subject potentially free in this endeavor, without any necessary connection to other subjects.

## Epistemological Irony

This detour through normative irony brings us to the critic whose irony most nearly embodies the abstraction without particular content that made Kierkegaard so uneasy. Paul de Man eternalizes the ironic moment and legitimizes Kierkegaard's notion of Socratic freedom through a process that demythologizes Kierkegaard's individualist Idealism. He is the apostle of an endlessly self-negating subject and reinforces the claim that irony can never be just local. By tracing the origins of irony to the constitutive fragility of the subject, de Man creates a parable of the rhetorical submission of the subject along with its truth. The passage from rhetorical irony through an ironic sensibility rejoins the two poles of "irony" in the recovery of the power of irony as a trope.

My own epistemological claims here are less far-reaching; I am more concerned with the implications of irony at an empirical communal level. Rather than engaging directly questions of Being and truth, I shall restrict myself to the consideration of irony as "the systematic undoing of understanding."[21]

The subject for de Man is inherently limited by the duplicity of language. It is ignorant in regard to what might be denominated as truth. Even worse, it is ignorant of the locus and origin of its own ignorance, hence also of any truth it might happen to speak. The subject is therefore unable to undo its ignorance, yet this very incapacity renders it especially prone to believing that it has indeed undone it. This occurs as the recurrent process of metaphoric totalization. The subject uses language to convert a world structured by the contingency of metonymic connections into one dominated by metaphoric necessity.[22] One can therefore always trace a metaphoric chain of substitutions, by which the world is unified, back to an illicit equivalence at its origin, a leap from metonym to metaphor. This original leap is the source of the incompatibilities that generate allegorical deconstruction.

Allegory tells the tale of this tropological displacement, of the self-serving domination of the world of experience by language. It reveals the fundamental noncoincidence of word and world that guarantees a failure of reference and a parallel breakdown of understanding. Deconstruction must therefore replace reconstruction. Nor is allegory any less subject to the incapacity of language than other modes of discourse; its tale is the record of its own unreadability.

Allegory takes the difference concealed or denied by metaphor and spreads it out over time. It is thus a "fictionally diachronic narrative," using a temporal continuum to articulate the loss and recollection of difference. "The fundamental structure of allegory reappears here in the tendency of the language toward narrative, the spreading out along the axis of an imaginary time in order to give duration to what is, in fact, simultaneous within the subject."[23] Allegory privileges the category of time, insisting on the priority of the temporal process of understanding over any intrinsic properties in the objects of its concern.

What allegory thus reveals is a pattern of repetition without coincidence that defines the operation of discourse, an ever-failing attempt to reenact the process of identification upon which language is based. "The meaning constituted by the allegorical sign can then consist only in the *repetition* . . . of a previous sign with which it can never coincide, since it is of the essence of this previous sign to be pure anteriority" (*BI*, p. 207). Nor is this noncoincidence confined to the incongruity of successive allegorical formulations. Divergences of meaning within a single text, born of its referential disjunction, serve to enlighten the attentive reader about the primacy of figural structures and their duplicity. These internal incoherences of competing structures extend to the foundations of subjective identity. "Allegories are always ethical, the term ethical designating the structural interference of two distinct value systems" (*AR*, p. 206).

Yet at the same time allegory enacts the process of mystification it set out to undermine. "Allegory can only blindly repeat its earlier model, without final understanding" (*BI*, p. 186). It is not as easy to learn from error as to learn how to repeat it. And allegory performs just this deception. As de Man noted in his essay on Lukács (*BI*, pp. 51–59, also pp. 103–104), the category of time can be made into a mediating force that denies the contradictions it has revealed.[24] Or without going even that far, allegory can reestablish the continuity and integrity of a text in its very self-incompatibility. de Man calls this resurgent coherence the "negative cognitions" of allegory; its truth is an awareness of the absence of truth. For this reason, even deconstructive allegory cannot serve as a stable resting place.

De Man paralleled allegory with its sister trope, irony, in "The Rhetoric of Temporality," seeing both as analogous demystifying procedures. "Allegory and irony are thus linked in their common discovery of a truly temporal predicament. They are also linked in their common demystification of an organic world postulated in a symbolic mode of analogical correspondences or in a mimetic mode of representation in which fiction and reality could coincide" (*BI*, p. 222). Yet the destabilizing tendency of allegory noted above serves to raise irony to a position of prominence, owing to a deconstructive rigor that would insist on putting words such as *truly* in the above quotation themselves into quotation marks. Even in "The Rhetoric of Temporality," de Man wavers in the equivalence he attributes to allegory and irony. "In this respect, irony comes closer [than allegory] to the pattern of factual experience and recaptures some of the factitiousness of human existence as a succession of isolated moments lived by a divided self" (*BI*, p. 226). Irony is both more constant in its vision of difference and more accurate in seeing it as a problem within the subject. So it is no surprise that the primacy of irony becomes increasingly evident in de Man's work.

It is not as much in overt discussions, however, as in methodological practices that irony asserts itself in de Man's work. Where allegory holds out the promise or remembrance of synthesis, irony reveals the rhetorical patterning of discourse to be inevitable and recurrent. Irony indicates the incongruence of word with word, the leeching of differential incompatibilities into the most basic levels of discourse. The anacoluthon on which de Man's analysis of *The Confessions* rests (*AR*, p. 289), a reintroduction of irrelevance and chance within the seams of Rousseau's tightly woven apology, becomes at the end of *Allegories of Reading* the type of an ironic parabasis to which all discourse is subject. The incompatibility seen by allegory in terms of a referential model depends itself upon a model of temporal continuity that the incongruity of competing rhetorical orders disrupts.[25]

Irony is therefore the fundamental trope, the trope of tropes, for it reestablishes incompatibility and discontinuity within the immediate presence of discourse. Or even more powerfully, it becomes the motor of the entire rhetorical system. "Irony is no longer a trope but the undoing of the deconstructive allegory of all tropological cognitions, the systematic undoing, in other words, of understanding. As such, far from closing off the tropological system, irony enforces the repetition of its aberration" (*AR*, p. 301). In the systematic undoing of understanding, irony reveals a passage from illusion to a disillusion that is at the same time a dissolution of the traditional notion of a subject articulating and defining itself in language. It becomes instead the idea of subject as language, as trope. "Selfhood is not a substance but a figure" (*AR*, p. 170). Or rather, the subject is the shifting among tropes that occurs as metonym becomes metaphor becomes allegory becomes irony. There is no metalanguage that one could invoke as a place from where understanding might finally be possible.

This tropological displacement is similar to the process I see in the novels of George Meredith, which I lay out at some length in chapter 3. Linguistic vision there becomes a limitation on further comprehension and even perception, blindly followed by deluded characters. But this process is not necessarily crippling for them, unless that vision is hoarded as private discourse. The linguistic turn does not, for Meredith, proscribe a return to hermeneutic adequacy. Such a return is in fact essential if tragedy is to be averted—this is the core of Meredith's insistence on what I term "hermeneutic responsibility." Linguistic vision, though blind, can generate a hermeneutic chain of displaced comprehension, not because another subject sees more or is in any sense the locus of truth but because that person necessarily sees differently.

De Man, however, insists upon that necessary misunderstanding. "Rhetoric is a *text* in that it allows for two incompatible, mutually self-destructive points of view, and therefore puts an insurmountable obstacle in the way of any reading or understanding" (*AR*, p. 131). Irony is therefore opposed to any interpretive authority (such as Booth's sharable norms); the rhetorical and the declarative are absolutely polarized. De Man thus breaks apart the particular and the universal, completing the task Kierkegaard assigned to Socrates. No generalized discourse can ever serve as the basis for particular discriminations, nor is irony an exception. "It can know this inauthenticity but can never overcome it. It can only restate and repeat it on an increasingly conscious level, but it remains endlessly caught in the impossibility of making this knowledge applicable to the empirical world" (*BI*, p. 222). The gap between literature and action, between fiction and the world, is permanent, a gap further inscribed within the subject itself. "Language thus conceived divides the subject into an empirical self, immersed in the world, and a self that becomes like a sign in its attempt at differentiation and self-definition" (*BI*, p. 213). So we return to the problematic Fichtean Ich that already had troubled Schlegel.

Yet all insights are subject to the same degradation, even ironic ones.[26] To articulate it (with respect to the past) is to blind oneself (with respect to its present recurrence). We, like Rousseau's Julie, lose control over the rhetoric of our own discourse at the moment when we gain a maximum of insight (*AR*, p. 216). The result is a relapse into metaphorical models of interpretation that bury the differences they had sought to salvage. "The rediscovery of differential moments, such as those suggested by the term estrangement, also signals the inevitable relapse into patterns of totalization" (*AR*, p. 255). At this point, naturally, we turn to writing. "We write in order to forget our foreknowledge of the total opacity of words and things or, perhaps worse, because we do not know whether things have or do not have to be understood" (*AR*, p. 203).

Yet far-ranging and self-conscious as de Man's analysis of the dynamics of irony is, it remains from Schlegel's perspective preliminary. For the notion it expounds of the subject is a very restrictive one, very much like Kierkegaard's detached, impersonal Socrates. De Man persistently reduces the relationship between subjects to a narcissistic one (*BI*, p. 196), itself resolved into a Nietzschean version of Hegel's master-slave relationship. Intersubjective feeling is immediately hierarchical, converted into a quantitative relation that abolishes difference, therefore essentially "conceptual" (in de Man's sense). As when it laughs at its empirical aspect's foibles, "in a false feeling of pride the self has substituted, in its relationship to nature, an intersubjective feeling (of superiority) for the knowledge of a difference" (*BI*, p. 214). Intersubjectivity is therefore a degradation, an evasion of the measure of truth to which the subject might, on occasion, be entitled.

De Man's analysis of language is equally restrictive, writing out from the start any communicative power of language, which he instead polarizes between its representational and figural roles. As the dominance of the writing-reading metaphor indicates, there is an intensely monologic quality to this discourse, a pulling back from Socratic elenchus. Even given de Man's insightful portrayal of the mechanics of irony, that process can continue and foster an awareness of the nature and dynamics of consensus, a procedure by which relative but adequate social, if not ontological, verities might be established.[27]

## Toward an Irony of Consensus

The process envisaged by the German Romantics was not a totalizing, teleological one. Instead they envisaged a nonsynthetic dialectic, one emerging from and reshaping social consensus. De Man recognizes this possibility, yet without giving it its full force, because he too easily assimilates it to a Baudelairean "vertige." "The dialectic of the self-destruction and self-invention which for him, as for Baudelaire, characterizes the ironic mind is an endless process that leads to no synthesis" (*BI*, p. 220). De Man goes on to quote from Schlegel's "Über die Unverständlichkeit," the essay that capped the Athenäum period, but he stops too quickly, clipping the citation of its full force. Schlegel speaks indeed of the dangerously vertiginous quality of the "Unverständlichkeit" arising from irony, but then immediately turns to the other side of incomprehensibility. In his view, the foundation of thought and society, and their continued creative and adaptive capacities, all depend upon the power of such ironic incomprehensibility to unify humanity.

It seems to me that the welfare of families and nations rests on it [irony]; unless I am totally deceived, states and systems, the most artful human works, often so artful, that one cannot sufficiently wonder at the wisdom of the creator therein. An unbelievably small portion is sufficient, if it is only preserved steadfastly genuine and pure, and no outrageous understanding is permitted to dare to approach the holy limit. Indeed the most precious thing that a person has, inner satisfaction itself, depends, as anyone can easily know, somewhere finally on such a point that must be left in darkness, but on the other hand, also bears and holds the whole.[28]

Schlegel's comments doubtless have a touch of ironic hyperbole in them, but we would be more victims of than participants in this irony if we were to infer from that any tentativeness in his commitment to the literal meaning of those words as well as their ironic turns.

Romantic irony thus does not prepare the way for an eternal non-dialectical polarity but relocates progress in progressive communalization, in the articulation of a history without ontological or teleological aim. It establishes the dependence of truth on the dialogic encounter, on the forum of the agora. It likewise establishes the dependence of the subject's identity on the web of social relations within which it exists. Irony is the active effort to locate one's place in a human world, in the emerging system from which one as subject emerged.

Schlegel here intersects with Jacques Lacan, to whom I turn in chapter 4. Lacan relates how the limits on the subject originate in its originary fragmentation. This is a division not between essence and phenomenon, nor between Being and Word, but between subject and society. The subject's ironic incapacity to grasp itself arises from the multiple roles it is forced to play, the multiple positions it must adopt within the Symbolic Order.[29] Lacan hints that the question of identity is in some measure resolvable at a social level, by following the Socratic turn from cosmology to the merely human. In psychoanalysis, one can see the diffusion of self-consciousness, where the words of one speaker need to pass through one or more other interpreters before being returned to their emitter with dynamic or curative force. Identity is social because the meaning of the communicative act can in this way exceed the conscious intentions of all the interlocutors. This excess of meaning, this abundance of alternate levels, is brought to the attention of the subject by the recognition of ironic incompatibilities.

Ethical irony can thus provide an alternative between indeterminacy and authority. It can prevent freezing them into a static polarity, where indeterminacy would itself become authority.[30] For irony is not just an attitude or an expression of some perceived truth but is also a reaction that endeavors to define a situational truth, what will suffice here and now. In avoiding absolutes, it attempts first to see other than before and thus to break open static situations. Self-consciousness may not coincide with social reality, but neither should it lag too far behind. Irony's role is to interrogate, not to establish, metaphorical equivalences.

Even more centrally, irony reconfirms the dependence of the subject on others. In the last analysis, irony is nothing more than a question designed to draw another subject into discussion of who and where one is. Irony enacts a providential blindness for the subject who has learned how and when to close its own eyes and listen. Its community is not a normative one of conventions, but one of reenacted modes of interaction. Nor is this a passive tie, because irony, in the act of querying the foundations of community and subjecting them to doubt, enacts, in its demand for attentive recomprehension of the other, a more positive and immediate notion of intersubjectivity. Irony refuses the immediate and personal, but also the neatly synthetic that would abstract from the particular.

This optimistic assessment, however, can well be tempered by the irony of Samuel Beckett, to whom I turn in chapter 5. The breakdown of the subject, seen in the fragmentation of the narrative presence throughout Beckett's work, liberates only at the cost of a heightened anxiety in the subject. Beckett forces us to confront the potential emptiness of the social gesture, the dislocation that results from ironic abstraction detached from historical grounding. He returns us to the fundamental incoherencies that we cannot and dare not ignore for too long. As the voice of conscience, he may take as his role the task of reminding us that all fictions and fictions of fictions can only remind us that they are fictions. It is only fitting, then, to return to the critical echo of the Beckettian oracle and to leave to him the final word, while pondering the ultimate impact of the looseness of the fit:

> Far from being a return to the world, the irony to the second power or "irony of irony" that all true irony at once has to engender asserts and maintains its fictional character by stating the continued impossibility of reconciling the world of fiction with the actual world. (*BI*, p. 218)

# Friedrich Schlegel's Irony:
# From Negation to Conscience

*What can indeed, of all that is related to the communication*
*of ideas, be more attractive than the question whether*
*it be possible at all?—KA II:363*

## Prologue

The modest, but long overdue, resurgence of interest in the work of
Friedrich Schlegel is encouraging; it suggests a growing recognition that
Schlegel anticipated many of the themes central to current critical debate,
such as the relations between discourse and authority, or between subject
and community. Yet if Schlegel is to be reconsidered, it is essential that
this be done by reference to the entire structure of his thought, not simply
by drawing on partial collocations of his writings that make his philosophy appear even more fragmentary than it really is. As the publication of
the *Kritische Ausgabe* is making clear, Schlegel's philosophy develops a still
not adequately appreciated non-Hegelian dialectic of intersubjectivity,
one not to be dissolved into Schelling's *Identitätsphilosophie*.[1]

This is especially true for the central concept of the early Schlegel,
Romantic irony. One cannot, in fact, account adequately for Schlegel's
concept of irony without addressing the full dialectical complexity of its
relation to other key operations in his thought. Recent studies of this idea
differ from one another not so much in their overall perception of that
irony as in the stress they lay on one aspect or another of the total ironic
operation. Two primary standpoints emerge, the first depicting irony as a
critical-negating phenomenon,[2] the second privileging its aesthetic-crea-
tive side.[3] The former group traces irony to its sources in the criticism of
Schlegel, especially as a critique of the philosophy and literary theory of
his time.[4] From this perspective, irony comes to be seen as a response to
and an expression of the incapacity of the human to ascend to the divine,
to transform finite history into an infinite totality. The pair "enthusiasm-

irony" is presented as comprising necessarily alternate moments, sequentially disjunct from each other.

The other viewpoint focuses on what Jochen Hörisch denotes as the universality-claim of poetry,[5] the capacity of a self-sufficient subject to actualize or to create the Absolute. Irony is then seen more as a means, as a stimulus to renewed creation of signification. It not only negates but in negating reignites the spark of the Absolute in the individual that leads it to strive again to attain that ecstasy. Its major task is to raise our attention from the particular to the Absolute lurking behind it.[6] This second approach is further characterized by a tendency to subjectivize irony, in that it stresses the creative act as the product of an isolated individual.[7] The emphasis is on its struggle to regain the experience of the Absolute from which it feels itself banished—the acquisition of aesthetic autonomy.

Although both analyses are indisputably correct and between them bring out the dualism inherent in Schlegel's irony, their emphases obscure another of its aspects, its ethical and consensual force. Schlegel's irony is an attempt to reformulate objective truth, both poetic and philosophical, as an intersubjective and suprasubjective attainment. What most sharply defines his unique position among the Romantics is the dialectical structure to which he submits the poet as legislator: "No artist should, alone and unique, be the artist of artists, central-artist, director of all others; instead all should be this to the same degree, every one from his standpoint" (*KA* II:267, frag. 114). The Romantic artist, for Schlegel, is possible only as part of a community of artists. The most crucial step in this aesthetic democracy will be the shattering of the isolation to which self-consciousness apparently condemns the subject, by means of a recognition of an already existing presence of the otherness of distinct subjects in the individual subject.

The mystery of the imparting of thoughts and feelings and the question of whether this is possible at all lie at the root of Schlegel's reflection on irony and come to expression in the central Lyceum fragment 108: "Socratic irony is the only fully involuntary, and yet fully self-possessed, dissimulation. It is equally impossible to feign it and to betray it. Whoever does not have it, to him it remains a riddle even after the most open admission. . . . It contains and incites a feeling of the insoluble conflict of the unconditioned and the conditioned, of the impossibility and the necessity of a complete communication" (*KA* II:160). That the communicative

problem of irony is given equal weight with its abstract binding of the Absolute and the finite is clear.[8] Meaning in discourse must therefore be seen
as a function of an attained harmony between interlocutors, a general
precondition whose full effect is felt in the ironic utterance and whose effects define the scope of any knowledge whatsoever.

This aspect of Schlegel's thought is articulated in his work as a stress
on ethics or morality equal to that on poetry and metaphysics.[9] The validity of the former is an intersubjective, not a logical or sympathetic acquisition; its claims are at least as essential as those of the latter activities, its
progress intimately interwoven with theirs. Schlegel goes so far as to note,
"Ethics [is] the real middlepoint of art" (KA XVIII:198, frag. 13), and later
parallels the moralization of philosophy to the romanticization of poetry
(KA XVIII:353, frag. 388). It should not be implied that irony is equivalent
simply to some ethical category, but it should not be forgotten either that
it comes out of this constellation of multiple and interdependent aims.[10]
Further, what is important is the *position* irony occupies in the total framework of Schlegel's philosophy. To trace the word *irony* alone through his
writings is to fall prey to the terminological fixity against which the entire
force of his own reflections was directed.

## Irony, the Absolute and Infinite Fullness

Despite their differences, virtually all studies of Schlegel's irony
coincide in their highlighting of two traits associated with it. Irony is a response to the unrealizability of the Absolute[11] as a tangible presence for
self-consciousness. The gulf between the Absolute and the mind that
seeks to actualize it, and in actualizing to comprehend it, is complete and
definitive. Though perceivable, the Absolute does not become conceivable
or explicable: "One can neither explain nor conceive the Universe, only
intuit and reveal it" (KA II:271, frag. 150). This implies, however, some
mode of access to it beyond that of empty desire. "True irony requires
that not simply striving after infinity, but also possession of infinity . . . be
there present" (KA XVI:126, frag. 502). "Pure striving is always a striving
after a known, but indeterminate, something" (KA XII:219). All such rap-
prochements, however, remain "tendential" in Schlegel's use of the term,
constricted by a taint of the solitary individualism he felt characterized his
age.

Nevertheless, the ironic human situation is secondly defined by the necessity of striving to portray the Absolute, as Mennemeier puts it, "to gain again the highest, to lead it back from transcendence into the here-present world of appearance."[12] In order to overcome the worthlessness of anything not informed by its relation to the Absolute, recourse must be had to the complex notion of representation: "The pinnacle of godly po-etry must also be a *representation of the Universe*" (KA XVIII:213, frag. 219). Furthermore, though our relation to it be aesthetic, it must still be verifi-able, objective, and therefore communicable.[13] Representation determines a reception-oriented and historical aesthetic theory. "Should, through rep-resentation, that occur in the other person which took place in us, then it has attained the aim of communication. In communication should be con-tained, not always a representation of the results, but rather of the manner and way in which it came to be" (KA XII:102).[14]

Schlegel's characterization of the Absolute is first shaped by the *Stu-dium* ideal of Sophoclean harmony, defined as a perfect order at rest. Schlegel later supplements this trait with an emphasis on the sublime, transporting nature of an Absolute in continual flux, and even comes to include the *interessant*, a quality initially denigrated as merely modern.[15] In all these forms, the Absolute appears as revelation, with the subject in an at least initially passive relation to it.

When self-consciousness tries to conceptualize the feeling reached in such a moment of revelation, its recovered impression of the Absolute is chaotic, perceiving it only as an endless and pointless activity. This should not be taken as meaning that the Absolute or even the Universe in any sense *is* chaotic for Schlegel,[16] only that to human senses it must nec-essarily *seem* chaotic—and that precisely because of its perfect order and interconnectedness, which exist on so many levels that they surpass lim-ited human vision. Schlegel metaphorizes the Absolute as an as yet un-perceived order, a chaos defined by its fecundity, its potential for giving birth to a world (KA II:263, frag. 71). Even the ability to see the Absolute as chaos would be progress, however, for then one would perceive at least the potential latent in it. This is the role to be assigned to irony in his sys-tem.

The human, however, is at a second remove from the Absolute, for neither is its world chaotic, nor can it even seem to be so. Chaos is what we can never see, only feel in enthusiasm and there as beyond any order-chaos dichotomy. For the idealist Schlegel, the mind inevitably structures its impressions, a process he calls "Tendenz," which eventually involves much more than the Kantian categories from which he begins. "Things do not exist at all, but rather only images" (KA XVIII:332, frag. 100) is his terse summary of his Kantian lesson. This is accomplished in various ways: by reason, by mechanical associations, by understanding, and by irony (as reversal into opposition or paradox).[17] Whereas the former two render the world static and the third is merely "chemical," the activity of irony is a higher illusion, a first approximation of the Absolute as it should appear to us. "Irony is clear consciousness of eternal agility, of the infinitely full chaos" (KA II:263, frag. 69). Irony allegorically stands for the possibility and necessity of any and all interrelations, for the totalized and perfectly ordered universe, by incarnating the most radical, apparently disorderly relations.

Yet the gulf between self-consciousness and the Absolute would still be absolute had not Schlegel undertaken to reformulate their relationship. The two are necessarily connected in that the former results from the Fichtean imperative that the Absolute realize itself, that it come into being as the Infinite or Universe, where the totality of presence of the Absolute is replaced by endless becoming. For chaos is not only agility, but energy as well. "*Energy* is more than force, is *active* force, not simply agility, but rather *determinate* outwardly active force" (KA XVIII:126, frag. 43). In consequence, as Anstett remarks, "That an infinite being becomes finite, allows the finite to become infinite" (KA XII:xvii). This return to the Absolute, however, is specifically exempted from the rational capacities of self-consciousness. "There is no reasonable and understandable crossover [*Übergang*] from the finite to the infinite" (KA XII:39–40).

Through this reformulation, the problem of access to the Absolute is reduced for self-consciousness to the necessarily relative terms of its own activity, to the temporal sphere in which its own finitude is overcome continually, if never definitively. "Time is itself, as regards its potential, an all-finitude overcoming power. But it overcomes it *in* the finite."[18] Rapprochement with the Absolute will be sought on this side of the dichotomy, in and through self-consciousness alone. "As though there could be things in themselves *outside* of all consciousness—*Things are in the consciousness*—on the other hand, the spiritual world is opened thereby" (KA XVIII:449, frag. 197). This position simultaneously restricts one to consciousness and opens out beyond it, operations indissolubly bound together by Schlegel. The Übergang denied above is immediately recuperated, in the manner described in the Jena Lectures: "But conversely, it is possible through the insertion of *allegory*" (*KA* XII:40).

Allegory, symbol, and image are alike in their double function of preserving consciousness from passive disappearance in an Absolute whose majesty it cannot comprehend (*KA* XII:344), while translating that revelation into a sensible form, accessible to the subject. "Symbols are signs, representatives of elements which in themselves are never representable" (*KA* XVIII:420, frag. 1197). Despite its this-side nature, allegorical discourse is "no empty appearance" (*KA* XII:148) as empirical speech would be, for it refuses to give itself up wholly to the interpretation of its formulator, to remain bound in a relative sphere by his intentionality. "Every allegory signifies God, and one can speak of God not otherwise than allegorically" (*KA* XVIII:347, frag. 315).

The reconceptualization of the Absolute as what Schlegel terms the "infinite fullness" or "Universe" makes more feasible the striving of self-consciousness for a totality of comprehension. Given that this infinite fullness is not just an abundance of elements but also of relations, the subject's activity can then be formative, a re-creation of the process by which the Universe came to be. This possibility of active formation [*Bildung*] is essential to Schlegel's conception of an accessible Absolute. "If, however, the highest is really not capable of any intentional formation [Bildung], then let us only give up at once every claim to any sort of free idea-art .... Mythology is such an artwork of nature. In its web the highest is really formed; all is relation and transformation, formed and re-formed, and precisely this forming and reforming its characteristic process, its inner life, its method" (*KA* II:318).

It may not be immediately obvious what has been gained in moving from an impossible to a merely infinite task of reconciliation between the subject and its Absolute. What Schlegel has done, though, is to render the experience of the Absolute accessible not only to feeling (via inspiration) but also to analysis (via reflection). For human understanding, the Absolute appears as *Witz*, an active revelation, a limited Absolute, a manifestation of apparent chaos as order. The passivity as well as the alienness of revelation is thus restricted, although wit still denotes an inner harmony with the Absolute that is only partially active, since wit is as much divined as made. "Wit, however, steps forth without any relation to what preceded it, isolated, wholly unexpected and sudden, as a deserter, as it were, or rather a flash from the unconscious world" (*KA* XII:393). Yet wit remains fragmentary, and incomplete as well, in that it does not comprise the self-representation that comes into being with ironic self-consciousness.

Irony may then be defined as the ultimate step to a representation or enactment by the individual subject of its *relationship* to the Absolute.[19] It implicitly conveys the entirety of Schlegel's analysis of self-consciousness, of both the necessity for and the inadequacy of allegorical discourse, and is only in this sense, in a mediated reflective fashion, to be understood in the following fragment: "Irony is, as it were, the ἐπίδειξις of infinity, of universality, from the sense for the cosmos" (*KA* XVIII:128, frag. 76). It does not directly represent the Absolute, although it stands in for it in human terms.

Irony mediates the finite and the infinite not synthetically, as both enthusiasm and wit do, but by demonstrating their dependence *as concepts* on one another. The *Wechselbegriff* is Schlegel's attempt to overcome the reductive monism of Fichte's subjective idealism and the obliteration of difference in Schelling's Identitätsphilosophie, an effort to contain continuity of development and radical contraries within a single system. Thus irony is not dependent on any one particular opposition, nor should it itself be fixed as one pole of any pair. The recurring formula of the Athenäum fragments, "to the point of irony [*bis zur Ironie*]," indicates the status of irony as a vanishing point in Schlegel's system of conceptual perspective. Yet the reversals that manifest irony are not random, but systematically rigorous. "*Irony* is regulated alternation, it is more than simple oscillation" (*KA* XVIII:77, frag. 392). Negation or undermining of particular relations is only a secondary and superficial aspect of its functioning.

Irony mediates not only abstractly, on a transcendental level (which would remain ever incomplete in that the two sides of the dichotomy remain ever inadequate to one another), but concretely—for part of its message is that only the allegorical can be true.[20] The key step in Schlegel's delineation of a form of irony that one could call ethical comes when the Absolute is taken as embodied in the totality of human subjects. Infinite fullness can then be reconceived as the manifoldness of the individual subjects in any group. "The article of faith for the philosophy of the Universe is *that* world.—As a person has an infinite sense for other persons, so humanity has a sense for THAT WORLD—for a beyond" (*KA* XVIII:285, frag. 1067). Society itself is actually a chaos analogous to that of the Universe

(*KA* V:34). The central aim of Schlegel's Romantic aesthetic is to make the deepest, most individual thoughts and feelings conscious and public through a sustained meditation on the dynamics of the intersubjective author-audience relationship.

It should be stressed that for Schlegel it is not the humanity-nature or subject-object relation that is central.[21] To overemphasize those pairs is to abstract from the mutuality inherent in the self-consciousness-Absolute relation and to privilege the part-whole configuration from which Schlegel constantly seeks to escape. "To become a god, to be a person, to form oneself, are expressions that mean one and the same thing" (*KA* II:210, frag. 262). As the "Gespräch über die Poesie" makes clear, the central human need is for a common, universally accepted mode of access to the Absolute, a tie between poet and community that locates the poem between them as a cooperative act. This priority is forced on Schlegel by his diagnosis of the endemic individualism of his age and the rigid dogmatism that corresponds to it, false subjective tendencies to be combated by increased hermeneutic self-consciousness. "Why does the highest now so often express itself as false tendency?—Because no one can understand himself, who does not understand his contemporaries. You must therefore first believe that you are not alone, you must everywhere perceive infinitely much and not become tired of forming the sense [*Sinn*], until you at last have found the originary and essential" (*KA* II:268, frag. 124). *Sinn für andern*, "sense for others," is what irony will endeavor to constitute and articulate.

To understand how this is possible, we need first to examine more closely the response of the finite subject to an experience of transcendence and to see how, for Schlegel, this necessarily leads to an awareness by that subject of its dependence on others. Vital to this process is the way Schlegel examines the subject-Absolute relation in aesthetic terms, thus objectifying an elusively abstract relationship.

## From Enthusiasm to Disillusion

It is as divine inebriation, called either enthusiasm or inspiration, that the Absolute first appears to the subject. The experience is felt as a surrender of selfhood in a transcendent unity. "The thought of *infinite unity* abolishes [*aufhebt*] all separation and difference, hence all personality. . . . the expression 'rapture'. . . describes the loss, the going-out from oneself very well" (*KA* XII:395). Enthusiasm is defined as "the feeling of the sublime" (*KA* XII:6), Kant's sublime seen in its deinstrumentalized state, without any practical aim.

But two problems arise in connection with this transport. Its occurrence is only transitory and its manifestation seems strange, alien when recovered by recollection. "Through [inspiration], the feeling of the infinite is admittedly very strong and stronger than that of finitude; because, however, it does not last, it is not suited to restraining thoroughly the ceaseless influence of the lower consciousness" (*KA* XII:396). "It makes, however, such a strong disparity with ordinary consciousness, that it really seems as if an alien I entered into our own [I]" (*KA* XII:394). These impressions strengthen the belief in a daemonic source of inspiration, subsisting independently, always already there. It thus seems, in its permanence, more than the subject is or could be. Sensed as inadequate to that experience, the subject reacts by withdrawing itself from its own transport.

This response is a temporary one, which then gives rise to the endeavor by self-consciousness to appropriate the experience, to assert control over it by being able to create it at will. In a standard Romantic transformation, *Poesie* becomes *Kunst*, the recollection of inspiration preserved as poetic creation. "This rediscovery of something lost is just what one generally calls *recollection*" (*KA* XII:348). "There is one eternal inner revelation—*recollection*" (*KA* XVIII:561, frag. 10). With recollection arises the "intuition" [*Anschauung*], the perception of the original unity, but only as that which has been lost. "The real genuine intuition occurs first in *recollection*" (*KA* XVIII:436, frag. 103). So these capacities are inevitably dualistic, split into seer and seen, past and present, and therefore unable to recapture completely the rapture they echo. But they do gain the positive capacity of being susceptible to direction by the subject via the will. From such applied concentration springs poetic creation, where the subject's intuited sense of the Absolute is first made accessible to it in an objective form, whose archetype is wit, the combinatory capability. The transcendent experience is thus translated into symbolic forms.[22] Nonetheless, the poetic rapture preserved in this way shares the two difficulties of the original inspiration—it is both hard to conjure and seemingly external in origin—which paradoxically serve to guarantee its genuineness.

The enthusiasm for the poetic experience gives way, however, to the reality and disillusion of the poetic artifact—a duality replicating the original and untraversable gulf between self-consciousness and the Absolute. The engendered accessibility of artworks leads to their undermining by reflective scrutiny. As noted in the analysis of the subject's relation to chaos, it is always tendential and therefore barred from the universal, a defect not obliterated by poetry. *"Productive force* is already limitation" (*KA* XVIII:24, frag. 63). It is inevitable that traces of the subject, its intents, and consequently its limitations, be sensed in the artifact. Furthermore, where transport seemed beyond the subject, the surviving creations seem beneath it, retaining only a part of the Absolute. Even worse, the subject itself seems only fragmentarily present there, not expressing all it felt. For the individual subject embodies only a part of the human spirit at which it hints. "Only the subject [*der Mensch*] is, in the individual, *not entirely* but only in a piecemeal way [*Stückweise*] present. A subject can never be there" (*KA* XVIII:506, frag. 9), states one of Schlegel's earliest notations, a point echoed continuously through the Cologne Lectures period (*KA* XII:337 and 392). Its inability to recover, to retain the Absolute thus *causes* the subject's recognition of its fragmentation and of its illusion that the active consciousness could ever measure up to the Absolute and the unity it experienced, or perhaps only intuited, there.

This process is simultaneously, though, a double appropriation by self-consciousness. First, the Absolute is internalized as an ecstatic self, exactly that which has seeped out of the artifact. And the act of creation itself is appropriated, now more clearly a product of the subject and not just handed down from the heavens, now fixed in the ambivalent status of the witticism. The proprietorship and the inadequacy of the poetic artifact are inextricably bound to each other.

The driving apart of the Absolute and self-consciousness causes a change in focus for thought, which concentrates now on the relation between the two, in an attempt to explain the inadequacy of the subject, why it fails to recover the Absolute, what separates it from that ideal. From an aesthetic of mimesis, early Romantic thought shifts not to the idolatry of originality and genius but to self-questioning, to wondering where the poetry has gone. For this aesthetic self-awareness, individualism is felt as a burden, if not an essential one. Its reality is implicitly negated as eternally flawed. The risk, or temptation, is to end in a disgust with reality and the self-isolation to which consciousness condemns the subject. It is inadequate simply to dismiss the Kierkegaardian critique of this aspect of Romantic irony. Regardless of his exaggerations and inaccuracies, Kierkegaard had an intuitive sense for the logical dilemma from which self-consciousness threatens to be freed only as negative irony. But Schlegel's perception of the risk was no less acute. "[The opposition of idea and reality] leads naturally now to the result that one disdains reality too much, as not corresponding to the ideal, while one does not believe in the idea [seen as] mere shadow-work" (KA XII:225). Whether disillusion is to go over into infinite negativity or self-elevation is the crux of Schlegel's entire philosophizing.

### Reappropriation of the Absolute as Negative Product of the Subject

The insight that permits the breaching of the intellectual barrier between subject and revealed truth results from that refocusing on the subject-Absolute relation, wherein it becomes clear that the Absolute does not exist apart from its manifestation in such a duality. "If, however, we now posit the infinite, and thereby abolish everything that is opposed to it, then there still yet remains something for us, namely *that which abstracts,* or *posits*" (KA XII:5). The restriction to this world implied in Schlegel's concept of allegory is radicalized when Schlegel concludes that the subject creates the *concept* of the Absolute through its own force, that is, makes its very appearance and recognition *as* Absolute possible. This remains, to be sure, a backward, negative process. "The consciousness of the infinite must be constituted—in that we annihilate the opposite" (KA XVIII:412, frag. 1095).[23]

Instead of a = a as the basis of philosophy, or even the "*Das Ich setzt sich*" of Fichte, Schlegel prefers to begin with "a *means* a" (KA XII:350). The proximity of the Absolute is conceived as an achievement of the subject, which recognizes the *meaning* of that Absolute as its own creation. In Schlegel's version of idealism, the entire structure of revelation is thus reversed, its untouchable transcendence used as a proof of the primacy of self-consciousness. "[The idealists] give the conditioned self precedence over the unconditioned, take the former as the highest reality, presuppose the unconditioned self simply as possible, it is for them simply a ground in order to be a ground, is not really, therefore in and for itself *nothing*" (KA XII:156). The subject thus has the potential to become the basis of its own self-consciousness.

Yet the Absolute remains incontestably the ground of a self-consciousness that can never adequately explain itself as a whole. The Absolute guarantees the integrity of the subject beyond its finite appearances and creations. Frank describes this as the circle in which Fichte's philosophy remains trapped. "The Absolute *is* therefore only as brought forth from me (otherwise it would not be for me)—on the other hand, it ought to be just that which posits me."[24] Self-consciousness remains a secondary phenomenon. It can never claim to have created itself, only to have found itself. "So as we are inconceivable to ourselves, appear to ourselves only as a part of ourselves, can we not possibly be a work of ourselves" (*KA* XII:343).

Schlegel's response is to reject the logical certainties upon which Fichte built his *Wissenschaftslehre*. "The two principles of the ground and of contradiction must be fully annihilated, as the limits of experience" (*KA* XVIII:409, frag. 1070). The principle of identity is no more inviolable, refuted both by becoming and by coming-into-being (*KA* XII:330–331). Hence it becomes possible for Schlegel to conceive the two Absolutes of revelation and poetic reflection as nonidentical, yet not wholly estranged from each other. As the Absolute splits into God and Universe, so the subject splits into a higher and a lower self-con)ciousness. "But insofar as it understands itself as its own ground, it is not I in the same sense, as if it understands itself as that which it actually is."[25]

The structure of duality is rooted in a perception of the inadequacy of the two constituents to each other. That Absolute reached through consciousness (or created via imagination) is only symbolically adequate to that Absolute experienced in recollection or revelation. Yet the intuition so central in Schlegel's thought is the perception of their absolute dependence on each other, more a feeling than a concept, but as informed by dualism as is reflection. "The *intellectual intuition* is nothing else than the consciousness of a prestabilized harmony, of a necessary, eternal dualism" (*KA* XVIII:280, frag. 1026). Due to its binding force, its necessary association with a dual relation, Schlegel even denies it the adjective *intellectual,* preferring the *spiritual intuition* that implies not a reflective dualism but a unity-in-separation that abides without being reduced (*KA* XII:355). Schlegel is evoking not mere opposition of contraries here but the juxtaposition of incompatibles, irreconcilable because on constitutively different levels.

Despite the intuitive reconciliation operated by the intuition, the Absolute per se remains accessible to self-consciousness only in its absence.

To think it, self-consciousness must not have it; the gulf between them is apparently uncrossable, even if their existences are mutually conditioned, even if they are respectively each other's first cause. This dilemma has a positive function as the initial spark to activity in the subject. "The cosmic I cannot be conscious of this unity, simplicity, without feeling an infinite *longing* to enrich this originary *emptiness* through multiplicity and fullness" (*KA* XII:429).

Yet this analysis emphasizes too single-mindedly the negative incapacity of a self-consciousness poised on the brink of activity. For Schlegel, the allegorical incarnations of the Absolute can be reliable guides. The good, true, and beautiful can give a sense of the Absolute, a faith Mennemeier refers to as Schlegel's "aesthetic optimism."[26] Second, the surrender of the omnipotence of Fichte's Absolute Ich opens up the possibility, indeed the necessity, of also eliminating the isolated subject of liberal political theory. For Schlegel's analysis of consciousness makes it seem presumptuous to stand as a limited being against the Absolute, while also insisting that partialness, a lack, is a necessary attribute only for such an isolated self-consciousness. The consequence of this realization is the acquisition of freedom, a benefit denied those already sure of their possession of the Absolute. "The infinite remains to us as freedom, whenever we abstract from everything and analyze our consciousness" (*KA* XVIII:408, frag. 1061). Intersubjectivity is the process that will allegorically enact the possibility implied here of a progress toward an Absolute subject.

For the problem remains: how it it possible that the feeling aroused by a manifestation of the Absolute should exceed the reasonable content extractable from that experience? How is relative, partial self-consciousness to be privileged with recollection of such a state? The semblance of the Absolute can even delude self-consciousness, what Schlegel calls a "meaningful appearance" (*KA* XII:149 and 152), and lead it to doubt its own verities. The premise that lies behind the Romantic audacity of undertaking to write a Bible is that the source of inspiration must be an intersubjectively valid consciousness. The risk of such an aim, heightened by modern isolation, is that private fantasies might be taken for public mythology. This aim, and this risk, provoke the rise of irony in Schlegel's system as a device to reintegrate the individual and society, to pass beyond the isolated creative consciousness and regain the sense of speaking to kindred spirits.

## Objectivity as Intersubjectivity

Irony in Schlegel's philosophy is thus applied to the process of re-gaining access to the Absolute as an objective or objectifiable phenome-non, for which poetry provides the first model. Objective in this context means not just realized, whereby the Absolute is subordinated to its showing-forth, but also means elevated to a general validity, whereby the subjective is raised to the level of that manifested total Absolute. The cen-tral theorem of the Jena Lectures is simply "All is in one, and one is all" (*KA* XII:7–8). This goal is not conceived as a purely negative process, how-ever endlessly it may stretch out, for the redefinition of the Absolute as a concrete Universe has made positivity possible. "The being and the real aim of idealism is *positive knowledge* [*Erkenntnis*] *of infinite reality*" (*KA* XII:126). This aim is perceived as part of the fundamental critique of Kant's exclusion of the transcendental from the sphere of human knowl-edge. "Kant introduced the concept of the negative into world-wisdom. Would it not be a useful attempt, now also to introduce the concept of the positive into philosophy?" (*KA* II:166, frag. 3). Though the task may fi-nally be unfinishable, it is still imperative to try to think the Absolute in positive terms; a positive irony is part of this effort.[27]

This requirement becomes increasingly evident as Schlegel's thought progresses. There is a shift from the use of *enthusiasm* to denote the contact of the human and the divine to a preference for *inspiration*. The subjective connotations of the former word are thus brought under control by the more objective and verifiable emphases of the latter term, where the external stimulus and not the reaction of the subject is determining. By the time of his Paris sojourn, Schlegel notes how religion, already a central concept of the "Gespräch," differs from enthusiasm. "*Religion* is not enthu-siasm, but *reaction* against this" (*KA* XVIII:474, frag. 32). He will later re-turn to the "Gespräch" before its republication in his collected works to edit out *Enthusiasmus* in favor of *Begeisterung*.

This increasingly objective emphasis necessitates a parallel privileg-ing of belief over reflection. "The *all in one* is revelation, and can only be *believed* (*KA* XVIII:303, frag. 1314). *Lucinde* and the "Gespräch" specifically set the attainment of poetic insight against the self-consciousness that rendered that acquisition a worthwhile goal. "For this is the beginning of all poetry, to abolish the course and laws of rationally thinking reason and again to displace us into the beautiful confusion of fantasy, into the originary chaos of human nature" (KA II:319). This evaluation is not, however, a leap of faith—the negation of reflection is not equivalent to its extinguishing, but only a beginning, a first step. Consciousness prepares the way for belief, but belief is never to be conceived apart from the knowledge of it that requires alert self-consciousness. "Belief without knowledge [Wissen] is not right—is limiting and hollow—belief is the highest blossom of perfected knowledge—namely of the positive knowledge that is itself the being of poetry" (KA XVIII:577, frag. 154). "What therefore first of all is an object of belief ought to become an object of knowledge" (KA XII:60), repeat the Jena Lectures, later echoed themselves by the Cologne Lectures. "A belief that is separated from knowledge and opposed to it is no longer philosophy" (KA XII:156). What is never to be forgotten is that all knowledge and belief are achieved, created by the subject. "Idealism, on the contrary, is entirely humanity's own product and gain, an attempt [at] what the human spirit without alien assistance, against all difficulties that could be opposed to it, might be able to bring forth from itself" (KA XII:162).

What this synthesis of belief and knowledge would be is not easy for Schlegel himself to define. Rejecting both recollection and intuition, he describes the act as Weissagung, prophecy. What it involves is the capacity to go out of oneself that makes possible the active adaptation to inspiration. "The infinite fullness, insofar as it is knowledge [Erkenntnis], is presentiment and prophecy; insofar as it [is] a bringing-forth, it is poetry" (KA XII:377). Both halves of the reception-articulation process are necessary, as checks on and supplements to each other to guarantee objectivity; their result is religious insight. "Is religion not really designated to cover the DEFICIT OF FULLNESS?" (KA XVIII:407, frag. 1042).

The direct consequence of the analysis of revelation is the ironic self-recognition that completes the development of self-consciousness, the realization that the experience of the Absolute is neither just subjective and incommunicable nor yet simply subjectively verifiable. The sense of otherness in inspiration comes from traces of the allgemeine, the general, in the process of recollection-creation, an unconscious accommodation of the subject to broader precepts and structures. The letting down of the barriers to intersubjectivity that ordinarily strain out the influences of others and permit a consistent, if restricted, view of the subject, is what characterizes inspiration. The corollary to this is that the otherness of revelation is an illusion arising from an incomplete self-knowledge on the part of the subject, a blindness to its constant capacity to be more than an isolated individual. The other is already in the subject, which as a consequence possesses permanent potential for inspiration. Anticipating Freud and Lacan, Schlegel develops this insight in an analysis between everyday thought and the dream. "Why do people find *only* their dreams so meaningful as they really should find everything? They then perceive that they are forever alien to themselves" (*KA* XVIII:150, frag. 323). The prophetic technique for assimilating the Absolute is analogy, by which discrete spheres are brought into harmony. "That a truth lets itself be *deduced* from other truths already presupposes that all truth is *in One*, all in one and one in all [is] the soul of analogy" (*KA* XVIII:415, frag. 1131). But the analogization of inspiration is only partial and happenstance; it needs to be made more conscious and active, approximated in the only way thought can, as self-contradiction. "Now if one once has a fondness for the Absolute and cannot let go of it; there then remains for one no other exit than always to contradict oneself, and to bind the most opposed extremes. The principle of contradiction is inevitably done for, and one has only the choice, whether one wishes on that account to behave passively, or whether one wishes through acknowledgment of it to ennoble necessity to free activity" (*KA* II:164, frag. 26). This act of self-contradiction is nothing more than the opening-out of an isolated subject to the contradictions and paradoxes, but also the consensual possibilities, of an intersubjectivity that far exceeds it.

So the subject-other barrier is breached and with it an eternally dissatisfying narcissistic pursuit of an elusive identity. Instead, the subject should maintain itself in a self-aware passivity, expunging its conscious revisions to let the communal perceptions through, from which alone creative mirroring can result. "The *dream* mirrors the world completely passively; hence its profound meaning" (*KA* XVIII:193, frag. 795). Contradictions are less created than perceived, inevitable consequences of an attunement to the Universe that does not distort the impressions it causes. It is in this sense that irony is an indifference point (*KA* XVIII:227, frag. 392), the creative rudder of enthusiasm. "Irony is the idea, Universe—It has fantasy, not she [*die Idee*] has it" (*KA* XVIII:206, frag. 114). For it directs fantasy away from the particular and tendential and toward the communal and general.

Objectivity is thus interpreted by irony as an intersubjectivity that can serve as a guarantor of general validity. "The infinite in relation to all humanity and all powers = Universe" (KA XVIII:260, frag. 795). The objective is a product of colliding subjectivities, termed Gegenliebe (KA II:286), where "only in the answer of its You can every I completely feel its infinite unity" (KA V:61). Strife is inevitable in such cases, to be combated by a communication whose model is the dialogue. "Who is right, and how can we become one? Only through development [Bildung], which broadens every particular sense to the general, infinite one; and through the belief in this sense, or in religion, are we already that, even before we become it" (KA II:263, frag. 80). The Socratic aims of Lyceum fragment 108 recur, even more central in the "Gespräch." "The game of communication and approximation is the business and power of life; absolute perfection is only in death" (KA II:286). Even misunderstandings are recuperated as a stimulus to a deeper communication (KA V:64), the goal and implicit precondition of which is the possibility of complete mutual understanding. "We take communication in the most general sense. If all objects of our reflection are only costumes for the related Opposite-I or You, then is reflection, as striving for understanding, indeed nothing other than a striving for unification, for communication with those disguised spirits" (KA XII:363).[28]

Art is not a uniquely privileged alternative in this system, though it does serve as the exemplar through which Schlegel's thought first develops itself. The artwork's presence for analysis and its fixing of patterns long enough to permit the dialectic of ironic self-recognition to occur do privilege it in the Athenäum period; poetry makes the Absolute, as dialectic of presence and absence, tangible in an indirect way, through representation. It is a stage on the way to the objective. "First through representation does mutuality come into knowledge and with this also the generally valid" (KA XII:366).

Insofar as poetry limits secondary revision, it facilitates access to the unconscious and to concrete intersubjectivity. This is, however, true only of that poetry that converts the subject-object relation into a mutual striving toward reconciliation and unity, providing Schlegel's "échappées de vue into the infinite." Yet poetry remains prone to monologic utterance. Given unity by individual tendencies, it is also pulled down from the ideal by them. So, far from absolutizing art, Schlegel seeks its integration with other human activities. Once the ironic insight into the self-insufficiency of the subject has occurred, the same patterns may be seen to be played out in all human phenomena.

## The Growth of Irony

Although consistently conceived as the enactment by the subject of its relation to the Absolute, irony is not an immobile or homogeneous term for Schlegel. By examining the transformations it undergoes, I hope to demonstrate more clearly its role in the development of objectivity into a concrete intersubjectivity. Schlegel regularly presents irony with an emphasis on self-possession, on an active, but not overactively distorting, mental alertness. Irony creates, it does not abolish, structures and relations. It is a negation that completes the partial by raising it to a paradox that confutes our notions of identity and thus incites us to extend them.

Irony was at various times associated by Schlegel with different conceptual clusters, as he emphasized one or another aspect of its functioning within his overall system. Tracing these shifts can also provide the beginnings of a schema to differentiate diverse kinds of irony along Schlegel's lines and thus to perceive possible contrasts in meaning open to the phenomenon of irony. Such a model will also make it easier to assess irony in literary works and to control the tendency of irony to seem to be everywhere and nowhere, capable of characterizing any and all texts—a point at which it starts to lose its theoretical usefulness.

Four primary stages in the process of Schlegel's thinking through of irony can be distinguished, whose succession should not be taken as a hierarchical assessment of their relative worth, but rather as a consequence of the deepening of Schlegel's concept of irony to include a number of disparate, but related, characteristics. With *dialogic* irony, it is the contrastive, polar aspect of irony that is emphasized, the juxtaposition of radical alternatives not reducible to any Hegelian synthesis. *Systemic* irony privileges the centrifugal quality of a consciousness seeking to include the manifold within a system that, however, never loses sight of a structuring center around which the multiple forms of the real insistently circle. *Negating,* or Socratic, irony, on the other hand, focuses on the ineffable, virtual existence of any such center, whose presence can be affirmed only through the destruction of the particular. The fourth type of irony, and the sort that is uniquely Schlegelian, is *ethical* irony, in which the consequences of his entire theory of the subject and the self-limitation incumbent upon the individual are drawn together. This engenders a movement toward the other subject who always serves as audience for any enactment and from whom that act must draw its final significance.

Much of the confusion endemic to the discussion of irony stems from inadequate attention to the different phenomena grouped under that rubric. For an ironic discourse or text might contain one, a few, or all the above traits, combined in various ways. And this composite definition might also include many texts not usually thought of as ironic, where ironic self-consciousness operates without utilizing specifically ironic statements or events. Yet the core of that self-consciousness seems sufficiently solid—a subject aware of and enacting its status of inadequacy in regard to an Absolute whose presence it can conjure only through engagement in a dialectic of intersubjectivity—to confirm the sensibility of ordinary language use, which finds it appropriate to denote a multiplicity of situations with the single term *irony.*

Irony appears early in Schlegel's notebooks in connection with the system-chaos complex of ideas, as a provisional approximation of their synthesis. "Irony is the duty of all philosophy that is not yet either history or system" (*KA* XVIII:86, frag. 678). Any system is perceived by Schlegel not as static but as "the fluid hovering [*das fließend Schwebende*]" (*KA* XVIII:37, frag. 207), itself based on alternation between opposites and hence held together by tension rather than synthesis. "*Two* foundations and alternation-construction, that seems to suit systematic philosophy and absolute philosophy" (*KA* XVIII:108, frag. 942). Like the fragment form (*KA* II:197, frag. 206), the individual is to be cut off from its environment to attain an internal self-perfection, much like a witticism. "Only through the sharpest directing at one point can the individual insight maintain a form of wholeness" (*KA* II:160, frag. 109).

This dialogic irony involves a sustained opposition between viewpoints not reconciled by the ironist. Though open in its nonresolution, at the same time it tends to give the impression of being all-encompassing, of being an exhaustive, final, and fundamental polarity. This suggests a permanent restriction to the given opposition and its particular terms, which is itself nonironic, appearing to position the ironist in a transcendent viewpoint with respect to his own ironic paradox. But as Schlegel's "Über die Unverständlichkeit" makes clear, any such claim to be above the fundamental conflicts of one's own discourse is the greatest (conscious or unconscious) irony of all.

As Schlegel increasingly realized, modern conditions render such a self-contained orientation dangerously subjective. "Systematic philosophy [is] completely subjective; absolute [philosophy is] completely objective" (*KA* XVIII:135, frag. 157), he says, demonstrating his awareness that any system reveals more than anything else the idiosyncrasies of its maker. The analysis of limited polarities provokes further examination of the preconditions for irony. "Can irony arise simply from the height of one form of formation [*Bildung*], or only out of the confluence of several?" (*KA* XVI:126, frag. 505). From this question stems Schlegel's receptiveness for Goethe, whom he will try to subsume under a broadened definition of irony encompassing Goethe's greatest virtue, his universality. "In addition, no idea is isolated, but it is what it is, only among all ideas" (*KA* II:265, frag. 95). Manifoldness was already praised in the essays on Forster and Lessing, equated in the latter to self-knowledge (*KA* II:116), but it finds its culmination in Goethe and in the *Wilhelm Meister* essay as a corrective to the earlier *Wechselbegriff*. "Universality must be *absolute*, hence simple adroitness in the alternation of standpoints is still nothing" (*KA* XVIII:380, frag. 716). "Sense for the cosmos" (*KA* II:131) is essential to raise irony from a merely logical, mechanical concept to a truly universal and intersubjective idea.

Hence the ideal of internal consistency, via differentiation from outside distorting elements, is supplemented by a notion of internal infinity. "A work is formed [*gebildet*], if it is everywhere sharply delimited, but within the limits limitless and inexhaustible, if it is completely true to itself, everywhere the same, and yet elevated above itself" (*KA* II:215, frag. 297). The individual becomes a microcosm, only apparently relativized in its isolation, for it possesses the structural capacity to transform itself into any shape in a world built on analogy.

> But to displace oneself intentionally now into this, now into that sphere, as into another world, not simply with understanding and imagination, but with the entire soul; freely to renounce now this, now that, part of one's being, and to confine oneself completely to another [part]; to search for and find one's one and all now in this, now in that individual, and intentionally to forget all others: capable of this is only a spirit that contains within itself, as it were, a number of spirits and an entire system of persons, and within whom the Universe which, as one says, should sprout in every monad, is fully grown and become ripe. (*KA* II:185, frag. 121)

Goethe's sublimity is that of an irony in absolute control, hovering over his characters and work (*KA* II:133), able to transform them into versions and echoes of one another, in a way that suggests he might well be able to complete all tendencies. Irony is here the ability to infuse the most disparate characters and events with hermeneutic unity (*KA* II:131). Irony acts as an integrative force, closely allied to the constructive poetic act.

This is the irony one could term *systemic*, an elaborate patterning with close affinities to Novalis's idea of the encyclopedia. The sense of being limited by the finite is resisted by an endless proliferation of mutually sustaining antitheses, no one of which is central and whose structural similarity (analogousness) is enriched by progressive extension into all spheres of human language and activity. Irony acts here to justify the juxtaposition of apparently unrelated contexts through its doctrine of the limited extensibility of polarities, that is , the idea that any set of terms can acquire systemic validity only through application to an ever-widening realm of situations, which necessarily leads to their progressive redefinition, if not outright replacement. Yet systemic irony runs a risk similar to the reductiveness of dialogic irony, insofar as the extension of spheres of applicability comes to be seen as mechanical application of a transcendent schema, instead of being itself the working out of the contours of such a schema.

Yet despite the attractiveness of Goethean universality, the subject's real position vis-à-vis the Absolute is more that of Wilhelm than Goethe, a realization from which a fatalistic, purely reactive disposition can spring, in the eyes of which irony is little more than parody. Schlegel later distances himself from the implied omniscience of the Goethean model, as early as in Athenäum fragment 118, where he argues for a republican, non-hero-centered text. If no artist can be the artist of artists, more than "sense for the cosmos" is necessary. "To many-sidedness belongs not only a comprehensive system, but also sense for a beyond of humanity" (*KA* II:262, frag. 55). *Lucinde* will in fact be specifically exempted from Goethean irony; its irony lies in the effort to create a more formal irony, an openness and uncertainty that only in subsequent parts was to go over into the content (*KA* XVI:238, frag. 78).

Hence the Lyceum-Athenäum period is already characterized by a greater stress on Socratic irony. The indeterminacy and doubt at the root of all philosophy are central in what one might term Schlegel's *fröhliche Unwissenheit*. "Skepticism is the condition of hovering reflection" (*KA* XVIII:400, frag. 955), and "Irony is the highest, purest σκέψις" (*KA* XVIII:406, frag. 1023). The Socratic method is to destroy any isolated opinion by bringing it into contact with a broader or alien context. Theoretical definitions are subjected to the limiting case that reduces them to stammering. What Socrates in his dialogic encounters does not know is how any particular case might manifest or be related to the Good without having first analyzed it, subjected it to the act of interpretation. What Socrates does know, however, is that all human beings are to be judged by their comparison with the divine. Irony here, then, acts as a disintegrative force, exploiting failed connections to intimate the Absolute.

This negating irony is an expression of the ironist's realization that he, too, is caught up in the process of interpretation and can never attain a position outside itself or himself. It is the contrary of systemic irony, its negative side that stresses the incompleteness and context-boundedness that provoke the idea of encyclopedic inclusiveness by way of compensation for the limitations of any part. What is important is the openness this negation adds to the ironic act, opening up conceptual gaps it fails to fill, creating a space for the other subject, the interlocutor. Where a dialogic or systemic ironist might easily get his audience to identify with the position he has adopted, a transcendent one, just that sense of being above paradox, even in the sense of being able to state it definitively, is here left out.

What Schlegel particularly admired in Socrates was his ability to translate this ironic consciousness into fertile inspiration of others, to provoke a manifoldness *outside* himself. "This free cultivation [*Ausbildung*] of self-reflection is the reason that out of his school such completely varied, such diverse and excellently cultivated systems have come forth" (*KA* XII:199). Socrates created not written works but dynamic, self-questioning human subjects. But Schlegel presses always forward, toward a more objective knowledge than ironic skepticism alone can provide, which in its focus on the inadequacy of the particular formulation provides no sense for how a more objective discourse might be made present. "Skepticism seeks to represent purely the subjective element (of philosophy)—dialectic demands the highest degree of objectivity" (*KA* XVIII:387, frag. 800). Schlegel's own thought will move itself in the direction of this higher objectivity.

The problem remains of how the finite, particular appearances of the infinite are to be evaluated. Their negation in itself is insufficient to determine how relatively adequate to the Absolute they might be, an essential condition if the idea of progress is not to be sacrificed and negation is not to be hypostatized. Negative irony, as Kierkegaard noted, would produce indifference, for any and all negated phenomena can equally well hint at the Absolute—or not. Irony does, in fact, virtually disappear from Schlegel's notebooks after 1800, a surprising development when one considers that it is related not only to his waning  poetic interests but to his philosophical ones as well. This suggests that other devices may have seemed to him more adequate in fulfilling irony's intersubjective impulse.

The mythology of the "Gespräch über die Poesie" is in fact a first attempt to transcend irony, replacing enthusiasm with an objective communal belief that would obviate the need for ironic completion of the individual. Irony here becomes the capacity to take the play of life as play, its association with contradiction minimized, as is its negating aspect (*KA* II:323). Even the Jena Lectures, however, still stress a dialectical, indirect approach to the Absolute, although the limitations of dialectic are astutely pointed out: "Namely there, where one is in agreement in spirit as to the essential, and only disputes over the letter, there is the dialectical form of disputing completely in its place" (*KA* XII:73). How that fundamental agreement is to be attained, what form it might take, is less clear. Yet irony seems to depend on such implicit prior agreement between subjects (or in some cases to test for such intellectual sympathy), rather than actually to constitute it. Irony seems to depend not just on another person but on some particular kind of other person.

So the Cologne Lectures mark a decisive shift in the development of the function of irony in Schlegel's thought, for here, where the term itself vanishes, its aspect of intersubjectivity becomes quite clear. Though still unremarked in the critical literature, a terminological shift occurs here that not only alters our understanding of irony but retroactively allows us better to see its significance in Schlegel's system. Irony, always perceived by Schlegel as a third mediating power between enthusiasm or fantasy and thought ("Irony is *menstruum universale* and synthesis of reflection and fantasy, of harmony and enthusiasm" [*KA* XVI:237, frag. 71]), here has its functions taken over virtually intact by *Gewissen*, conscience. The parallels are so close as to be startling, not only in terms of function, but in a surrounding descriptive vocabulary retained almost without change. "Conscience . . . is entirely at rest and clear. It relates itself not to a particular form of the finite and the infinite, but rather, as mentioned, to the relationship of the two. . . . it leads, as the feeling of relationship accompanying all thinking, to self-possession . . . . It is the most characteristic, most inner, freest and most active activity in us, the kernel of consciousness, as it were; it hovers as the feeling of relationship in the middle between two worlds" (*KA* XII:397).

Besides acting as mediator of the finite and the Absolute, conscience displays even more clearly the intersubjective impulse always present in irony for Schlegel. "[Conscience] draws us, as our most characteristic, most inner activity, back toward ourselves, back toward our person and individuality; not however toward the Individual simply in its limitedness, but toward the *general Individual* and its opposite; not toward the earthly alone, but toward the relation and opposition of that to the divine." Like irony, conscience preserves the subject from loss both in the sensual particular and in the overwhelming majesty of the Absolute. "It saves us from the mastery of the world of sense and preserves us from the superior power of higher spirits" (*KA* XII:397–398). In sum, conscience is "the consciousness of consciousness, the life of life itself" (*KA* XII:399).

Conscience exhibits precisely those traits I have been arguing are central to ironic self-consciousness. It displays the vacillation characteristic of irony between a character disposition and a specific event of discourse.[29] It is the recuperation of an outer dictum as an inner, self-imposed voice or, rather, as the propensity to compare the two voices, to spot divergences between them. Conscience recognizes that the subject and the suprapersonal are so inextricably mixed that their reconciliation must be the primary task of self-consciousness. Their correspondence is always tentative, for every formulated ethical theory will be in constant tension with a praxis whose complexity far exceeds it. But it is always a particular outer voice, one that separates and judges, ever there, the core of our humanity. "*Judgment* [is] a capacity accompanying all other capacities, pervading all of them" (*KA* XVIII:46, frag. 278). "The human being is completely conscience" (*KA* XII:85). This terminological transformation makes it evident that irony all along has had an ethical as well as an aesthetic potential. The vanishing of appearance leaves an imprint of the divine on the individual, whose contact with the divine is to be certified only through mutual striving for communal standards, and mutual submission to the endless necessity of such striving.

What this ethical irony adds is a reminder of the limited, even inessential, status of the individual subject. It counterbalances the self-centeredness possible with dialogic or systemic irony and the relativism implicit in negating irony—all of which can suggest that the ironist is in some sense at the end of his pursuit of knowledge. To the possibly empty or despairing openness of negating irony it adds an invitation to the other to participate in the process of self-unfolding that moves out beyond the individual. In this sense, ethical irony is at the center of Schlegel's own system, although it, too, is not to be taken as absolute and converted into dogma.

For even though positively formulable as conscience, irony remains an endless regress, an eternal process. There is no absolute spirit in Schlegel's world. The sense of paradox as permanent, even though only apparent, is part of the ironic self-consciousness, of dilemmas of conscience as well. "Paradox is the *conditio sine qua non* for irony, the soul, source and principle" (*KA* XVI:174, frag. 1078). The pretensions, either of reason or of fantasy, to unity are always denied by "the principle customary in ordinary life and taught by experience, that *life* and everything whatsoever rests on contradictions" (*KA* XII:321). So it is essential for irony that it be informed by an Absolute that it cannot contain; only "one who has sense for the infinite . . . whenever he expresses himself firmly, speaks nothing but contradictions" (*KA* II:243, frag. 412).

The endless becoming of the human world and of self-consciousness is an erratic, not a smoothly continuous process. "Every development, every ascent, every self-strengthening becoming that hastens its own growth *must finally reach its goal; if once this is reached and becoming is still however necessary, then it springs, since it* cannot go further, either *back into its own, but transformed, beginning, or over into its opposite*" (*KA* XII:417). Only through expression of this imperative, through the cultivation of Unverständlichkeit, can the forgetting of apparent truth be maintained as process. "All highest truths of every kind are thoroughly trivial and just for this reason is nothing more necessary than to express them always anew, and where possible, always more paradoxically, so that it not be forgotten, that they are still there, and that they can never be completely expressed" (*KA* II:366). Whether these are expressed in a dialogic, a systemic, a negating, or an ethical fashion will depend on the individual ironist.

As such, irony is a logical relation that takes precedence over all determinate contents, eventually even over itself as mere term. "Truth is related to *relationships*, not to *things*" (*KA* XVIII:410, frag. 1076). Irony, the "logical beauty" (*KA* II:152, frag. 42), desubstantializes the world, but even more significantly, self-consciousness itself. To the definition of irony as enactment, then, should be added the purpose of all irony, especially in its ethical form: an intentional decentering of the subject that operates as an opening out to the other. Novalis puts this well in a specifically literary context. "The true reader must be the extended author. He is the higher tribunal, which receives the matter from the lower tribunal already preworked" (N II:470, frag. 125). Communication is therefore not a function of intentionality or rhetoric alone. "[The synthetic writer] wants to make no specific effect on [the reader], but he enters with him into the holy relation of the most inner symphilosophy or sympoetry" (KA II:161, frag. 112). Schlegel's goal here, I would argue, is pursued in forums as diverse as Lacan's psychoanalytic theories or Meredith's novels. To speak of irony, with irony, one must recognize its essential bond to some form of intersubjective consciousness, what Schlegel here terms *conscience*.

This goal requires above all the "sense for others" that transcends reflective understanding. "Not understanding comes most often not at all from the lack of understanding, but from lack of sense" (KA II:176 frag. 78). It involves a renunciation of egocentricity that permits a divination of meaning, of common purpose in the other. "Divination is perhaps the principle of all experience—also inspiration—all understanding and discovery occurs thus" (KA XVIII:306, frag. 1352). To be able to pass to this stage, to be capable of communication or *Sympoesie* is the practical consequence of having sense for the Absolute. "All human beings are originally . . . things for us. To hold them for spirits is an original image to which we can approximate ourselves only in the infinite. Only in the proper relations do we spring over the stages up to the goal, and posit all human beings simply as spiritual" (KA XVIII:26, frag. 85). Out of such sense for others arises the initial fermentation in the subject from which a knowing and known self-consciousness can result. "The spiritual intuition is an immediate displacement into the other, where the *I* becomes the *You*; it is the sole creative element in consciousness" (KA XII:375). Intent, self-conscious linguistic interchange is the place where this mental agility comes to be realized, a process whose necessary transformation to awareness Schlegel sought to hold momentarily frozen in the concept of irony, a permanent perception of the time it takes for the growth of understanding: "That one person understands the other is philosophically inconceivable, doubtless, however, magical. It is the secret of divinization; the blossom of the one becomes seed for the other" (KA XVIII:253, frag. 713).

# The Subject in Romantic Narrative

*Without letter, no spirit; the letter only thereby to be overcome,*
*in that it be made flowing.*—(KA XVIII:344, frag. 274)

### Irony, Conscience and the Romantic Absolute

The entwining of irony and conscience accomplished by Schlegel's Jena and Cologne lectures is especially significant because it makes explicit the connection between irony and the status of the subject, the problematic nature of self-identity. This focus permits one to move irony out of the aesthetic realm to which it has generally been banished and to see it in the full complexity of its operation. Although it is true that Schlegel develops a conception "in which irony is understood as a special possibility of artistic shaping and as a means to and a sign of a special form of art,"[1] it must still be kept in mind that irony, as we have seen, had a variety of overtones for Schlegel. As we shall later see, irony retained these additional overtones—in explicit theory or implicit practice—for a series of writers concerned with the ironic subject. Much confusion in regard to Romantic irony, and irony in general, comes from not adequately discriminating these alternate emphases, which it is especially important to keep separate if one would analyze the entire Romantic project from an ironic perspective.

Irony is above all a certain way of dealing with the problem of the subject in language and its apparent communicative isolation. The confrontation of private and public perspectives was already evident in the opposition of Socrates, the first philosophical ironist, to the Sophists and recurs wherever irony comes to be treated in a philosophical and not merely rhetorical fashion. For irony is necessarily an intersubjective act of confrontation with and mediation through an other subject. Different varieties of irony, however, can engender radically different perspectives on this encounter and correspondingly divergent ideas of the status and limits of the individual subject.

What an exclusively aesthetic focus on irony perpetuates is the model of an isolated Romantic artist confronting nature,[2] in which the Romantic dilemmas can come to be seen as versions of an existentialist anguish or affirmation. Given this focus, the Romantic revolution is then seen as a shift from a depiction of surface to that of an inner essence, and as a shift from a mimetic to an expressive use of language.[3] The premise on which the latter must rest if it is to convey universal truth is that of a mental or spiritual congruence between humanity and nature, forcefully expressed by Wordsworth in the Preface to *The Excursion:*

> How exquisitely the individual Mind
> . . . to the external World
> Is fitted:—and how exquisitely, too—
> Theme this but little heard of among men—
> The external World is fitted to the Mind.

This attunement bridges gaps between the individual subject and nature, between part and whole, mortal and immortal, material and spiritual.

Conceived in such terms the problem of language to which irony responds is the adequacy of language to preexisting thought, or to an intuition whose maintenance is put into question by its very expression.[4] The initial problem for communication, then, is that of sincerity, the faithfulness to that which one intuits. However, this remains problematic in that all creations attempting to convey this are necessarily inadequate, for language inevitably partakes of the material. Such an outlook was already excoriated by Kierkegaard, who criticized Romantic irony as infinite absolute negativity because of its reliance on an unverifiable private criterion of truth.

Even the recent stress on a creative, romantic side of Romantic irony, its association with the imagination as its necessary correlate, has not really provided an adequate response to Kierkegaard's original charges. Though not pure negativity, the subject in its creations remains negative with respect to any absolute, as representation is to presence. Ironic creation is an evocation of that which, if it were present, would not need to be evoked. This creative irony attempts to recuperate that gap by employing self-representation, that is, the representation of the act of representation, in which the limits of that activity can be indicated and the Absolute sustained via implication.[5] What is actually represented by the subject, then, is its own illusion, and its essence becomes self-abnegation. Yet at the same time, the ironic subject seems to be fully adequate to its dilemma, absolute in regard to its own finite flounderings. Kierkegaard's critique remains valid. If all is conceived as process, which acquires a nonteleological structure when the Absolute is conflated with a Nature already complete in itself, and if the role of the subject is the repetitive utterance of the unchanging truth that truth is inaccessible, then the particular terms of that restatement, of that process, become irrelevant, and all evaluative and ethical distinctions vanish. Why privilege any one creation, any one irony, over another? What remains to be accomplished once the ironic transcendence has been achieved? An aesthetic ironist remains hemmed in by the bounds of a self-contenting narcissism.

To counter this, theories of Romanticism have also frequently stressed the positive gain in self-consciousness more characteristic of Idealism—Abrams's "spiral journey back home."[6] The stability of Romanticism as a critical term has been well established, most notably in the work of Wellek and Abrams.[7] Yet their separate responses to the reservations of Lovejoy about the coherence of the term *Romanticism* tend toward the homogenization of Romanticisms, and even of Romanticism and German Idealism. The Romantics generally share a common attitude toward Enlightenment reason and Kant's critique of that, above all in their reiteration of the limits of a materialist philosophy. Coupled with this reaction is a sense of the loss of universal truth and a perception of the individual as a fundamental unit.[8] The Romantics, however, reject Kant's severing of the transcendental realm from that of practical experience and share the consequent idealist inclinations. Yet it makes an enormous difference how they endeavor to reattach this realm and to what degree they make the individual a measure for all things, distinctions that the pursuit of a uniform Romanticism can easily blur.

Despite its stress on the individual, Romanticism, insofar as it remains ironic, is a critique of the isolation of the subject that anticipates the drift of much modern philosophy and criticism. Both irony and the imagination are associative capacities, however different their consequences may be. Yet Romanticism is not simply a version of either a Judeo-Christian or a Hegelian synthesis; it is never static, but an unending search for the positive value to be found in the maintenance of difference on every level, in process. The conflating of distinctive versions of Romanticism tends, however, to subsume the entire movement to a doctrine based on a transcendental ego and a maximum of self-presence which that implies. The isolation of the subject is combated by its extension to universal status, generally through the recovery of some more fundamental part of itself. Critics differ, to be sure, as to whether this synthesizing point is an accessible goal or a receding limit for various Romantics, but both creative and expressive theories maintain the centralizing focus of a stable ego, the synthesizing subject of Kant.[9] Given some basic insight into its own developing nature, its reach can be quantitatively, but not qualitatively, altered. For it always stands in the present, outside of the process of its own development, yet unable to see beyond that. Irony, especially ethical irony, is an alternative solution dispensing with the transcendental ego by fragmenting, rather than hypostasizing, the individual subject.

Behind this grappling with subjectivity is the Cartesian dualism of subject and object, now seen almost exclusively from the stance of the finite subject. Kant's philosophy had aggravated the split between subject and object by removing the latter from the realm of cognition as a *Ding-an-sich*. Consciousness, therefore, seems necessarily a fall from unity accompanied by a yearning for its restoration, what Abrams calls "the compulsion to closure."[10] The task for consciousness, then, is to reconcile itself with its object, to restore their reciprocity by canceling in some way the difference between them. The most obvious solution is that which we already saw privileged by theorists of creative irony—self-representation. The irreconcilability of dissimilar subject and object can apparently be avoided by converting the object into a relation, precisely the relation of subject and object, now unified in a reflective or intuitive act.

The transcendental ego emerges as the agent of relatedness and reconciliation, a self seemingly not caught up in the fragmenting subject-object dualism. It is grounded in a feeling of unity beyond discursive expression, so that a split may be conceded on the level of empirical (creative) consciousness, but only as a step toward the transcendental ego. Consciousness, taking as its object the subject-object relation, attains self-consciousness. It sees the object through itself and therefore as subjectivized, while the empirical ego absorbs the burden of materiality as an illusion. Put another way, the subject-object split is internalized as the difference between a demystified absolute subject and an illusion-bound empirical subject.[11]

The isolated subject is thus replaced by a universal one, but only by means of an absorptive monism, for the incongruence of the original terms has not been eliminated. Without having developed a reciprocity between the terms, any Romantic theory will tend toward a repression of one term or the other, whereby the transcendental ego comes to be identified with one or the other side of the original subject-object split. When merged with the object (Nature), it will remain opposed to finite consciousness, which retains a purely functional status. When identified with the subjective side (spirit or imagination), it will remain divorced from a material nature of similarly functional importance. One term is merely accommodated to the other.

In art, this split is replicated by the image of the poet as creator. The poetic work is both a creation out of nothing and an expression of the self, but a "heterocosm"[12] complicated by the fact that what it takes for its material is the self. Like the empirical subject, however, this self is materialized or fixed by being projected into the past. In the sublime distance maintained by the creative ego and the ability to treat even itself as mere material for shaping, the artist seems much nearer God than humanity.

Contrary to the resolution typical of either expressive or creative theories of Romanticism and Romantic irony, irony as conceived by Schlegel works toward dispersion of the transcendental ego. Unless it is recognized that a central strain of Romantic thought sought to leave behind expressive as well as mimetic theories of the subject's role in favor of a communicative theory of intersubjectivity, the full significance of the Romantic enterprise cannot be made clear. Schlegel was emphatic that every subject-object distinction must be attacked at its root. "Given a total difference between spirit and matter, the common product of both, the mental representation [Vorstellung], must be explained either entirely out of the one, or entirely out of the other" (KA XII:265).[13] The key romantic insight shared by Schlegel and Novalis is that there can be no subject-object division for the mind. "Where there is no self-recognition [Selbsterkenntnis], there is no recognizing at all; where there is self-recognition, the subject-object correlation is abolished, as one might say: a subject given without object-correlate."[14] All objects are already subjects insofar as they can be recognized at all by the subject and are subjects in the full sense of the term, as self-cognizant. "Every becoming-recognized of a thinking being presupposes its self-recognition."[15] Everything is subject, so that, in Schlegel's terms, the object is "potentialized." No independent subject can be isolated or stable, for it exists in that constant condition of dispersion that is relationship. Hence the subject, in its individuality, is fundamentally dependent on other self-consciousnesses for its development. It must enter into relation with them.

Relation is established in thought via reflection, which is a necessary mode of experience, in no sense simply a sickness.[16] Nor is reflection to be seen as a divisive activity, however dualistic its structure may be. "Identity of reflection—that it is not the case that one strand runs over into the other, that it is one thread" (*KA* XVIII:363, frag. 507). Since the terms *subject* and *object* arise simultaneously, there can be no precedence, temporal or intellectual, between them.[17] But reflection remains dual, both deriving from and deriving anew an originary difference that penetrates into being itself. "It is an absolute relation. Nothing in the world *simply is:* being does not express identity" (*N* III:378, frag. 622). Kant's Ding-an-sich as an identity is thus abolished from the realm of thought, not by its exclusion from the purview of reason, but through its interpenetration as subject with the entirety of things, its subsumption into relationship both with itself and with other things. This being-in-relation constitutes the subjectivity of the object, which Benjamin relates explicitly to the constitution of ironic consciousness. "To observe a thing means only to move it to self-recognition. . . . . One ought to name this magical observation in the Romantics' sense also an ironic one. That is, it observes in its object nothing particular, nothing specific."[18] That observing stance involves a restraint on the part of the subject of the desire for unity, the wish to occupy the place of a transcendental ego. What it necessitates is a renunciation of the possibility of knowledge in favor of recognition. Fichte's *Wissenschaftslehre* becomes *Erkenntnistheorie.*

The act of reflection goes one step beyond self-consciousness to take self-consciousness itself as an object, opening up the double possibility of an infinitely regressive ego and a dialectic of intersubjectivity that can serve to provide limits for it.[19] This reflective repetition is characteristic of Schlegel's and Novalis's terminology, where *Poesie der Poesie* and the representation of representation are more than narcissistic self-elaboration. The subject is not just materialized (represented), but spiritualized (displaced) through the interpretive act of an other subject, because it is representing itself for that other.[20] The communication involved in (ironic) creation involves a progress toward making tangible the virtual unity of all self-consciousness. For the premise that everything is subject does not directly eliminate the partial character of any individual subject, whose task is to realize a condition of total subjectivity that exists only in potential form.[21] The subject has no direct access to such an Absolute, which hence cannot serve even a regulative function, for ideal unity does not preexist its coming-into-being. The subject's relation to it is that of faith or belief, a religious, but nontheological rapport. Aesthetic activity is no longer a place of impartial and detached observation, but a realm of practical ethical interaction.

The dispersion of the transcendental ego is accompanied by a parallel denial of any transcendental terminology. From the standpoint of Romantic irony, no particularity is valid, even that opposing self and universe.[22] Any definition by which these terms are made precise will itself lead to a new duality. For dualism is fundamental and irreducible, though infinitely reformulable, since it reflects the essential fragmentation of the self.[23] Not in merging or synthesis, but in reversal, is that ironic insight maintained. Yet that may be the most difficult demand of all, given the logical disposition of the mind toward unity, toward being wholly there where it is, however partial and one-sided this location may really be.[24]

Given the situation of the individual subject and the untenability of universalization, there are two possible exits from isolation. The first is temporal: to contain over time, successively, what consciousness cannot conceive simultaneously.[25] Yet this tends toward a valorization of the present, as sooner or later the locus of wisdom. The past ego can be embraced by the current one in a way the former can never contain the latter, which mounts inexorably toward transcendental status. Alternatively, the duality characteristic of the self can be sustained by projection of a portion of the self into something external—be it a work of art or another subject. Hegel criticized the former alternative as Romantic aestheticism, arguing that it is impossible to compensate for the deficient subjecthood of the artwork, and inaugurating the series of repudiations of the self-duplicity of Romantic irony.[26] Yet his argument, in that it stresses the materiality of the artwork, misses (as do even subsequent defenses of Romantic irony) the important way in which irony can draw otherness into the act of projection. The other subject, implicitly in the ironic text or explicitly in ironic enactment, serves as the ideal locus of projection, for its refusal to be made material reflects back to the self a truer analogue of its own nature as process, as necessary and eternal dualism, as irony.

Irony is this enactment by the subject of its relation to the Absolute.

Though all four of Schlegel's ironies in some measure fit this definition, they do not do so in the same way.[27] But only that text will be fully ironic that depicts such enactment, focusing on the effort of the subject to comprehend itself through realization of its necessary interpenetration with otherness. Without unironically restricting the fluidity of the elements of the above definition, some precision of their content may prove useful before proceeding to their application on particular Romantic texts.

The Absolute may comprise the unification attained either as total consciousness (truth) or total self-consciousness. It represents the most radical contrary to the individual subject in its finitude and relative ignorance, and consequently operates more as a goad than a goal, almost inconceivable to the subject. "Self-consciousness in the larger sense is a task—an ideal—it would be *the* condition, *in which* there were no progression of time, a timeless—*persisting*, always identical condition" (*N* III:431, frag. 832). As Novalis's description implies, the Romantic ironic relation to the Absolute is different from that of Idealism. The Absolute is ineffable and decentered, at least for discursive reason; it does not exist. "What would be absolutely transcendent cannot exist" (*KA* XVIII:82, frag. 634). The subject remains in a position of dependence with regard to the Absolute that implicitly contains it, yet it is not necessarily cut off from it, for it is also true that "that world is already here" (*KA* XVIII:285, frag. 1067). *How* that other world of unity is here is precisely the problem irony, with its ability to convey incommensurables, must be invoked to resolve. Since the subject is that which is *nur Stückweise da*, access to the Absolute can be achieved only in human terms, as that mixture of fantasy and logic that is human understanding.

Enactment is the presentation for another in a particular dramatic or interactive form of the epistemological dilemmas of the subject as relevant to this particular relation between subjects.[28] It involves the conversion of the subject's relation to an ineffable Absolute into a relation with a much more effable, but still ambiguous, other subject. "*Irony* is, as it were, the ἐπίδειξις of infinity, of universality, from the sense for the cosmos" (*KA* XVIII:128, frag. 76). This epideictic indirection of irony is based on the premise that there is no passively intuitive access to the Absolute. Representation, unlike conceptualization, is not inherently monist, for it always implies two centers, and aims at communication, not simply expression. "Should, through representation, that occur in the other which occurred in us, then it has reached the aim of communication" (*KA* XII:102). But even this is not enough, for enactment must also raise the other to the status of authority in an act of generosity that is a surrender of its own centrality. Parabasis is not the core of irony, but merely literalizes what always occurs in true ironic interchange. Its essence is not the interruption of illusion, but the opening up of space for the response of the audience and their inclusion in the communicative act.

Enactment is the only way the subject can realize its status—the self-contradiction of being both self and other—without the temporal hiatus of conscious reflection. It makes the successive duality of the self seem simultaneous and permits a continual regaining of difference for and in the subject. Full self-consciousness is attained through the internalizing of the other as difference, so that the subject comes to see itself as a locus of difference. For the integrity created by synthetic consciousness suggests that the Absolute is, or could somehow be, in the subject, or alternatively, that it is wholly inaccessible. In the communicative act, this integrity expands to include the other, but first only as a facet of its own unity. So the response of the other is crucial, for there consciousness is reflected back as an other's consciousness of my consciousness, a restructuring of the self that is sensed initially as continuity, for the subject continues to project its initial integrity. Only the full reabsorption of the reflected consciousness and its comparison with what was originally projected makes difference evident, along with the recognition that the subject has, however briefly, been in the position of the other in looking at itself. This is an ironic and not empathic shift of roles, for what makes it effective is the temporary adoption by the other of the reflective position, its endeavor to catch and reconvey what the subject originally projected, now necessarily altered in perspective. From this interaction, regardless of where the "correct" view may lie, the subject emerges with a recognition of the possibility of active restructuring, at least insofar as it remains ironically aware of the alterations that have taken place. The other is therefore finally an embodiment of the Absolute as *possibility* and not as presence. This permits the reappropriation of the Absolute as a creation of the subject (though not identical to it), which it created by performing the initial act of generosity. The Absolute is not hypostasized out there as a synthetic moment, but the fundamental dualism of reflection is transformed to a monism of process, an active and total dialectical interpenetration.[29]

The Absolute must then be rediscovered in its movement and continual absence if the subject is not to be pushed toward one pole or the

other of its epistemological continuum. It is torn between what it feels it is
(as object) and what it senses it could be (as subject), but the true ironist is
not more one than the other.[30] His subjectivity is comprised by a *schwebende* (hovering) and not a transcendental ego, not even a transcendent
ironic ego. Despite this, there is always the temptation to move toward
either one pole or the other, the visionary or the sophistic stance. For the
visionary, the Absolute is tangibly present (though how it is present divides, for example, Wordsworth from Blake), a position tending toward
systemic irony. For the sophist, the Absolute is postulated with no guarantees of its presence in any form, so that all is relativized and he culminates
in negative irony. But both alternatives leave out a key aspect of irony—
that it has to do with communication and consensus. Irony is for another
person; one cannot be ironic with oneself (except insofar as the subject is
already fragmented), for one already knows what lies behind any ironic
utterance, and the process of explication that constitutes irony cannot
therefore take place. Irony is the realization that the opposite of whatever
one says may be just as true—or there would be no need to be ironic. Full
irony never obliterates an alternative; it is the condition of being between.

The ironic conscience, then, is an Absolute irreducible to specification that can still serve as a basis for human interaction. It relativizes the
Absolute by posing a universality-claim for life itself based on the intrinsic absoluteness of every experience. It is the practical presence of a polarity between an outer voice and an inner dictum, "an inner independent
power and a condition outside of *ordinary* individuality" (*N* III:448, frag.
934) where the subject's role becomes their harmonizing. Where the visionary tends to equate conscience with the absolute law of duty, the
sophist privileges the inner dictum of desire. Ethical irony, however, is
born of the recognition of the mutual dependence of self-consciousness
and a force outside it whose validity, however, it guarantees—a necessary
yet provisional authority. Without identifying the force with any other
subject or fixed creed, the subject remains in constant search of it, what
Hörisch calls a *Dialogzustand*, a condition of dialogue.[31] Ironic conscience is
the displacement of the dependence of the subject on an ineffable Absolute into the realm of intersubjectivity, the conversion of a negative epistemological dilemma into a positive socializing one.

How conscience can be both an outer voice and an inner dictum and
whether the balance between them can be maintained are the questions
that will focus my analysis of a set of Romantic texts. All four are varia-

tions of the *Lehrjahre* model, yet differ from it in that they lack a *Turmge-sellschaft* to serve as a final guiding force. Schlegel's *Lucinde*, Novalis's *Heinrich von Ofterdingen*, Wordsworth's *Prelude*, and Carlyle's *Sartor Resartus* all depict apprentices without masters; as a group they demonstrate a range of ways of locating the Absolute and the consequences of this for the subject. My concern will be for the patterns of intersubjectivity enacted within these texts and the modes by which they put conscience into practice.[32]

    *Lucinde* depicts an irony of relationship that is based on the double presence of the self to itself in role-exchange. As such, it is the model for all ironic intersubjectivity, a dialogue format where lyric effusion provokes communicative breakdowns, thus forcing investigation of the mechanisms of relationship. Lucinde is here the outer voice that channels Julius's growth into self-consciousness. *Heinrich von Ofterdingen* stresses a hermeneutic act of mutual completion that opens out beyond the particular relationship and beyond the text. It is perhaps the most successfully ironic of these texts, for it moves beyond the immediacy of the subject to a generalized notion of conscience. The novel continually relocates an outer voice displaced from one source to another, but always there. This displacement allows Novalis to confront the most radical type of otherness, death, and to question the adequacy of any human resolution via replacement. *The Prelude* internalizes the process of imaginative enactment so that the subject becomes the site of the whole drama of duality. Wordsworth's polarity of man and nature seems continually threatened by the disproportion between its terms, which pass between isolation and absorption as Wordsworth balances between dialogic and systemic irony. *Sartor Resartus* indicates the difficulty involved in Wordsworth's effort to contain an ironic dualism within a single subject. Carlyle formalizes dualism, operating with metaphoric analogies that collapse its tension and lead to a valorization of its terms. His irony is basically a negative one, directed at replacing an inadequate reality with an unnameable Absolute. The outer voice is incarnated for him by the hero, whose shadow stretches over and eventually blots out the spirit of irony, there fully transformed into conviction.

### *Lucinde* and the Irony of Love

    The publication of *Lucinde* in 1799 was notable mainly for the book's *succès de scandale*. Viewed as a paean to sensuality, and an autobiographical one at that, it was widely read and nearly as widely censured in Schlegel's lifetime. Serious attention to the complex philosophical, aesthetic, and ironic issues with which it deals was further deterred by the chaotic structure of Julius's letters to Lucinde and meditations on love.[33] Nor was the reaction entirely unjustified, for the Absolute here takes the form of love, portrayed as the meeting point of spiritual and physical.

Lucinde concretely manifests this absoluteness for Julius, serving as a projection of his own ego into the world that makes possible a dramatic treatment of the psychological dynamics of the subject. "You feel everything entirely and infinitely, you know of no separations, your being is one and indivisible" (*KA* V:11), says Julius, recognizing that she has sated his *Liebe ohne Gegenstand*. Her ability to merge opposites and display a unity is what attracted Julius to her, who creates himself as a unity by drawing all his thoughts and actions back to her. Lucinde mediates the distance between the individual subject and the absolute subject as "the mediatress . . . between my fragmented I and the indivisible eternal humanity" (*KA* V:71). But her role is a complex one, for she also tends to move from mediator to the place of the Absolute itself, to be identified as an adequate goal in herself. "First of all, that I idolize you, and that it is good that I do so" (*KA* V:71).

This latter aspect is especially in evidence in the beginning of the novel, where the absolutizing of Lucinde serves as a counterpoint for Julius's own narcissism, either of which can undermine the dialectic intersubjectivity and the irony of the text. The ostensible aim of Julius in *Lucinde* is the recovery of the feeling of an absent totality, a loss born of Lucinde's unexplained absence. Julius anticipates no problems in this and chooses to recount to her his own ascent from egoism to wisdom and harmony through love. He undertakes to provide her with a lyric celebration of his concluded *Lehrjahre*, a spirit now so ordered in its content that he feels impelled to create disorder in the structure of the letters, lest monotony intervene (*KA* V:9). Julius wishes to become a composite Wilhelm Meister–Goethe, both observer of and participant in his own past.

Yet, in its faithfulness to the dynamics of relationship, *Lucinde* moves beyond this expressive, celebratory Romanticism toward the possibility of ethical irony. As the novel progresses, it becomes increasingly evident that the ascended height of love can be maintained only insofar as both subjects remain equal and separate, with neither absolute. For the metaphor of organic wholeness, where Julius and Lucinde become flowers or leaves of a single plant (*KA* V:12), must come to be supplemented by a fuller organic myth, one that comprises the necessary diversity implied in fertilization. "Love is higher than charm, and how soon would the bloom of beauty wither fruitlessly without the completing formation [*Bildung*] of opposed love [*Gegenliebe*]!" (*KA* V:60).[34] What unity presages is a recognition of separation and of its necessity that will blast apart the unitary subject and its pretensions to sublime omniscience, while giving Julius occasion for writing the novel itself.

There are hints even early in the novel that totality involves some sort of repression or exclusion. As in the mind "one thing represses the other, and what just now was entirely near and present, sinks soon back into darkness" (*KA* V:11), so, too, in relationship is total presence of consciously understood experience a myth. There are multiple possibilities for the subject, but they are all partial and finite.[35] In consequence, the most beautiful situation, whose description makes up the first chapter of the novel, is the exchange of roles, "when we exchange roles and compete with childish pleasure, [to see] who can more deceitfully mimic the other" (*KA* V:12). The full significance and the dynamics of this role-exchange are not yet clear even to Julius, but what is clear is that Schlegel's model is far from an Identitätsphilosophie. The characters clearly are not meant to merge into one another or into a shared understanding. Schlegel persistently moves from a posited or desired unity to the reality of an ironic, partial subject and seeks those modes for its completion that are actualizable.

When one looks more closely, in fact, the harmonious texture of the novel begins to unravel, and the lyricized rapture of unity becomes suspiciously similar to narcissism. Unity may be an attainable state, but the normal human condition here is separation. Lucinde, in fact, is absent from the text except as addressee in all but three of the thirteen chapters. The introductory lyric of love breaks down and indicates its role as a mere prelude to the realization that Lucinde is not there. Nor is this absence innocent, for Julius continues to attempt to fill it up with his own personality, as the lyric has already done. The dialogue of love is in reality a text composed of one-sided letters, where Lucinde never acquires an independent voice. Its function is to enable Julius to form his own past and through that narration to attain self-knowledge. Though Schlegel insisted that Goethean irony was not characteristic of his novel,[36] that sort of systemic overview is exactly what Julius, in concluding his autobiography, claims to possess. "It became light inside him, he saw and looked over all the masses of his life and the articulated structure of the whole clearly and correctly, because he stood in the middle" (*KA* V:57). His third person narration of his own life, as though above and beyond it, further reinforces this impression.

The risk of such self-narration is that even though Julius concedes a role to Lucinde as impetus to his self-development, he refrains from granting her an integral identity as other than himself. The other subject becomes an aspect of his own ego and loses its otherness in the narcissistic self-extension of fantasy. Lucinde recognizes this absorption in the second of their two encounters, at the very moment of Julius's rhapsody. "Not I, my Julius, am the one whom you so holily paint. . . . You are it, it is the wonder-flower of your fantasy which you in me, who am always yours, then catch sight of, when the tumult is veiled and nothing ordinary distracts your high spirit" (*KA* V:78–79). This lapse at the very height of their love suggests that the subject, however far it may extend itself, remains limited by its own nature and hence cut off from the Absolute except as an abstract ideal. Julius seems locked into a narcissism akin to that by which he first defends his overexuberance, that of the child Wilhelmina, whose self-sufficiency and naive mimesis are far from fully developed role-exchange. Wilhelmina hears only the inner dictum. Kierkegaard criticized exactly this in the novel, though he focused on the self-indulgent sensuality of Julius's earlier lover, Lisette.[37]

Schlegel himself, however, suggests that limitation on narcissism, for Lisette falls in love with Julius and, lost in his narcissism and without an independent self-identity, commits suicide when she feels he has renounced her.[38] Indeed, the further action of *Lucinde* makes an identical judgment, for when Lucinde is actually present, she and Julius enact an ironic intersubjectivity that goes beyond and negates Julius's epistemological hubris and lyricism. Julius, and even the events of the novel, are not themselves ironic, but the text nonetheless exhibits the mechanisms of the ironic consciousness so prominent in Schlegel's thought at this time. The process by which this occurs is actual role play, by which a more than intellectual or sympathetic relation with another subject is established. Role-exchange involves actually taking the place of the other, by which the hero is decentered, his own proclaimed aim and self-knowledge undermined.[39]

This strategy is most clearly brought out in the "Treue und Scherz" chapter, near the center of the novel, where Lucinde makes her first physical appearance. This chapter precedes and implicitly comments on the "Lehrjahre" chapter, for unlike *Wilhelm Meister*, the "Lehrjahre" here do not constitute the whole narrative, but are instead enclosed by expanding frames of signification, a mobile context of six preceding and six following chapters which keep its meaning fluid. "Treue und Scherz" reveals the nature of conscience as a force governing intersubjective relations, acutely demonstrating how subject and other interact in practice. The meaning of the chapter emerges in the fragmentation of the self by conscience, the prior existence of the other in the self. The subject depends for its recognition of this, however, on involvement with some specific other. Furthermore, a part of the subject that seems to lie at its center, desire, is shown to produce effects alien to the presumed integrity of the self. Irony, then, is the recognition of the consequent ambivalence of the simplest interaction. It demolishes the model of a transcendental ego possessing full access to its own intentions and motives.

"Treue und Scherz" opens with Julius breaking in on Lucinde and begging her erotic attentiveness to him. He is responding to the inner voice of his own desire, so preemptory that it will not even permit her to speak. Lucinde, however, reacts in a withdrawn manner, adopting a position the subject never can vis-à-vis itself, that of the enigma, or here, the coquette. She hides behind conventional morality, setting the stage for a confrontation that will be both serious (Treue) and playful (Scherz), both particular and universal, thus providing multiple perspectives on a particular situation that lead not to fragmentation or relativism but to consensus. This confrontation is also ironic, in that the positions are not stable but reversible; the agon is prized as the fullest interaction, and not for its outcome alone.

The lovers first accomplish a preliminary resolution, which is flawed, however, in that it deals only with the here and now. Lacking a reason in the immediate situation to resist, Lucinde gives herself over to Julius's desire, but not without significant byplay. Julius compares her to a judge, a role she refuses at this point. As she gives in, she makes the startling shift to the formal *Sie* form in addressing Julius, as Schlegel indicates even on the grammatical level the inequality of the relationship at this moment. It is a master-slave dialectic, the full surrender of Lucinde who is overcome by the scent of hyacinths in the room, a tangible manifestation of Julius's narcissism. Her forgetfulness of herself in his narcissistic desire extends even to remorse for her earlier resistance.

This initial reconciliation, however, does not permit the canceling of the past and of its disquieting disharmony. Julius's continual editing out of difference from his text is no longer so secure once Lucinde is there. She brings out the real fragmentation of the subject, which is a temporal one, that which one, in time, forgets. As prelude to the subsequent deepening of intersubjectivity, Lucinde's recalcitrance is discussed in terms of the will, which has an uncontrollable and dual nature, either good or bad. Lucinde's annoyance, and her independent identity, reemerge when Julius attempts to explain her behavior by using conventional sexual roles. She recalls that her actions are not exhaustible by any such reductive theory and converts the abstract discussion of Will into a dramatic test of wills.

The specific cause of her earlier coldness remains concealed, however, until Julius takes the first step of commenting on her pathos and eloquence. His request for an explanation of her conduct is his recognition of her and of her enigmatic status. He perceives the limitation of his outside knowledge of her and acknowledges her status as subject via an implicit acceptance of her integrity, her ability to provide an explanation of her behavior. What emerges as the source of the disharmony is that Julius's behavior the prior day remains inscribed, but unresolved, on Lucinde's mind. She thus possesses a portion of him that his own ego refused to acknowledge or remember.

So Lucinde accepts Julius's offer to reverse roles, putting him in her own initial position; he played the coquette at the prior night's party. She censures not his flirtation per se, however, but his impoliteness and unresponsiveness to her, the signs of his guilty conscience. Her earlier behavior replicated or parodied precisely that in Julius which annoyed her. Julius was divided against himself, made awkward by Lucinde's visible displeasure, when her disapproving mood passed over to him, and hence he ignored her. He displayed an inability to reconcile himself as isolated subject with his larger role as part of a couple. He ignored the voice of conscience and forgot Lucinde, as in fact the entire novel has been doing.

His response is yet another self-creation, but one that for the first time includes Lucinde without absorbing her. This self-justification is an ironic one, based on the contrast between Treue and Scherz and an affirmation of a necessary dualism. It is also a denunciation of bourgeois love relationships, where others become appendages of an omnivorous ego and passion is repressed.[40] After asserting the inviolability of fidelity, he develops a defense of flirtatious wit as well, basing it on the fundamental difference between men and women. Differences, and not the least sexual ones, need to be acknowledged and brought to consciousness, at least in Scherz. At the same time, Julius rejects the jealousy evidenced by Lucinde as an unwarranted restriction on relations within the human world, an unjustified limitation of difference to a single couple.

This acknowledgment is essential because desire and self-will lie at the root of human nature. "The human being is by nature an earnest beast" (KA V:34). Elsewhere, Schlegel locates the essence of individuality not in reason or even the imagination but in passion. "*Fantasy* is a too general character. Our determination must lie more in passion" (KA XVIII:430, frag. 42). Scherz, by bringing these divisive elements into the open, makes them accessible to consciousness, just as enactment brings out the fundamental split within the subject. In both cases, the directive force of that which remains in the unconscious is diminished. The effort to repress the multiplicity of forces within the subject, on the other hand, leads to errors like that of Julius at the party. The acknowledgment of difference in aims, in feelings, in beliefs, is what permits consensus to emerge. "Society is a chaos, that is only to be formed and brought into harmony through wit; and if one does not jest and flirt with the elements of passion, it balls itself into thick masses and darkens everything" (KA V:35). One might also add, that unless these expressive acts are mediated in ironic interplay, full integration remains only potential.

But the specific content of Julius's explanation is less important than the recognition that it implies of Lucinde's status as a partner in interpretation. The resolution of discord is a linguistic one, where behavior is converted into an understanding that can then be reapplied to future behavior. The initial disagreement, and Lucinde's refusal to surrender it, serve as an impetus to a heightened self-consciousness, a subject more aware for having passed through otherness on its way to a self-estimation. One problem remains unanswered, however, for the final reconciliation depends not so much on the speech of Julius as on an already existing agreement to which it pays tribute, a willingness to restore and work from the basis of love in the relationship. The use of language and of the whole dialectic of self-representation seems dependent on some extralinguistic basis.

This is a paradox of irony, one built into the theory of the subject on which it is based.[41] Two subjects must already be attuned for it to work, actively displaying the mutuality it is ostensibly creating. Irony reinforces a preexisting harmony; it does not create a new one.

This analysis of "Treue und Scherz" may seem to overstress one particular aspect of Schlegel's fragmentary novel. Yet Schlegel himself indicates the centrality of this chapter by weaving into it religious elements notably absent from the remainder of the text. A full communion with the gods can be made possible only through the resolution of difference into understanding. Thus, the libation to the gods which Julius wishes to make before his discourse on jealousy is held off, at Lucinde's request, until that speech has restored the equilibrium between them. Once again her sensitivity to the fragility and importance of full, dual harmony seems greater than that of Julius.

Furthermore, the image of love as born of strife and maintained as difference is sustained throughout the balance of the novel and in Schlegel's philosophical writings. The chapter entitled "Metamorphosen" follows the "Lehrjahre" and with "Treue und Scherz" frames it, reinforcing in an allegorical form what has occurred on the narrative level in Julius's and Lucinde's encounter. In it, the child begins as the echo of its own desire, a narcissism reminiscent of both Wilhelmina and Julius. But by passing through a sea of forgetfulness, the metaphorical equivalent of a fully enacted role-exchange where the unconscious can appear, the child emerges into a new golden age, one not of unity but of *Gliederbau*, reticulation. This construction incorporates the division and difference that alone can give the subject a measure of its own status. In terms of the novel, the divisive power is love, for the longing for unity that begets it should not be allowed to obliterate the difference fundamental to subjectivity which it brings to light. "Not hate, as the wise say, but love separates beings and forms the world, and only in its light can one find and look at it [the world]" (*KA* V:61). Only the assumption of harmony between subjects leads to the recognition of the difference fundamental to each. Hence misunderstandings and strife are good, for they permit the internalization of difference and the recognition of the fundamental dispersion of subjectivity attained in love. "Misunderstandings are also good, so that the holiest things may once come into speech" (*KA* V:64).

This conclusion is carried over to the philosophical systems of Schlegel and Novalis. Both insist that the unity of an Absolute is something that lies before us and emerges only out of division; their novels provide us with a model for the intersubjectivity by which that can be reached. "The crossing over from monotony to harmony will admittedly go through disharmony—and only at the end will a harmony arise" (N II:546, frag. 111).[42] In terms of the subject, this means that only the fullest ironic recognition of its own fragmentation and resultant interpenetration with others can serve to elevate it out of an illusory transcendental status toward a positive and perpetual reenactment of difference.

The second half of *Lucinde* displays a more pronounced dualism, both in structure (two-part chapters) and theme (an additional quarrel with another friend). Yet in a real sense, the novel remains at the level of dialogic irony, what Schlegel himself calls an irony of form alone, which he hoped in a continuation to bring over into the content (KA IX:238, frag. 78). For Julius continues to tend to absolutize particular differences—as between himself and Lucinde or between men and women—without leaving space for the full exchange of traits between them. As it stands, *Lucinde* also restricts the play of irony to a particular pair of persons, though Schlegel considered this text to be a fragment he hoped to expand, which his notes indicate might have emerged very differently had he ever completed it. For a concrete instance of how that completion might have appeared, we can perhaps turn to Novalis's more fully articulated though still fragmentary novel, *Heinrich von Ofterdingen*.

## *Heinrich von Ofterdingen* and the Irony of Awakened Conscience

Despite the closeness of both their personal relationship and philosophical speculations, the aesthetic production of Schlegel and Novalis is markedly divergent. *Heinrich von Ofterdingen* can be read as an implicit critique of *Lucinde*, the appearance of which served as an additional incitement to Novalis's own novel. For the intersubjectivity of the couple depicted in *Lucinde* is at best a limited dialectic, and Schlegel's own hero demonstrates the perpetual tendency of any such fixated duality to collapse into one or the other pole. Even were it possible to sustain that duality, the resultant subjectivity would remain incomplete, "for also the inwardness of private happiness is only an anticipation of that cosmic happiness, which poetry must lead up into the world."[43]

Novalis therefore pursues a broader perspective, going so far as to reject the Lehrjahre model outright. "The word *Lehrjahre* is false—it expresses a specific *whither*"(*N* IV:281). Though Heinrich embarks on a journey, it is an endless one that takes him *immer nach Hause*, without ever arriving at that residence of a transcendental ego. This openness extends to the subject as well, radically altered by the recognition that any individual is replaceable. So Novalis's novel will be the story of the discovery of self not in love but in its loss, through which a yet more complete dispersion of the Absolute is effected. Yet Novalis builds on Schlegel's foundation; as Heinrich says to his love, Mathilde, echoing Julius, "My eternity is indeed your work" (*N* I:284). This dispersion to which the love relation is subject is possible because of Novalis's full assurance of the omnipresence of an outer voice that speaks in all things, an assurance the love relationship serves to confirm. Separation or isolation are momentary lapses, from which the subject always recovers.

*Heinrich von Ofterdingen* is also more strongly allegorical than *Lucinde*, for the products of imagination and the events are exhibited in constant, kaleidoscopic interchange.[44] The novel has a curiously dreamlike quality to it, for all levels of imagination and fact are blended together, reinforcing and mutually conditioning one another. Yet the influence of Novalis's mystical tendencies, his pursuit of a "magical Idealism," should not be overemphasized, because for him vision counts only to the degree that it becomes part of life, and hence of interpretive approximation. "Dream and fantasy are to be forgotten—one ought not to abide there—least of all *eternalize* it. . . . I, too, cannot avoid *sleep*—but I still rejoice in the awakening and would *secretly* wish always to *be awake*" (*N* IV:280).[45]

The juxtaposition and integration of oppositions take place here not only on the intellectual level but also on the narrative one, making *Heinrich* a more successful novel than *Lucinde*. It is epic, enacting the approach to the Absolute, rather than the lyric celebration of its presence. The poet activates the latent unity in everything around him by mediating contradictions through their analogical restatement, by confronting and restating apparent contradictions.[46] This possibility of continual terminological displacement reveals that indeterminacy and paradox are only relative consequences of a stable point of view. The insistent repetition of patterns within the novel is not only recurrence but also always extends them into a new realm of significance, which renews the stabilizing patterns.

Despite Novalis's mysticism, or perhaps because of it, the Absolute never appears absolutely in his text. It is always caught up in a process of signification and application, which enriches rather than diminishes its value. As several motifs, such as the frequent question-and-answer format or the Sphinx in the "Märchen," make clear, the novel is oracular rather than visionary. In addition, any appearance of the Absolute is mediated for Heinrich by some specific other; it finds its origin as well as its applicability only with and through another. These visions are deepened and displaced throughout the novel into an increasingly personal, but also increasingly wide-ranging, frame of reference. The same is true of characters, who recur in later guises that can blend several prior personages, continually expanding the relevance of each element in Heinrich's life. His own experience is a similar broadening, as he passes from son to lover to mourner to father, where each stage absorbs prior ones without negating them. Visions serve, then, not as culminations or transcendental foci of significance but as an impetus to parting and a new stage of experience, which can serve to attach their indeterminacy. Mahr points to a sustained split between the subject in his private and in his public role. "Of a dissolution of reality, of an eternal love in the loveliest covering . . . Heinrich speaks only in regard to his love and his personal happiness, never in connection with poetry."[47] The vision must not be given any permanent subsistence, but must be worked into life, into communal relevance, which is a constant *Übergang zum Endlichen*, a going-over into the finite, not into paradise.

The Absolute always poses for Novalis the hermeneutic question of application. Self-consciousness is acquired through the internalization of an outer voice, its harmonizing with that subject attending to it.[48] This interaction with an outside, an other subject is the most striking trait of all of Novalis's philosophizing. For him, it is the only way to self-knowledge. "One studies alien systems in order to find *one's own* system" (N III:278, frag. 220). This mediation of the subject by an other can occur only when that other is seen as also being a subject and hence capable of full role-exchange, complete dialogic interpretation of another. "We should transform all into a You—a second I—only thereby do we raise ourselves to the Great I—that is *one* and all alike" (N III:314, frag. 398). This equality permits the self-representation that is the real content of any vision to be mediated via its communication into an adequately generalized expression of a more than subjective truth.

This interpretive process necessarily seems endless for the individual, for its conclusion would abolish the duality characteristic of the subject.[49] It typically begins as a response to some excitation from outside, some concrete appearance that the subject takes for absolute. Responding to this stimulus with a heightened imaginative energy, the subject converts it into a personal allegorical vision or fantasy. This, in turn, acts as a motivating force on the subject, a reaching out into the world to make sense of its vision. Interpretation then follows as a confrontation of the ego with the restructuring of its model by some specific other; Heinrich's development into a poet is in large part a measure of how well he succeeds in reaching a point of balance between inner and outer. Since Novalis lived only long enough to complete part 1 and one chapter of part 2, Heinrich seems more often passively receptive than actively engaged in this interpretive act. The Golden Age would be brought toward reality by being made an intersubjective possibility, in which what was first sensed as foreign to the subject would become fully integrated with its own expanding self-consciousness.

The risk of this engagement with another in interpretation is that the result will be reductive, that the vision will be brought too fully down to earth and become significatively fixed. This is made evident in the first of the four visionary experiences in the novel, the dream of the blue flower.[50] The mysterious stranger, whose tales seem to strike only Heinrich as exceptional, acts as a stimulus to Heinrich, whose senses pass over into an imaginative riot that attains clarity only when he slips into dreaming. After a chaotic vision of his own future life, the dream acquires stability in a narrative structure of ascent, penetration, immersion, and slumber, whereupon the vision in the vision comes to him as a dream of a wondrous blue flower that contains a face at its center. On being awakened, Heinrich exhibits no nostalgia for his dream, but engages at once in a debate with his parents on the significance of dreams. His father denies their relevance to real life, seemingly negating their meaning by describing them as purely subjective fantasies. This is the question interaction must answer: whether that vision emerging from the subject can be given any objectively valid status as more than mere self-representation.

Reminded by his wife of a dream of his own, the father proceeds to recall with remarkable clarity a dream nearly identical to Heinrich's own.[51] The function of this repetition, as throughout the novel, is to break down the coherence of self-identity and to demonstrate the already existing elements of intersubjectivity. The difference between the dreams lies in the responses of father and son. Where Heinrich leaves his dream interpretively open, deliberately undetermined, his father filled his dream at once with determinate content—the image of Heinrich's mother, whom he then sought out and married. His restriction of its play of signification is typified by his entire life, that of a not entirely contented artisan who might have been an artist.

The father thus provides a negative model on how the Absolute may be brought into life, which Heinrich's second dream begins to correct. Arrived in Augsburg at the home of his grandfather and already in love with Mathilde, Heinrich has a dream that makes more explicit the proper mode of access to the Absolute. He dreams of Mathilde's drowning, his despairing search for her, and the sudden recovery of her beneath the water, where she seals their eternal love with a kiss and a word. "She spoke a wonderful secret word into his mouth, which rang through his whole being. He wanted to repeat it, when his grandfather called, and he awoke. He would have liked to give his life, still to know the word" (N I:279). But it is of the essence of the Absolute that the word be irrecoverable, that the subject engage in an endless effort to pronounce it.

Its image, however, has become clear and real in Mathilde, whose mediatory role in conveying the word to Heinrich is evident. The dream itself is structured by ironic reversals—passive to active, over to under— which presage the active power Heinrich must seek to enact and to acquire. The dream also corrects a too optimistic estimation of the adequacy of private bliss. The problem that will necessarily confront the subject is the nonsubsistence of any individual, itself included, and the tendency to view that condition as one of irreparable loss. Mathilde drowns in time, which is both the condition of possibility for self-consciousness and the medium of its obliteration.

Death, as Novalis's own life made him feel acutely, is the one obstacle insurmountable by the individual subject, so that his philosophy necessarily focuses on the possible modes of response to that unalterable fact. The dispersion of the subject at which he arrives is an anticipatory enactment of death itself and works itself out in the implementation of ethical irony as the basis for a bond between subjects. Death is the pervading motif of the novel, dominating both the Atlantis tale and the "Märchen," striking the spouses of both poet figures, Klingsohr and Heinrich, as well as the queen in Atlantis. Its necessity is the only question Heinrich asks of Sylvester in the last completed portion of the novel. "But did the mother have to die, so that the children could flourish, and does the father remain in eternal tears sitting alone at her grave?" (N I:327). Sylvester has no direct answer, though he will gradually steer the conversation around to the one compensatory device he recognizes. The avoidance of death is the tendency that the novel seeks to overcome, along with the related overvaluation of an integral self. The ability to accept death is a recognition of the completeness with which the individual can come to permeate his universe. "Death is transformation—*repression of the principle of individuality*—that now goes into a new, more durable, more capable binding" (N III:259, frag. 100). That new and superior connection, that one compensation Sylvester can offer to Heinrich, is conscience *(Gewissen)*.

The intimation of the centrality of death for the subject is shortly converted into the more abstract "Märchen" told by Klingsohr at Heinrich's request. Accepted by Mathilde as betrothed and by Klingsohr as apprentice in poetry, Heinrich is at the summit of his private bliss, which prepares him for a fuller recognition of his own status as subject. The "Märchen" is far too complex to analyze completely here, but a consideration of those elements relevant to the imagination and to death can demonstrate the widening scope of Novalis's perspective.[52] The fable opens amidst the apparent tranquility of a familial ideal, whose members represent allegorically the aspects of the mind, so that the tale serves as a depiction of the individual subject as well. Above this sphere is the realm of Arcturus, the star-king, and below it that of the Fates, spinning death. What the initial disconnection of the three levels indicates is a myth of self-sufficiency and personal immortality, which the "Märchen" will gradually transform into the awareness of the inadequacy of any isolated system to maintain itself. As long as the heavens and hell, eternal life and death, are kept apart by the mind perceiving them as negations of one another, their dialectic integration will remain impossible. The tranquility of the family scene is soon disturbed, however, by a loss of power in the heavens and an intimation of death, two versions of the single problem confronting the subject—the possibility and mode of its own subsistence.

The realm of the Fates is concealed behind the altar in the house, an attempt by the mind to use religion to repress any recognition of the inevitability of death. This was likewise the source of instability in the earlier tale of Atlantis told by Heinrich's fellow-travelers. The paradise in Atlantis was inevitably disturbed by the problem of the succession of the king, for his pride in his own heritage led him to perceive any suitor for his only daughter as inadequate, an inferior replacement for himself. The king, unifying force in his domain, became over time a hindrance to the continued mediation of opposites, an attitude grounded not only in pride but in a refusal to recognize his own mortality. To accept any heir is to move one step closer to death. Schwaning's song at the feast plays on the same motif from the other point of view, the resentment of youth at the repression forced on them by their elders, who refuse to admit the inevitability of succession.

The action of the "Märchen" begins with a signal from Arcturus to the earth, whereupon Eros embarks on a quest to restore the upper realm, which will finally be accomplished by his marriage to Arcturus's daughter in an elevation of desire to a cosmic perspective. He is led astray, however, by fantasy, and the separations between the levels and the resultant disorder widen, culminating in the burning of the Mother on a pyre constructed by the Writer (Reason) who has taken over the middle realm. The proper relationships are finally restored by *Fabel*, who alone can pass between the realms and integrate them. The final fulfillment occurs when the ashes of the Mother, mixed by Sophie (Wisdom) in her bowl, are drunk by all. "All . . . perceived the friendly greeting of the mother inside themselves, with unspeakable joy. She was present to everyone, and her mysterious presence seemed to transfigure all of them" (*N* I:312). Death is overcome by the internalization of it, and Fabel gains rights over the kingdom of death.

What emerges from the "Märchen" is a new concept of the subject, now seen as connected with others in multiple, intangible ways so that its own limits begin to blur. "The more manifoldly something is individualized—the more manifold is its contact with other individuals—the more variable its boundaries—and neighbors" (*N* III:261, frag. 113). *Berührung,* contact, is the condition of ironic interrelation, for "contact is separation and binding alike" (*N* III:293, frag. 295). Death and loss permit the extension of the subject to a view of the whole and of its insertion in that, an awareness of the nonmaterial basis of spirit.[53] They overcome the sense of self-importance characteristic of the ego in its desire to attain transcendental status in the present, and press it to reinvolve itself with other subjects. So it is appropriate that the Fabel who defeats the Fates is a child, a successor. As the king of Atlantis sensed, the hardest replacement to accept or imagine is that of oneself.

The vision of Mathilde which opens part 2 reinforces the idea of the self as a conduit leading to and from other subjects. This waking vision supplants both dream and fable, as the outer voice becomes for the first time a fully inner one, converting allegory to a practical model for Heinrich. The second part opens after Mathilde's actual death, where Heinrich is filled with a sense of violent and permanent separation, of personal diminution. Yet though the world swallows persons, they will be seen to continue to exist and to speak. First the belief that a rock he sees is his old teacher and then the vision of Mathilde convert his sorrow into joy. Mathilde's reappearance is marked by a disjunction of voice and image. Heinrich perceives first a voice and then an image, but it will be up to him to join the two, to convert her presence to him into tangible poetry, to speak for the Absolute to others. "First in the word arises out of sympathy a community which can gain duration in time."[54] Mathilde charges him to commemorate the vision in a poem, whose topic turns out to be the general validity of his experience, for it foretells the erecting of a shrine where all may share the comfort Heinrich received at this scene.

The poem makes possible the enchaining of replacement that redefines the subject; it calls forth the tangible response of a girl, who arrives as surrogate daughter to replace the lost mother. The mother must die, but survives as possibility in the child. "My little child has overcome death" (N I:321). The dialogue between Heinrich and the child plays on the expanding frame of reference, as family ties are made multiple. There is no fixity of identity here. Heinrich is ready for an initiation into conscience. With the child and with Sylvester, Heinrich enacts the otherwise abstract claim that the dispersion of the subject and its interpenetration with otherness is truth.

This occurs as the vision is again submitted to interpretive specification in the dialogue with Sylvester, which moves out from the question Heinrich found in the vision, whether the Mother must die.[55] The conversation between them is not the confrontation typical of dialogic irony, but more like a mutual working out of a single position through the back-and-forth movement of ethical irony, where both personalities in their individuality are brought into play. They speak not of Nature per se but of its lessons, its signifying power. Conscience eventually moves to the center of the discussion as a recognition of human nature and a necessary integrating force among subjects.[56] The question it raises is of the extensibility of the subject and the nature of consensus. Sylvester states that it is awoken by violent nature, that is, a sense of the fragility of the self and its fear of death. It suggests the infinite and immortal as well, but though understandable seems incommunicable in language. Heinrich asks, "Would one only understand a thing when one had it?" (N I:331), thus posing the question behind all communication, whether the truly different can ever be made explicable without some prior understanding of it.

Sylvester's response develops a notion of the subject based upon scope as the measure of self-consciousness, a schema of gradations by which the subject comes to comprise more and more of the world around it, which is actually a multiplicity of worlds. "The cosmos falls apart into infinite worlds always encompassed by larger worlds." Conscience is the "creating ground of all being," by which all personal tendencies become widened through reflection into worldviews that reshape conscience itself. But the final question of how far any subject can finally succeed in extending its capacities is one that Sylvester leaves open. "It is hard to say whether within the sensory limitations of our bodies we can really increase our world with new worlds, our senses with new senses, or whether every augmentation of our recognition, every newly acquired ability is only to be accounted to the development of our present world-sense" (N I:331). What the subject can at most attain is a higher standpoint in this world through its integration, as experience and not as abstract thought or rules alone, with other subjects in a common conscience, which is finally seen to be identical with Fabel, poetry itself. "The idle conscience in a smooth, nonresisting world becomes the binding conversation, the all-narrating fable." It is "the inborn mediator of every human being" (N I:332).

This dialogue completes Heinrich's ascent to what I term the stage of ethical irony. He achieves in the discussion with Sylvester a balance absent from the conversations of part 1 and enacts with him the mutual pursuit of some common basis for understanding in reflection born of experience. Where the first half of the novel showed an absorption of the self into various absolutes, the second half can be foreseen as the vital reassertion of the subject through its ironic involvement with others and its ethical extension into multiple spheres of human endeavor. As the Paralipomena make clear, Heinrich is to become all things and all men on his journey toward Mathilde (N I:348). The wholeness of the subject resides in its immersion in such process and in its ability to take from other subjects a sense of itself. Only through the most radical dispersion of self, which this implies, can the individual escape from an overriding fixation on death and the self-limitation that entails and finally hear the unspeakable word. Starting from a sense of a finite and partial human nature, transience can come to seem a boon. Once the self is displaced and the transcendental ego is denied, immortality itself as subsistence of something wholly individual becomes an ambiguous good and death a source of positive value. "Death makes ordinary life so poetic" (*N* I:343). And, one might add, so ironic.

## Wordsworth's *Prelude* and the Elided Middle

*He is the most isolated figure among the great English poets.*—Geoffrey Hartman

With the shift to Wordsworth and English Romanticism, we encounter a conception of dualism that is very different from the dialectical dualities with which Schlegel and Novalis worked. What made the maintenance of a split within the subject tolerable for these German Romantics was the presence of a mediator, with that role being filled by another subject. Thus the confrontation of the subject with loss and death was mitigated by its breakdown and interpenetration with other subjects. The ironic subject saw itself as fragmentary and finite, but was compensated by a heightened awareness that any individual, even itself, is replaceable.

When this mediating element is removed, however, time and not self-consciousness becomes the central problem for a now isolated subject, whose fate is seemingly exhausted by its personal destiny. The Absolute is conceived not in terms of a totality of consciousness but in terms of immortality, which Nature is wholly adequate to represent. Yet time must seem an irresolvable dilemma for any individual consciousness, which at some point will necessarily recognize its own end. Wordsworth's topic, of course, is neither the mind nor Nature alone but the mind responding to Nature. Yet the self-sacrifice typical of the mind in responding indicates an underlying epistemological dualism that will hinder their reconciliation, though their separation may be sensed as intolerable. Wordsworth's poetry is marked by the alternate inability to distinguish and to yoke his two terms, for with the mediating other subject vanishes the possibility of dialectical interchange and the ability to be in two places at once.

The focus of Wordsworth's poetry is the mind in time and over time, two states whose juncture is problematic for him. He is therefore a poet of the dramatic peripeteia, disinclined to imagine becoming except as a total transformation. Unlike the German Romantics, who began with finitude and reflection, Wordsworth took feeling and infinity as his starting points. From this perspective of immortality, transience will seem to be degradation, change a loss. Time is that which ends. His individual subject will come to founder in time because it lacks the ability to see it as a truly historical sequence.

This disjunctive dualism results in a rejection of the kind of replacement we saw in *Heinrich von Ofterdingen*; though the mind may come to terms with it, any loss still remains absolute. "The Two April Mornings" dramatizes the clash between a finite human and an infinite natural truth, showing in Matthew the mind incapable of hovering between them. The two girls of this poem are far more different for him than the two April mornings, so that the attempt at their metaphorical synthesis falls short. The human here is the realm of the individual and hence of mortality, represented by Matthew's daughter as a memory, while immortality and unity are projected into Nature, which imperceptibly replaces things without any loss, one morning by another identical to it. The juxtaposition of these two alternatives may or may not force one to choose between them, but in any case their reconciliation seems impossible.[57] As Hartman put it, "There is an exclusion of intermediate (mythical, humanizing) links in favor of the equipoise and occasional strange blending of two immutables."[58] This blending, I would argue, is ultimately inadequate to break down the isolation of the subject. The practical consequence of this split is the response of Matthew to the second girl who meets his eyes as he turns from his child's grave. " 'I looked at her, and looked again: / And did not wish her mine!' " He refuses both replacement and consolation, preferring a permanent and undiminishing sorrow in which he says he loves his daughter more than before. His response is made despite the fact that the second girl has already actually replaced the first one, for she, and not his daughter, provides the fullest image in the conversation and in the poem. Sorrow like Matthew's provokes the ascent of the subject to a transcendental, natural purview, embodied by the final image of Matthew in his grave holding "a bough / Of wilding" to signal his unity with Nature.[59] The inability or unwillingness to allow replacement of the subject leads to the eventual replacement of poetry itself by a philosophical Stoicism like that of *The Excursion*. This is transcendental realism, but seen from the position of the isolated subject, who retains a consciousness of the human that foresees for itself only an immortality of the kind Matthew grants his daughter—a recollection by others that gradually diminishes her to a mere voice and a dull pain. His refusal to surrender her is a reflection of his own insistence that he not be surrendered, that he preserve in the minds of others the same substantial status as image that she has for him. Wordsworth's poem, of course, obliges. As a result, however, there is no possibility of affirming death or mediating it in any way with lived social experience.

The association with Nature, even in its joys, is equivalent to the sacrifice of individual human life.[60] The adult of "Peele Castle" sees only death in nature, where the child of "We Are Seven" cannot even conceive the discontinuity death implies as long as she remains in Nature, undifferentiated. Wordsworth's attempt to overcome this gap within the mind centers on the power of the imagination, the possibility that it, in poetry and books, might extend the scope of the individual subject and by anticipating it, defuse its own death. He seeks to locate some mediator, often depicting the restorative power of some solitary figure in Nature. Yet these mediators lack the essentially active metamorphic power that can preserve dualism and hence do not refract back to the subject some recognition of their involvement with it, the ironic interplay that sustains the subject outside of itself.[61] Though provocative, Garber's claim that encounter always provides extension for the subject seems suspect, for confrontation is not the same as dialogue, much less equivalent to the role-exchange envisaged by Schlegel in *Lucinde*.[62]

Despite the earnestness with which Wordsworth reiterates his dilemma, his poetry has often been seen as containing ironies, albeit unintentional ones.[63] This irony is based on the radical discontinuity of the self over time, as illustrated by poems like "A slumber did my spirit seal." Such poems depict the passage from an illusion about the positive and permanent unity of humanity with nature to a fuller recognition of the implications of that unity, an awareness of the profound difference between infinite natural and finite human processes. The disappearance of the speaker's own attitude from the second stanza suggests a full acceptance of the transcendental perspective it invokes and a negation of the past in its naiveté. This recognition that conscious experience of a sublime Absolute is identical with the experience of separation from it parallels the fundamental dualism in the German Romantic subject. But Wordsworth's response is to hypostasize the Absolute, projecting it impossibly far from mortal life. The voice of Nature becomes more and more the voice of destiny or duty, unaltered by circumstance.

Wordsworth's "wisdom" in this poem is a systemic irony above all the vicissitudes it beholds, at one with Nature in the place of transcendental indifference. Dialogic irony arises, as Brooks notes, when the reader recoils from the sublime indifference of the second stanza to reassert the claims of the first stanza's "human fears." A balancing between the two is perhaps most typical of Wordsworth, who in his best poems displays the ability to portray two impossibly contradictory perspectives on a single plane, in necessary conjunction with each other. Thus the first view of Lucy is both a delusion and a higher truth to which the mind longs to ascend. As elsewhere, Wordsworth's ironic tone is established by playing with the multiple and opposed connotations of key terms. He undermines terminological fixity by passing back and forth between significations, as with a "Nature" that is both eternal changelessness and continual process.

But the dynamics of irony are wholly within the ego here, subjectivity wholly internalized. Lucy is first one and then another kind of thing, but never a person at all, absorbed more fully by the narrator than by the earth itself. This internalization tends to force on consciousness the choice Ferry insists must be made between contraries, or at least to require the projection of the two states over time in order to maintain the self-identity of each alternative, its exclusion of the other.

Wordsworth's poetry delineates an ego that is ideally a transcendental and self-present entity, one well described by Novalis in his Fichte studies. "The unity that accompanies it everywhere, that it is completely *there, where* it is—this is the highest, essential character of its subjectivity" (N II:136). This ego is characterized by its integrity and wholeness, especially insofar as these imply that it has access to its own past. It is unified over time (as any more than ephemeral self would have to be) by atemporal moments, and its existence is actually maintained only insofar as it can conjure those moments in a recollection of them that must be always identical. Since the self-identity of the ego even in the present is dependent on its access to the past, the fear of loss is an overwhelming one; not only its pastness but also its present integrity would disappear were forgetting to take place. Matthew's unending sorrow is exactly analogous to "Tintern Abbey"'s renewed joy; either is too precious to sacrifice.

Vision is a moment of apparent juncture between that mind and Na-

ture, where the mind itself seems to become immortal. Time, and with it
the possibility of death, is abolished. These atemporal "spots of time" blot
out the human temporal continuum and stand isolated, like the peaks that
rise up above the mist in the vision of Mt. Snowdon.[64] However well prepared for by the section leading up to it and interpreted by what follows,
Mt. Snowdon remains a singular experience, replicable only as an identical recurrence in an individual mind. Such spots of time are "unmediated"
in their access to a domain of absolute wholeness which abstracts from
any determinate relations.[65] The vision typically comes as a surprise,
breaking in on a subject forgetful of itself owing to its concentrated attention on some particular thing that circumscribes it. That attentive expectation is diverted by an initial disappointment, but salvaged by the inrush of
a peripheral revelation.[66] The subject seems wholly dependent here, for
although its active response is essential, it cannot really invoke the vision.

These moments become functional, however, only insofar as they
remain accessible to the imagination, which necessarily involves providing
them with a context. The feeling of a sublime emotion, by being bound to
images drawn from Nature, is tied to Nature and thus made eternal. *The
Prelude* first attributes this action to Nature: "didst thou intertwine for
me / The passions that build up our human soul; / Not with the mean and
vulgar works of man, / But with high objects, with enduring things—"
(I:406–409), but the outcome is the same whether Nature or the imagination or both effect the binding. Once imagistically fixed, the recollection of
such moments must be integral if they are truly apart from time, so the
poet must refuse transformation of any kind. The Nature to which they
are bound is an immortal one, complete in itself and in no need of the
kind of interpretive realignments to which Heinrich submits his visions.

The "spots of time" are substantialized intimations of a wholly transcendent power, absolute appearances of the Absolute. What confirms
their validity is the continuity of their psychological force for the individual, not any cumulative process of understanding that would gradually
load them with communal resonance.[67] The only change they might un-
dergo would be to fade in intensity. Even *The Prelude* creates a sense that it
is not about development at all but about a poet untouched by process
who moves inexorably to his goal or, in fact, is always there.

Hence one needs to ask if such moments succeed in mediating the
human and the divine, if they do indeed bind the personal to the universal, or whether they simply drown the former in the latter. The "spots of

time," on the one hand, are cut off from other persons by their singularity and, on the other hand, become generalized as any incidental external elements are stripped away.[68] The necessity for this reduction indicates the incommensurability of the two terms. Nature exceeds the conscious self precisely in its immortal and nonmaterial basis. Wholly to identify with it is to sacrifice the distinctively human, for the mind is always dependent on a mortal garment. If that insight is not repressed, every approximation of the eternal will be an intimation of the death of the self: its status as seen from an eternal viewpoint. Unable to see itself as replaceable, the subject must see obliteration as the only imaginable outcome of death. It will therefore resist any apocalyptic overcoming of the finite, or any imaginative complicity with that act, yet at the same time resist its own severing from Nature and restriction to the finite.[69]

Book V of *The Prelude*, "Books," examines just this problem of the status of the vision as image, and the consequences of that for the subject and its own mortality. This section raises the question of why books should receive special attention at just this moment in the poem. It interrupts the chronology of the work more thoroughly than has heretofore been done, ranging back and forth in time, displacing a natural with a human order. It attempts to mediate the human-nature, finite-infinite split by inserting books, the tangible embodiments of spirit, between them.

Books I–IV have argued for a dualism that would be an idyllic unity of forces; the two aspects of consciousness flow into one another and the mind abides between them. After the introductory search for a theme, the first two books display the double working of Nature, both pleasant and sublime, and the corresponding double response of a mind attuned to either. Wordsworth would have these two seen as aspects of a single force, and so childlike joy flows into an awe before Nature. The early visions are powerful, but only vaguely frightening. They are associated with misdemeanors, as though Nature somehow cared even about the human moral code. Nature also balances the loss of Wordsworth's mother (II:276–288), acting as a surrogate mother so that loss hardly ripples across the mind. Singleness even reinforces the harmonious intercourse with the cosmos (III:185–188); this is the summit of the "egotistical sublime," but already moving toward a descent from it.[70]

In books III and IV, there emerges a split between the empirical and the transcendental egos, and a parallel drifting apart of the pleasant (now associated with frivolous joys, too) and the sublime (full communion with

Nature). First in Cambridge, and then on return to the valley, Wordsworth remarks disturbing discontinuities across time. The increase of a "human-heartedness" in his love is accompanied by a sense of mortality, of the now vacant nook where an old acquaintance used to sit. Neither this nor the transcendent perspective is dominant here, however, for the mind inconstantly moves from one to the other. "Strange rendez-vous my mind was at that time . . . Of inconsiderate habits and sedate, / Consorting in one mansion unreproved" (IV:338–343). Yet the movement is sensed as "an inner falling off" despite the fact that "I loved . . . more deeply even than ever" (IV:278–280). That love is no longer so harmonious and all-embracing once the human and divine (or natural) orders begin to grow apart. Thus conformity to God results in the indifference to human fate, even one's own fate, which characterizes the veteran at the end of book IV.

Book V dramatizes the effect of this split on the subject as an apocalyptic fear the mind struggles to keep down. For that mind differs from Nature in its necessary dependence on perishable embodiments; the image is not quite what it represents. The question raised at the opening of book V is whether books can survive. Wordsworth envisages an earthquake or fire that would destroy not an absolute and regenerative Nature but only the evidence of the mind's ability to relate itself to that, both to partake of immortality and to recognize mortality.

> Oh! why hath not the Mind
> Some element to stamp her image on
> In nature somewhat nearer to her own?
> Why, gifted with such powers to send abroad
> Her spirit, must it lodge in shrines so frail? [V:45–49]

There is evident here an imbalance between the two poles of consciousness: an ego rooted in ephemeral particulars and an Absolute indifferent to them. Though it partakes of the Absolute, a "spot of time" is not replaceable in the way the things of Nature are. That the mind moves between the two realms is evident, but unless it can mediate their radical difference it is fated to be always caught on one side or the other. The desired harmony between the two forces is destabilized by the threat of a disproportion between the two terms.[71] The confrontation of two unequal terms must result in either isolation or absorption, the subordination of one term to another instead of their integration.[72] The reciprocity on which Wordsworth so frequently calls is a response to this felt danger of collapse, if not a solution to it.

For the problem is that Nature is not, even for Wordsworth, a subject in the full sense of that term. To identify with it is to sacrifice one's own subjectivity, since the truth of the self is finitude. So no role-exchange or reversal of positions is possible; the Absolute is fixed in Nature and can be achieved only by surrendering to it. Nature is already complete and therefore has neither goal nor need for development. It requires no self-consciousness to complete it, and the finitude self-consciousness implies is irrelevant to natural processes. Wordsworth's preference for a static, eternal object is a concession to what he deems essential in Nature. Looking at this kind of Nature, as in the image of book IV where someone hanging over a boat observes the reflections of his surroundings, the individual subject recedes to the evanescence of light itself. The reflection "now is crossed by gleam / Of his own image, by a sunbeam now" (IV:267–268), where the self disappears as a mere momentary gleam in waves of things. This distance between subject and Nature actually makes total imaginative projection onto the object easier, for no imaginative absorption can alter a nonresistant object, unconcerned what tales may be woven upon it.[73]

Humanity, then, has the total ration of subjectivity, a separation that is not, however, a completion. Interpenetration is to be feared as a loss of identity; the subject as subject is forced to embrace isolation, for obliteration of difference in contact would equal the obliteration of the self. Isolation in Nature becomes isolation from it, a subordination of unity to the division characteristic of the ego.

This model is carried over to relationship with others as well. An encounter is often of the type in "Resolution and Independence," where the other subject becomes a nature image effectively distanced from any empirical subject. The extent to which Wordsworth has to go in order to maintain the discreteness of a human object out there by rendering it strange indicates the threat that merging with it poses to the integrity of the subject, which can only foresee the twin dangers of isolation and absorption. Such other subjects are generally passive to the imaginative charging of them with significance, so effectively other that dialectical communication is unimaginable. Wordsworth's world is a place without any ground for comparison, a place of the elided middle, where terms are so excessively other as to drift apart if not forcibly jammed together.

So book V is fundamental to Wordsworth's project, since its argument is that books may indeed serve as the mediating term. The initial apocalyptic vision gives way to a dream where the same problem will be worked out further. The texts of Euclid and the Ode, borne by the desert Arab whom the dreamer encounters, embody the harmony between the mind and the Absolute. Their survival is threatened now not by fire but by a deluge (water continuing in book V to be associated with death). The Arab seeks to bury and thus to save them, but it may be that they are already irreparably damaged. For Wordsworth's imagination has reduced the spiritual side of humanity to its material basis, and the outcome is in a sense already decided. The books are represented by a stone and shell, which, did they not partake of human mortality, would be unlikely to be damaged by a flood. The irony of this alteration is especially prominent in that the book the dreamer was reading before his slumber was *Don Quixote*, a tale of how the spirit of books acquires an immortality, however skewed, not in its substance but in the minds of others.[74] What has occurred is that the individual subject's own fear of death has been displaced onto the books, the tangible embodiments of spirit. Even the tale told by the Ode is one of irreducible separation between human and natural and of its own complicity with the former. The mind's access to the Absolute serves only to allow it to foretell the destruction of mortals (and mortality), the dissolution of its own condition of possibility. The infinite and finite cannot be mingled, nor is the latter a place of reproduction and replacement, but only of death. Even the transcendental ego aware of this fact cannot escape from it.

Yet this pessimistic conclusion is disputed as book V continues and Wordsworth praises the power of books to mediate human and natural, to speak of Nature itself. They are "only less, / For what we are and what we may become, / Than Nature's self, which is the breath of God" (V:219–221). The duality that threatened to split books from Nature reemerges within the class of books, for these elevated texts are contrasted with an inferior kind. The latter sort, which limits the mind's growth by filling it with knowledge, is contrasted with Wordsworth's mother's faith in the goodness and adequacy of the human order. In this first of the particular death images of book V, the possibility of positive replacement is effectively evoked. The doctrine the mother leaves behind does adequately substitute for her in her children, convinced "that in the unreasoning progress of the world / A wiser spirit is at work for us"

(V:359–360). This is a spirit more beneficent than death; yet death has still not been recognized in relation to the subject and its own personal death.

This positive restoration shifts immediately to the other side of Nature, the problem still unresolved by books of how the individual can deal with death. The human sphere is ultimately not divorced from the natural one but implicated by it, for it is Nature that brings death. The Boy of Winander is Wordsworth's example of this and the beginning of a final movement where Wordsworth will seek to recuperate death in a fully infinite perspective.[75] The Boy of Winander's immersion in the natural order is a premonition of his death, but a death that seems like fantasy and blends into an image of an endless succession of children playing near his grave. Books will be realigned with Nature as effective instruments for rendering death benign, for accomplishing the effortless slipping away performed by the Boy of Winander.

What succeeds this segment is the tale of the drowned man, a reimagining of death that depicts it as the removal of mortal garments and a descent to the full depths of immortality, disturbed only by the annoying prodding of grappling irons. The young Wordsworth's response to this event is conditioned by a kind of book far removed from the Ode of the dream, fantasy tales that detach even the experience of death from reality and make it less ominous. Books here are treated not as things but as intersubjective acts, the focus of joint purchase projects and participatory declamation. Their function is not to depict the characteristically human, and hence they remain untainted by it. They provide instead dreams and fantasies of omnipotence, easing the transition from childhood, "ere we learn to live / In reconcilement with our stinted powers; / To endure this state of meagre vassalage" (V:516–518). The dualism running through *The Prelude* is resolved not through mediation but through temporary vaporization of one of its terms, personal death. Books are a transitional isthmus where immortality still seems possible, as is *The Prelude* itself.

But the image of shared joys is an illusory one, for the subject does not succeed in passing beyond itself and reverts to the stance of an individual ego. Wordsworth laments, "Poems withal of name, which at that time / Did never fail to entrance me, and are now, / Dead in my eyes" (V:549–550). Books, as the original dream made clear, also die and force the poet to a recognition of the final nonintegrity of the subject over time, of the failure of the shared vision that books imply. Wordsworth characteristically conveys not the possible life elsewhere of these books, or even their integration into later lived experience, but only his *personal* loss of an experience he would have wished eternal. Here the immortal is sacrificed to preserve its human truth, for the two are radically discontinuous. Their integration succeeds only in the realm of fantasy, detached from limitations of the real.

One final image remains: the compression of literature and Nature that closes book V, a reconciliation attained by cutting off reflection and surrendering the problem of the fragmented subject. The myth of reciprocity in *The Prelude* is an impossibility born of and sustained in metaphor, a juxtaposition of irreconcilables in the faith that they might merge, despite the recognition that they will not. Wordsworth's poetry will increasingly speak the tale of the Ode, the death of the imagination as the consequence of its very success in reaching out to the Absolute, for any human voice, though it speak with "a glory not its own," can never be anything but its own—individual and mortal.

> Visionary power
> Attends the motions of the viewless winds,
> Embodied in the mystery of words:
> There, darkness makes abode, and all the host
> Of shadowy things work endless changes—there
> As in a mansion like their proper home,
> Even forms and substances are circumfused
> By that transparent veil with light divine,
> And, through the turnings intricate of verse,
> Present themselves as objects recognized,
> In flashes, and with glory not their own.     [V:595–605]

Wordsworth's conclusion is ironic in its refusal to soften the paradox of the human state, to ignore one or the other alternative of the duality that defines the subject. But the repudiation of mediation consequent on the isolation of the subject leaves irony behind in a plunge toward one version or another of single vision, and even Wordsworth proves unable to bear the burden of an unceasing dialogic irony. What such irony lacks is a sense for the dialectical interchange possible between equally charged centers, an activity that takes for its measure not the expression of any absolute but rather its enactment in the forms of human communication. The elided middle absent from Wordsworth's poetry is the other, as subject.

## *Sartor Resartus* and the Irony of Subordination

Despite its hortatory tone, Carlyle's *Sartor Resartus* is the only one of the four works dealt with in this chapter that is usually conceded to be ironic. By creating a disproportion in role and understanding between the English editor and his subject, Diogenes Teufelsdröckh, Carlyle dramatizes the essential split existing within the subject. Yet the question whether the ultimate result is ironic, or perhaps instead comic,[76] depends for its answer upon the success with which the narrator can first create and maintain a viable alternative perspective and then succeed in ironically integrating that with the higher wisdom of German Idealism, Teufelsdröckh's Clothes Philosophy. Irony depends upon the maintenance of a clearly articulated and integrated structure of opposition, but Carlyle's thought shies away from the uncertainty such sustained dualism requires. That *Sartor Resartus* is not a novel, and thus is not structured by dynamic interaction of characters, is usually conceded, but equally significant is the form of the philosophy to which it would persuade us.[77] Harrold's assessment of Carlyle's debt to German philosophy concludes that "the result of this eclectic assembling of doctrines into a rough unity of thought is that Carlyle's general 'Weltanschauung' is lacking in internal cohesion, symmetry, clarity, logical structure. Its only philosophical unity rests on the informing concept of 'Offenbarung,' or dynamic revelation."[78]

The consequence of this is that even the dialogic tension between alternatives of Wordsworth's poetry is difficult for Carlyle to sustain. He converts this to a reductive, subordinating dualism that extends the ethical implications of *The Excursion*. The material and the spiritual are sharply divided, with the individual firmly housed in a finitude that, along with mortality, is mere illusion. Wordsworth's problem of books, which can speak truth only when they speak of death, is here resolved in the form of silence: "Speech is of Time, Silence is of Eternity."[79] Yet speaking, though it cannot articulate the Absolute, cannot really damage it either and can assist in turning us from the medium of its own possibility, an illusory finitude. What lies beyond is a romantically ineffable Absolute, "what there is at present no name for: The unspeakable Divine Significance, full of splendour, of wonder and terror, that lies in the being of every man, of every thing."[80]

The problem *Sartor Resartus* confronts is not the need to join these two spheres but rather their too facile mingling into a single continuous order. Since Carlyle's "Divine" is absolutely extended into all things, there can arise a tendency to ascribe independent validity to reality without recognizing its inevitable deviations from the spiritual pattern, its wholly inferior status. There arises the delusion that the subject can somehow mediate this gap and purify the real of its realness. This is the perspective embodied by the English narrator, who comically entangles himself in the idiosyncrasies of the garment, as though he could there observe the lineaments behind it.

What does mediate the gap for Carlyle is the symbol, which unites silence and speech. "In a Symbol there is concealment and yet revelation: here therefore, by Silence and by Speech acting together, comes a double significance" (219). But symbols are not thought images which could be fully spirit; they are solidly material, the reality of human life and action itself. Thus the highest symbol is the biography, and the highest biography that which tells the life of a prophet (224). Recognition of their higher significance, however, succeeds in overcoming this materiality and in raising the real to the ideal. The function of the symbol is to draw our attention and then to pass away. "In the Symbol proper . . . there is ever, more or less distinctly and directly, some embodiment and revelation of the Infinite; the Infinite is made to blend itself with the Finite, to stand visible, and as it were, attainable there" (220). This description, hedged around with qualifications and limitations, conveys the problematic status of the symbol, the question of exactly how the infinite can be in the finite at all. As with Wordsworth, mortal accessions to the Absolute prove tainted by their origin; they, too, grow old and die, thus revealing the intractable separation of spirit and letter. "[Time] at length defaces, or even desecrates them; and Symbols, like all terrestrial Garments, wax old" (224). In Carlyle's world, symbols do not give birth to other symbols in a process of historical growth but pass away wholly to make room for new flashes of divine inspiration. Even those books that seem most divinely inspired, such as the Koran, are relevant only to a limited human context. "Nothing but a sense of duty could carry any European through the Koran."[81] Symbols are not self-subsistent, do not contain spirit in any way that would alter their materiality, and hence are wholly relativized and, like all things real, need to be sacrificed.

*Sartor Resartus* converts this epistemological dualism into the human relationship between Teufelsdröckh, the prophet of a new philosophy of clothes and of a new age, and the more tradition-bound, prosaic English editor presenting this to an English public. The text itself is a symbol of their interaction, a measure of the effectiveness of their juncture. The editor is characterized by his tendency to ascribe significance to the real in itself, mistakenly believing that it transparently reveals the ideal, that it can be a literal manifestation of the divine. Though he perceives the primacy of spirit, he persists in treating garments as though they were analyzable in themselves. He awaits Teufelsdröckh's biographical materials impatiently, convinced that these facts will unlock the spirit behind them, that their reality is wholly permeated by the ideal. He thus undertakes the abolition of the realness of the real, attempting to reconstruct it as a continuous stream of plums of insight. "So here we endeavored, from the enormous, amorphous Plum-pudding, more like a Scottish Haggis, which Herr Teufelsdröckh had kneaded for his fellow-mortals, to pick out the choicest Plums, and present them separately on a cover of our own" (292). The editor is unaware of the recalcitrance of language, its symbolic deceptiveness. *Sartor's* comedy arises from the opaque, patchwork nature of the garment with which he is provided—the lack of unity in Teufelsdröckh's biography, philosophy, and style. To attempt to separate the plums from the pudding reveals a fundamentally erroneous attempt to deny dualism and render words back into spirit.

Teufelsdröckh, and Carlyle with him, sustain instead that intractable duality of the human situation and the inability of reflection to resolve this. "Metaphysical Speculation, as it begins in No or Nothingness, so it must needs end in Nothingness; circulates and must circulate in endless vortices; creating, swallowing—itself. . . . everywhere there is Dualism, Equipoise; a perpetual Contradiction dwells in us."[82] Contradiction here is a dualism not susceptible to dialectical integration. It must instead be defused by making one term primary. It is a reductive dualism, resulting in the either-or absolutism of single vision, where the subject, insofar as immersed in the real, receives the lesser role. "This great mystery of a Life and Universe . . . is larger than man, not to be comprehended by him; an Infinite thing."[83] The finite and the infinite are so opposed that the former is in no sense a microcosm, but an element on a sundered chain of being.

Hence there is no question which term is granted priority; Carlyle's assent to a transcendental perspective is complete. He provides a scale ranging from Divine Idea to Teufelsdröckh to editor to implied reader, according to how completely that Absolute is recognized. The recognition of the Divine is indeed something of a problem, for its inaccessibility to discursive expression means that it can be sanctioned only by revelation or intuition, apparently private and incommunicable modes of knowledge. The editor's reaction to the Clothes Philosophy acknowledges the resultant dependence of knowledge on character. "For it seems as if the demonstration lay much in the Author's individuality; as if it were not Argument that had taught him, but Experience"(52). Access to the Absolute is therefore strictly personal, passing through unconscious channels to a passive identity with it. Activity, which is the subsequent outward directing of this force, is evaluable only in terms of its sincerity, its fidelity to that Absolute all subjects sense individually. "I should say *sincerity,* a deep, great, genuine sincerity, is the first characteristic of all men in any way heroic."[84]

Carlyle's solution to the incipient solipsism of this doctrine is the hero figure, who institutionalizes a scale of inspiration. Access to the Absolute is a question of gradation; though all possess it, some possess it more completely than others and are therefore suited to guide them in the interpretation of it. All who are not heroes are best advised to attach their insight to the concrete mediation provided by a hero, an acceptance that necessarily is all or nothing.

"A Hero ... has this first distinction ... That he looks through the shows of things into *things.*"[85] The hero perceives more clearly the fundamental dualism of garment and idea and is hence more fitted to guide others in shaping the former. Embodying the Absolute for others, he relieves them of the doubt and confusion into which they might otherwise fall. Carlyle has shifted the idolizing of another from the private relationship of *Lucinde* to its public replication across the breadth of society. "Only in reverently bowing down before the Higher does [man] feel himself exalted" (251). Only the hero is his own mediator. Conscience, in its ironic sense, is inoperative in the hero, for with no higher visible standard, he cannot suffer from doubt or hesitancy. That this arrangement will work out is something Carlyle, however, bases on a benevolent fatalism. "Meanwhile, observe with joy, so cunningly has Nature ordered it, that whatsoever man ought to obey, he cannot but obey" (251).

Irony, then, in most of its forms must be relegated to a subordinate position, for it is identified with sarcasm and, even worse, with doubt about the adequacy of the Absolute's ability to extend itself into the finite and into human beings. "An ironic man, with his sly stillness and ambuscading ways ... may be viewed as a pest to society" (129). Yet Carlyle's faith is itself parent to an insistent negative irony, his typical mode and one to which the editor himself will finally be subjected.

For the real must be negated actively; its positive worth is nothing more than its being there to be abolished.[86] Not its existence, but its significance, is what Carlyle attacks in Teufelsdröckh's claim that it exists only as garment. "He has looked fixedly on Existence, till, one after the other, its earthly hulls and garnitures have all melted away" (255). Facts are hieroglyphs, whose function is to vanish into their signification or, insofar as they do not do so, to demonstrate their own inadequacy. Their relations are not to be multiplied, as Novalis urged, but all subsumed in a direct line back to the Absolute. To take their concreteness as meaningful would be a dangerous illusion.

A parallel decomposition of the subject into its basic dualism is at the center of *Sartor Resartus* in the tripartite passage of Teufelsdröckh from despair to sublime faith. The first stage, an Everlasting No of despair born of a sense of the limitations of the real, is ended by an act of courage (what *Heroes* will call "valor"). The subject passes out of despair by seeing that it is spirit as well as matter, hence in some sense free of the limitations of the latter, of life. This self-assertion leads at first only to the Center of Indifference, a place of pride and isolation for the subject that believes it can be wholly spirit and ignore its own materiality. Its experience with the world conveys the lesson of the ephemerality of even the human products of spirit (like Wordsworth's books), for they can survive only transiently, in partial actions. The pride of self-liberation gives way to the humble perception that that effort weighs not at all on the scale of the universe. This self-annihilation and renunciation of the mortal ego permits the final ascent to an Everlasting Yea, where Teufelsdröckh attains a "diabolico-angelical" indifference that speaks as apocalyptic prophecy. Here he proclaims his phoenix view of history and the doctrine of natural supernaturalism.

His salvation has come from the rejection of the expectation of personal happiness; a subject bound into a finite condition can never expect fulfillment from that condition. It is a perception of the incommensurability of the human and the divine, whereby desire can never, but always must content itself with mortal things. Where this insight turns Novalis toward the depiction of a more multifaceted and elaborated enactment between subjects, to realize more completely the possibilities of the human, Carlyle moves toward a renunciation of expectation, a wholesale uprooting into the divine. "It is only with Renunciation (*Entsagen*) that Life, properly speaking, can be said to begin" (191).[87] This translates into a submission to fate, to the Law of the World, tinged by the shades of individual pessimism. The conversion process for Carlyle is singular and one-way, bound to a chronology in which one is lifted to the tranquility of systemic irony.

Though the consequences for the individual subject are wholly negative, since it as an accomplice of the real must be annihilated, Carlyle's vision still permits a historical optimism. The world can be seen as process, humanity as a race, promising a reconciliation beyond that accessible to the individual, and equally beyond its anticipation. "But whence?—O Heaven, whither? Sense knows not; Faith knows not; only that it is through Mystery to Mystery, from God to God" (266–267). One wonders, though, if a subject would even recognize this paradise were humanity, eventually, to arrive at it. The tangible goal is to be attained apart from human assistance, then, and the individual's role is only to act, which is to work, which is to follow directives. This philosophy of work indicates again how Carlyle reverts to a reductive dualism of subject and object, the one serving as material for the other. Harrold has noted the parallel to the Fichtean idea of work. "The world is merely the object and materials of our duty, awaiting the plastic operation of our wills in action."[88] Carlyle's sphere of action bears much resemblance to Fichte's *Nicht-Ich*, to which the shaping mind can do no injustice since it is both mere materiality and an emanation of self. The "felt indubitable certainty of Experience" is available only to a transcendental ego, able to dominate a recalcitrant reality that can exert no claims of its own.

The problem is that practice, even when informed by the ideal, can never live up to it, for that would deny their mutual opposition. Action, then, is more a question of proving oneself worthy than actually changing the world. Real change is an inner and not an outer phenomenon. "[Paradisal visions] are parables of the spiritual life of mankind that demand as much as they promise, with both demands and promises being, first and foremost, spiritual conditions."[89] Real progress hardly matters; to assume it did would be to fall back into the error of taking the garment for the essence.

For the Absolute in Carlyle remains finally unknowable and unassimilable to the world. It is "the Deep that is infinite, without bottom as without shore" (257). Though it is in the real, it is not visible there except as miracle. The effort to find it there will necessarily seem ironic, though only in a negative way. A corollary to this is that the spirit even in another subject must remain equally unknowable, as the editor wishes to be for the reader. "It is a voice publishing tidings of the Philosophy of Clothes" (13), no tangible, fully exposed subject that can involve itself in interpretive interplay. There can be no explicable mechanism of communication for Carlyle, for only the surfaces could thus be laid bare. Nor can there be any mutual assistance in the merging of partial visions, for insight is one, a matter of degree and not of perspective.

So the editor's pursuit of truth about Teufelsdröckh provides a fixed polarity of master and disciple, where the authority clearly falls on Teufelsdröckh's side. The editor resists the lack of order, the chaotic style, and the contradictions he finds in Teufelsdröckh, but these are clearly, especially for Carlyle, matters of secondary import. In his enthusiasm, the editor prefers the facts of biography, a far distance from Carlyle's use of that genre to describe spiritual essences. Yet he does most completely merge with Teufelsdröckh in the biographical middle portion, where he shares the certainty an older Teufelsdröckh would have of the inevitably successful outcome of his own pilgrimage through life.

The climax of the relationship between them occurs when the editor comes to realize the truth of, and to find explicitly expressed by Teufelsdröckh, a metacomment on his own editorial enterprise. After concluding the biography proper, its very perfection, its ideal assimilation of the real, lead the editor to suspect the fabrication of its elements. As he reshaped it to structure it within a coherent transcendental teleology, so has Teufelsdröckh also done in his prior compilation of its elements. It is the act of the mind upon them, and not the facts themselves, that provides a pattern no material things could ever possess in themselves and a pattern common in its abstractness to all things and all persons. Hence Teufelsdröckh can assimilate any and all facts, however trivial, to his philosophy; for him the six bags would all speak in a single voice.

Still unable to perceive that such restructuring is inevitable and essential, the editor reflects his dismay. "Our theory begins to be that, in receiving as literally authentic what was but hieroglyphically so, Hofrath Heuschrecke . . . was made a fool of, and set adrift to make fools of others" (202). Yet hieroglyphs are the only truth; there are no facts, as the editor proceeds to quote from Teufelsdröckh himself. "Wilt thou know a Man, above all a Mankind, by stringing-together beadrolls of what thou namest Facts? The Man is the spirit he worked in; not what he did, but what he became. Facts are engraved Hieroglyphs, for which the fewest have the key" (203). With his recognition of the importance of this statement, the editor is indeed retailored, made aware of the ludicrousness of his own efforts to tailor a Clothes Philosophy he should have treated as whole cloth, the essence of a man with access to the Absolute, and hence as pure revelation.[90]

It is impossible to know the other in this purely spiritual world except as a type. Teufelsdröckh himself vanishes into a romance biography, so that the frequent refusal of critics to call this a novel at all serves as some measure of its lack of the concrete particularity on which ironic interchange would have to be based. The mystic desire for a merging into oneness that permeates Carlyle's writings is enacted here as the merging of the editor into Teufelsdröckh, with a loss of ironic tension, as the editor himself finally realizes. "Even as the smaller whirlpool is sucked into the larger, and made to whirl along with it, so has the lesser mind, in this instance, been forced to become portion of the greater, and like it, see all things figuratively" (293). Though the editor still erroneously sees his assimilation only on the level of style, as he persists in reading the garment, his subordination to Teufelsdröckh is conveyed by the image itself, which swallows his difference on every level.[91] There is only one absolute scale among human beings.

Biography and history are for Carlyle a matter of stripping off the inessentials of place and time in which the editor continues to believe, the recognition that facts reveal the abstract pattern only insofar as they are subordinated to it and even manipulated to fit it. Carlyle's style is frequently characterized as metaphoric, but the obsessive extension of a single metaphor (such as the Clothes Philosophy) is more properly analogic in function, for it serves to align the universe into a pair of contrastive and all-embracing orders.[92] The tangible basis of metaphor gives way to the abstract relation of analogy as a particular relation expands over an increasing domain. This serves not to join or mediate the terms but to lock them into opposition and all oppositions into some primary opposition. Hence it differs from Novalis's use of analogical restatement, where every analogy is absolute in the context of its consideration and displaced in any other context.

The reduction to a pattern brings with it the elision of difference in a juxtaposition of unequal terms. Carlyle's own practice is revealing, for his appropriation of terms from the Romantic vocabulary was accompanied by a disregard for any connotations beyond his own. In consequence, his thought failed to draw from them the enrichment of multiple and ironically competing frames of reference. "Though the author of *Sartor Resartus*, he never adequately retailored his own convictions."[93] Given his epistemological premises, he could hardly be expected to do so, for the tailor cannot and does not retailor himself; the subject cannot change and expand by taking in otherness, unless it confronts an otherness so excessive that it itself vanishes. The impetus must come from the outside, for the ego alone could hardly know where, consciously, to begin.

The use of metaphor is expressive of Carlyle's refusal to speak directly of the spirit, of his sense that referential language is necessarily inadequate for dealing with spiritual matters. It is a submission to the limits of the real, an attempt to reinforce the materiality of language, and a recognition of how the problems of the ironic subject are finally problems of language. Conceiving language use in expressive and not communicative terms, however, Carlyle employed an irony that could only be negative. His writings speak the death of mortality as loudly and persistently as Wordsworth's shell-ode. Yet *Sartor Resartus*, as a text that takes as its model the translation, looks forward to a modern sense of the complexity involved in all communication. Had the editor observed Teufelsdröckh instead of trying to gaze through him, Carlyle might have made a greater contribution to the development of ironic discourse. Nonetheless the letter writer of *Lucinde*, with his tendency to identify narcissistically his ego with the Absolute he would convey, has been replaced by a recipient-reader, intent on conning an Absolute that seems, somehow, not to make the kind of sense it should.[94] The other remains confined, though, as in Teufelsdröckh's biography, to the realm of indifference, a place where subjects share only their common sense of human insignificance. Like Teufelsdröckh himself, communication moves along mysterious paths of manipulation whose workings cannot be sounded. How language, in irony, acts to communicate more of the subject than the words themselves express, and how that comes to be reflected back to and to expand the subject in the dialectical play of enactment, are topics whose fuller analysis necessitates our occupation with a further development of the ironic text in the works of George Meredith.

# ◄§ 3

## The Irony of the Ego: Meredith's Novels

### I: Linguistic Blindness and Ironic Vision

Irony has often been treated as a device leading toward the subjective assertion of self. Yet this focus is an incomplete one, stressing the corrosive aspect of Socratic wit, while ignoring the equally essential Socratic ignorance and dialectic. As Schlegel realized, these latter factors imply an inherent limitation on the scope of knowledge of any individual subject and the consequent necessity to be involved with and rely on other subjects. It is this consensual sort of irony that is particularly operative in the novels of George Meredith, which display an acute awareness both of the intersubjective nature of knowledge and of the linguistic detours through which alone such knowledge can be attained.

Meredith criticism has traditionally relied on external factors to organize his texts—most often biographical information or Meredith's own fragmentary theorizing.[1] Like recourse to the *Essay on Comedy*, however, these approaches can unduly constrict the achievement of his novels to fit an often didactic and narrowly Victorian theory of literature.[2] Nor are the comments on literary practice in his novels to be taken as the last word on those texts, as the novels themselves will be seen to demonstrate. Meredith is constantly aware that no one, not even an author, can be fully ironic with himself.

Much Meredith criticism has also tended to read the novels in terms of individual character and characters, when for his ironic awareness it is the interaction of characters that is determinative. "They are essences or forces."[3] So concludes Pritchett, underestimating the dialectically determined nature of character. Meredith instead focuses on the changeableness of character, especially prominent in youth, but persisting throughout life.[4] Even more important, however, is his insistence on the dependence of character on the ebb and flow of relationships.[5] For with Meredith, the novel is in the process of shattering the idea of an integral self, of an individual consciousness and agent. An important consequence of his ironic sensibility is that this occurs without removing, in fact by intensifying, the sense of individual personal responsibility.

There has been, in sum, too little attention to the integrity of Meredith's work on any level besides that of the thematic. My intent is to take Meredith as a case of irony, as a novelist of the blindness and vision involved in the interpretive act from which meaning and identity emerge. Meredith is ironic, to be sure, in his undermining of literary conventions and current ideas, but this is not the irony with which I am most concerned.[6] The irony of the subject begins with the humility arising from a sense of inevitable human imperfection, evident already as a principle in *Richard Feverel.* Yet this is only the precondition to that irony involved in and constituting the process of understanding. Blindness and vision shape a hermeneutic and linguistic problem for Meredith, whose test for the value of words is their revelatory expansiveness.

Irony exists in Meredith's works as a hermeneutic and intersubjective phenomenon, embodied in a particular mode of interaction, linguistic though not necessarily conscious, between subjects. The revelations of self-identity which Meredith explores in dialogue illustrate: (1) the ironic limitation on the capacity of any individual to acquire complete self-knowledge, (2) the equally ironic mediation of any potential self-knowledge through the often subconscious patterns of language, even in the apparently most trivial utterances, and (3) the communal consequences of this epistemological irony, for the words that permit self-knowledge must be rearticulated on the plane of a second person's awareness in order to be activated for the initial speaker. Full irony involves not just the perception of someone else's blindness, as in dramatic irony, but an enacted awareness of the factors that make everyone subject to repeated bouts of blindness.

Meredith studies the leaping in and out of the self that makes understanding possible, an understanding that is always situational and mediated by some particular other, therefore perspectival. Vision always brings with it a new blindness to be sought out. Hence it is characteristic of Meredith's work that there are no sustainable isolated characters.

Those who pursue this path inevitably end in total blindness (Richard Fe-verel), madness (Richmond Roy and Victor Radnor), or self-obliteration (Sigismund Alvan, Lord Fleetwood). The missed human connection is a sufficient condition for tragedy because of the hermeneutic imperative in all human life.

Ironic awareness, then, is the recognition and enactment by the sub-ject of its reliance on others for self-understanding, and hence also as a basis for effective action. Judith Wilt's study is among the best on Mere-dith, because its argument recognizes this intersubjective imperative. "Re-ality, 'comic' reality, is connection, the impingement of one being upon another, the flow of one man's feeling toward another for the sake of the other's response."[7] Vanity, on the other hand, is the belief that one can be one's own ironic corrective. This is the fault of Meredith's first hero, Shibli Bagarag, whose need of Noorna is repeatedly stressed in what is necessar-ily a dual quest for the overcoming of illusion. Self-consciousness is not to be had simply by willing it, nor even by understanding the conditions that govern its attainment.[8] "For who beguiles so much as Self?"(HR, XXVIII: 308).

The self-knowledge essential to irony comes from the outside or not at all. Irony defines a form of social consensus that combats the inevitable blindness of individual vision, without being any definitive final state-ment.[9] Joseph Kruppa acknowledges the centrality of just this process in Meredith's late novels, which I would argue runs through all of them. "In Meredith's world, this positing of values cannot be grounded in any su-pernatural force, but can only be found in the meeting of consciousness with consciousness. It is only in another that we find ourself."[10] It should be stressed, however, that the nature of this meeting is hermeneutic, based on an ironic reflectiveness, and not basically intuitive or instinctive. Laughter, the saving gesture in many of Meredith's works, is the expres-sion of that internalized outer perspective.

At the same time, the apparently restricted social sphere of Mere-dith's novels remains somehow disturbing. One wonders if the truths he is at such pain to unravel are indeed applicable to broader philosophical and social concerns, if his irony does indeed provide an effective impetus to-ward community. Beer speaks for most readers of Meredith when she states, "Meredith is always interested by the individual will towards free-dom rather than by responsibility within society."[11] Yet I would argue that the question of understanding self and other at the center of Meredith's works and its necessarily intersubjective resolution provide an essential basis for any social bond. The mutual material self-interest of liberal models was too uncertain, the sympathetic interpenetration of romantic models too intermittent, for Meredith to have faith in their efficacy. His interest instead is in a spiritual bond, irony, that can establish a form of mutual intellectual self-interest, binding individuals together in a community of reinterpretations. Whether Meredith has indeed succeeded in interrelating private and public values is the question we need to keep in mind as we sketch his ironic vision in three central novels, *The Egoist*, *The Ordeal of Richard Feverel*, and *One of Our Conquerors*.

### *The Egoist*: Blindness in Revelation, or Rough Truth

The blindness of Sir Willoughby Patterne is an appropriate focus for the discussion of Meredith's presentation of character. He has proven almost infuriating to critics in his mixture of undeniable skills and fatuity, an "aberration" in van Ghent's terms, with whom it seems impossible to identify.[12] Worst of all, he is not corrected by the Comic Spirit hovering over the book, nor even directly designated an egoist to his face.[13] Even so, the reader must wonder at the end if even an egoist could be so totally blind to his own nature after its public exposure.

This blindness is most glaringly illuminated in the chapter, "In Which Sir Willoughby Chances to Supply the Title for Himself." This chapter and the several succeeding ones contain Clara's double revelation of Willoughby and Vernon Whitford. They focus her awakening vision in such a way as to make the situation at Patterne Hall evident to all the principals involved. The key self-appellation scene in this chapter serves, moreover, as a paradigm for the mode of access to knowledge in the text.

Enacted here is a movement from vision to blindness in Willoughby that apparently sets off a contrary movement in Clara. It begins with Willoughby pondering some way of avoiding the threatened breakup of his domestic circle that would damage his own sense of identity. Vernon has made known his wish to depart for London, but also wishes to have Willoughby's assurance that he will send Crossjay to naval school. Willoughby, however, plans to use this double desire to permit a trade—Vernon's future for Crossjay's—and to bind Vernon further to Patterne Hall by marrying him to Laetitia.

This is more than a plot, however. It is also an enactment for Clara's sake, an attempt by Willoughby to transmit his vision to her and thus to tame her admiration. Already sensible of her still inarticulate rebellion, he seeks to defuse it by this display of power and benevolence. Clara herself has begun to sense her discontent, but is still blind to any flaw in her fiancé that might justify it. What Willoughby reveals in sharing his plan, however, is not so much his insight into others as his blindness to himself. He admits his faults, such as pride, but revels in them, a curiously impotent form of self-knowledge that springs from his view that character is integral and fixed. "I am what I am" (E, X:107).[14] Confession, in fact, becomes self-justification, a measuring of self against the world in which the nature of the world is second best.[15] Clara, however, focuses on a different level of the discourse, seeing for the first time how Willoughby's vision of the world is a reflection of his own nature. "Her teacher had brought her to contemplate his view of the world. She thought likewise: how must a man despise women, who can expose himself as he does to me!" (E, X:111). Meredith's point here is that one's vision of the world serves as an excuse for one's behavior. It is a purely subjective impression and projection of oneself that fails, however, to enlighten the self.

The consequence of this effort at shared vision is that Clara begins to think differently. "Miss Middleton owed it to Sir Willoughby Patterne that she ceased to think like a girl" (E, X:111). She thus sees Willoughby more clearly, but is beginning to go out of focus to herself (nearly perfectly repeating Willoughby's own status in this conversation). She becomes alienated first from her own past, the origin of their courtship. "And she . . . [had] become barred from imagining her own emotions of that season. They were so dead as not to arise even under the forms of shadows in fancy" (E, X:111).[16]

Prior to examining the epithet scene, we do well to recall Meredith's introductory chapter, where he specifies the nature of the comedy he will give us. "The Comic Spirit conceives a definite situation for a number of characters, and rejects all accessories in the exclusive pursuit of them and their speech" (E, I:1). Meredith makes two important points here: (1) the objects of the Comic Spirit are plural ("them"), and (2) the process of analysis will focus not on acts alone, but on linguistic revelations ("their speech"). One needs to keep these comments in mind in order to avoid equating Clara, or anyone else, with the corrective Comic Spirit. Individuals are at most the occasional agents of it for others; there can be no one

Comic Spirit for everyone, and no one can serve this role for himself or herself.[17]

During the dinner scene, Willoughby is mocked for the blindness of his generic simplification of national character. He revenges himself by appropriating the discourse with an anecdote—a monologic verbal act—about a gentleman whose only concern as his wife lies desperately ill is that he might be forced into the inconvenience of seeking a new wife to replace her—the "loving husband of any devoted wife." "Now there, Clara, there you have the Egoist" (E, X:115), concludes Willoughby, handing her his own definition, whose first element is the absorption of others into the framework of one's own needs and drives. Willoughby's self-exposure is again a linguistic one.

This title serves as the key revelation for Clara, clarifying her perception of her fiancé. The immediate result is to justify her revolt, arming her self-defense and nerving her to action. But Meredith stresses that this is an alienating vision as well, a private one seen by no one else, that divides Clara from those around her. "She looked at Vernon, she looked at her father, and at the ladies Eleanor and Isabel. None of them saw the man in the word, none noticed the word; yet this word was her medical herb, her illuminating lamp, the key of him" (E, X:115). The dangerous consequence of such private vision is contempt for the blindness of those who cannot or do not share it.[18] To adopt it fully is to assent to a view of consistent character very much like Willoughby's own. The reader, sharing Clara's vision here, is close to sharing her sense of omniscient discovery. The subsequent extension of the term, as all in turn proclaim themselves egoists, makes its explanatory power seem that much more compelling.

Yet it ought to be more disconcerting than critics have generally felt it to be that we lose sight of Willoughby here, just when one would most like to see inside him. Why tell this particular anecdote? Why at this particular moment? Does Willoughby see the significance of what he relates? We, like Clara, are in interpretive limbo, uncertain whether the words are a warning or an instance of Willoughby's fatuous self-satisfaction. The blank we are given of his mind here is a function of Clara's and our own blindness toward him, as the text enacts the limitation of linguistic vision. Clara terms Willoughby an egoist; we agree, and the case is settled.

The succeeding consequences of Clara's insight, however, are curious. Armed with her epithet for Willoughby, Clara for the first time imagines requesting her release from the engagement. In so doing, she turns him into an "obelisk," an "immovable stone man." He becomes The Egoist. Thus, although all the main characters declare themselves egoists, he remains the measure for it and in a sense their justification. This world of egoists is much like the worldview Willoughby has been endeavoring to pass on to Clara, so that she is most like him as she begins to wield the temptingly abstract and multiapplicable word.

This transformation for the subject of character by epithet is characteristic of the functioning of epithets in Meredith's work. Their tendency to freeze their objects is a prime concern of his, drawing together the epithet, image, and comparison as essentially analogous in their operation on reality. "A single word is too broad a mark to be exactly true" (*V*, XXXII:109), notes the narrator in *Vittoria*, and the generalization holds throughout Meredith's novels. Epithets seem partial and distorting, a one-eyed vision of the aspect for the whole, which can nonetheless be correct in a sense, and troubling until one has extracted the grain of truth in them.[19] The role of such linguistic abbreviation in the functioning of interpretation is summarized by Meredith in *One of Our Conquerors*, where its role is equally pronounced:

> We are indebted almost for construction to those who will define us briefly: we are but scattered leaves to the general comprehension of us until such a work of binding and labelling is done. And should the definition be not so correct as brevity pretends to make it at one stroke, we are at least rendered portable; thus we pass into the conceptions of our fellows, into the records, down to posterity. (*OOC*, XI:110)

Beneath the deprecatory tone of the narrator is the disquieting sense that such terms are in a sense constitutive of identity.

Clearly uppermost, however, is the idea that epithets are delusive because they masquerade as full knowledge. The clearest victim of their power in *The Egoist* is DeCraye, whose vain dreams of picking up an unattached Clara are fostered by his own linguistic self-manipulation. "Regarding her sentiments for Willoughby, he had come to his own conclusion. The certainty of it caused him to assume that he possessed an absolute knowledge of her character: she was an angel, born supple; she was a heavenly soul, with half a dozen of the tricks of earth. Skittish filly, was among his phrases" (*E*, XXII:261). The risk is that the satisfaction such phrases provide will allow one to stop thinking, to cut short the hermeneutic process by blinding one to further reflective efforts.[20]

Epithetic discourse also conceals from the subject the element of personal bias involved in its construction. "Shun comparisons. It is the tricksy heart which sets up that balance, to jump into it on one side or the other. Comparisons come of a secret leaning that is sure to play rogue under its mien of honest dealer" (*BC*, XXIV:252). Such language use is favored by the sentimentalist, who employs it as a tool in his evasion of personal recognizance. But the epithet differs from the image perhaps in its deterrence of the sort of precipitate action into which a Wilfrid Pole plunges. The epithet is the mode of the detached ironist, first appearing in Meredith's work with Adrian Harley, whose "two ears were stuffed with his own wisdom" (*ORF*, VI:51). As Wilt has effectively demonstrated, Meredith is radically suspicious of just this sort of detached intelligence, whose embodiment here is Mrs. Mountstuart.[21] Vernon's evaluation of her is a warning to all of us. "You see how easy it is to deceive one who is an artist in phrases. Avoid them, Miss Dale; they dazzle the penetration of the composer" (*E*, XXX:77). Even vision should not be too brilliant, lest the observer himself be blinded.

Yet Vernon's judgment here, springing as it does from an epigram flung at *him*, errs perhaps in being too scrupulous. Epithetic discourse is the most consistent trait of Meredith's own style, and is a crucial aspect of his epistemology. He recognizes that the mind will think in images and abbreviations in any case, and that one therefore needs to learn how to employ them.[22] They are necessary, because there are parts of the psyche to which we only have access thus. While Meredith's understanding of the unconscious was hardly explicitly developed, his recognition of the role of a "submerged self" (*SB*, XXXVIII:121) made up of repressed sensations and his willingness to explore the resultant mysteries contribute to the unusual depth of his characters. The psyche for Meredith is not just a set of relations, logical or otherwise, but also the emotional intensities attached to particular relations, which account for the half-willed evasiveness of language, where flashing insight and disguise are virtually simultaneous. "I am sensible of evasion when I open my lips," says Diana (*DC*, XXXVIII:428), different from Meredith's other characters only in that sensibility.[23] Once pressed into language, however, such evasions are hard to dislodge, since their elements are constituted below the level of reflective awareness.

Epithets and figurative language can nonetheless work positively in the mind, by keeping at the level of consciousness elements that might otherwise be wholly repressed, and by communicating ideas that are not yet formalized. Unresolved, they serve as a focus for psychic concern, as does the "rogue in porcelain" description of Clara, whose significance reverberates through Willoughby's mind precisely because it has not been reduced to a determinate signification. Epithets and images provide "a tart measure of the truth" (DC, I:14) for one who knows how to interpret them. After providing a simile to describe Wilfrid Pole, Meredith pulls himself up and says, "This simile says more than I mean it to say, but those who understand similes will know the measure due to them" (SB, XVIII:179–180). The key to interpreting such language use is not so much to determine what they mean, but rather how far they mean what they say. It is neither by accepting nor rejecting an epithet that one approaches truth, but by fitting it into a system, an embedded hierarchy of discourse.[24]

Returning to Clara's use of egoist, it is clear that she sees more by employing it, but also less, due to the hermeneutic overconfidence it engenders. She not only freezes Willoughby linguistically, but grows literally blinder to his nature. Apparent discrepancies between his behavior and his tag—his deference to her wish not to wear the family jewels, for instance—act to inhibit her free action. She cannot anticipate him and, even near the end when she knows of his duplicitous proposal to Laetitia, is incapable of outmaneuvering him. It is Vernon who is able to rout Willoughby then, for he sees him as a cipher, not an epithet (E, XXX:76). Clara, however, fails to see the cunning in Willoughby's egoism's readiness to compromise, that is, his particular pragmatic species of egoism.

The epithet scene also marks the beginning of Clara's blindness to herself, not only to her past, but to her present behavior as well.[25] Clara is absorbed by the very term she has created, possessed of a deeper, but correspondingly narrower, vision. Already in chapter XI she justifies, by anticipation, whatever hypocrisies she might find it necessary to use. Her encounter with Laetitia in chapter XVI brings her transition from vision to blindness full circle and links up the next participant in the interpretive chain.

Here Clara enters into a confession of her situation, acknowledging her own egoism. This is a revelation exactly parallel to Willoughby's, for it indicates her similar refusal to envisage clearly her own practice of egoism and the privileged position of the hearer who sees most obviously just what is being concealed. Clara's summation is worth quoting at length as an illustration of her willful blindness:

> "Here is the difference I see; I see it; I am certain of it: women who are called coquettes make their conquests not of the best of men; but men who are Egoists have *good* women for their victims; women on whose devoted constancy they feed; they drink it like blood. . . . They punish themselves too by passing over the one suitable to them, who could really give them what they crave to have, and they go where they . . ." Clara stopped. "I have not your power to express ideas," she said.
>   "Miss Middleton, you have a dreadful power," said Laetitia. (*E*, XVI:191)

What Clara's scrupulous adherence to a balanced abstract theory obscures is the personal reference immediately clear to Laetitia. Critics have generally followed Clara in making a distinction between good and bad varieties of egoism, without adequately stressing that it is not self-assertion alone but the commitment to an alternate view of relationship that frees her.[26] But is her egoism here wholly positive?

What her confidante recognizes is that Clara's egoism and sudden power to express ideas, to manipulate language, are ruthlessly aiming to sacrifice Laetitia on the altar of Clara's own freedom. She treats Laetitia as a counter, seeing her as she would have her be. After portraying her grim picture of Willoughby, to give Laetitia to this vampire is surely as heartless as anything Willoughby has heretofore contemplated. Clara lacks only his power, though that lack makes her seem less culpable. And she possesses a power of her own, using Crossjay and DeCraye with a nonchalance hardly more commendable for being thoughtless rather than consciously manipulative.

More important here, however, is the vision transmitted to Laetitia out of Clara's blindness; her eyes are opened to the horror and pervasiveness of egoism. Seeing it in Clara enables her to read Willoughby much more clearly, which ironically lays the foundation for her later refusal of him that threatens Clara's escape. But she sees Clara as well, well enough to begin to trace the directions of her particular egoism. As for Clara, what began as vision becomes the blindness of self-revelation as soon as it contacts the web of her own needs and desires.

This pattern of blindness and vision is expicitly laid out by Meredith later in the novel. The "Egoist" label is what the characters come to term a "rough truth." Each of the principal participants in turn defines rough truth, in the process of which they enact the very definitions they propose. To give Dr. Middleton's initial effort precedence, we may say with him, "A rough truth, madam, I should define to be that description of truth which is not imparted to mankind without a powerful impregnation of the roughness of the teller" (E, XXXVI:150).[27] Here indeed is Meredith's view of all language that aspires to truth; it is an effort at knowledge that acts as a self-revelation, concealed as an abstraction, or as the soldier DeCraye puts it, "A rather strong charge of universal nature for the firing off of a modicum of personal fact" (E, XXXVI:151). Each further definition aids Clara's concealment only by a linguistic revelation of each of the speakers in turn, culminating in Willoughby's claim that rough truth is caricature (which he is fast approaching), and Laetitia's that it is realistic directness (from which she, too, is not far distant). The roughest truth of all may be that of Mrs. Mountstuart, who does not contribute a definition, but admires herself for her assumed full knowledge and adroit manipulation of the situation.

Rough truth, like epithet, is partial truth slanted toward the personality of the teller. Given this vision of language, it seems less remarkable that Meredith should be, as Wilde wrote, "breaking his shins over his own wit," when all speakers are doing just that. Like Willoughby's vision of the world, rough truth externalizes and thus justifies the vagaries and inconsistencies of personal behavior. Egoism is Clara's projection of her current state on to the world. It, like all egoism, is nourished by the abuse of linguistic possibilities, a confusion of intent with meaning.

This label thus blinds Clara to the second aspect of egoism, which not only tries to absorb others, but uses them for personal ends, treating them as counters in the belief that one has a special ordeal. Such a vision is a self-induced evasion of personal responsibility, of conscience's assertion that responsibility extends to being accountable for others' development and knowledge as well as for one's own. The silence born of this self-blinding is not the neutral limit of a language bordering on the inexpressible but the edge of moral irresponsibility. The lack of words for what one would express, for one's interpretation of the world, does not absolve one from the obligation of seeking them.[28]

Yet Clara retreats into just this kind of conscious inarticulateness, sure of her vision, but unwilling to communicate it to others. She refuses to accept the responsibility of calling Willoughby an egoist. She endeavors to create attitudes in others without confronting them and constantly conveys either more or less than she means. In her first effort after freedom, she twists Willoughby to make him strike "the very point she had not named and did not wish to hear named, but wished him to strike" (E, XIII:148), namely the possible replacement of her by Laetitia as bride. Her epithet, like all private vision, remains powerful only when held in reserve. "What could she say? he is an Egoist? The epithet has no meaning in such a scene" (E, XLI:212). So she invents and evades, not only with Willoughby and her father, but with Vernon and Laetitia (at least at first) as well. The danger of vision, then, is that it seems so clear and self-evident that she thinks all should see it, which obviates the need to speak. The consequence, inevitably, is misapprehension, the tangle of misperceived motives that make up the fabric of the remaining four hundred pages.

Most human misconnections in Meredith's novels arise from this refusal to speak or from taking refuge in allusiveness. This is in part a rightful fear of the power of words—"a thing once spoken of attracts like a living creature, and does not die voluntarily" (RF, XXX:324)—but it is more often an attempt to protect oneself from the self-revelation in all communication. At the same time, there exists an expectation that the other person can read through this silence and see one's state of mind. This refusal to engage in dialogue and interpretive probing is based on a belief in the essential sameness of minds and a blindness to the complexity of the hermeneutic act. Irony appears in Meredith's work as the recognition of the need to communicate, to speak what one conceives to be the case, while knowing that the other will see one's self imprinted in it. But it is necessary to leave that interpretive space for the other, as the point where an alternative meaning can emerge that the subject can then strive to envisage. Irony is the "diversity in the companion throbs of your pulses," whereas egoism is "the malady of sameness, our modern malady" (E, I:2,4). That malady of sameness, of interpretive orthodoxy, has been Meredith's target since Shibli tackled the Identical and is the ultimate crime attributed to Willoughby. "What he revealed was not the

cause of her sickness . . . but the monotonousness. He slew imagination"
(*E*, XXXIX:183). This is not the Romantic aesthetic imagination so much as
the creative apprehension of difference in others. Clara's own language
becomes Willoughby's accomplice here; her term of liberation becomes
more and more constrictive of her identity as well as his.

In contrast to this gathering blindness stands Clara's second revelation, which immediately follows the epithet chapter as a counterpoint to it.
Her vision of Vernon sleeping beneath the cherry tree gives her a positive
anchor to cling to, although this imagistic summary is initially no more
able to break through her obscurity than her linguistic one was. Yet the
difference is notable, for the vision here is mobile, both delimited and
controlled. "Wonder lived in her. Happiness in the beauty of the tree
pressed to supplant it, and was more mortal and narrower. Reflection
came, contracting her vision and weighing her to earth" (*E*, XI:135). It is
important for Clara's developing sensibility that the image and feeling are
not idealized (as was the epithet), but are absorbed by reflection. Her
greater detachment from Vernon at this point, since she anticipates no
great aid from him, permits the conversion of image into interpretation,
where particular relevances replace and limit its sentimental thrust.[29]

This vision, then, serves as an aid to freedom, as the appellation did
not. It counteracts her earlier, limiting view of Vernon, even her resentment at his aloofness. It thus facilitates her speaking to him and through
his advice to Laetitia, which sparks the trail of illumination in the novel.
Yet this vision also falls short of a fuller development because the personal element, her observing self, is left out. The cherry tree remains a
private vision, whose roughness as truth Clara does not quite grasp.

This limitation permits another aspect of Clara's blindness to develop. Partially blind to Willoughby and to her own egoism, she is also
almost totally blind to her own desires. She spends most of the novel
evading them, unconsciously acting in response to Vernon without acknowledging or understanding this. Part of the reason for this blindness is
the endemic influence of her fixation on egoism. That sets up a polarity of
absorption and liberty, easily translated into sexual terms, that artificially
narrows the terms of her situation. For Meredith, opening one portal of
vision always closed off other ones.

This fixation is to some degree inescapable. Characters in Meredith's
novels are never isolated, but identify instead with someone else. As Clara
is here attached more psychically than legally to Willoughby, so do

Meredith's characters display identities that are inextricably intermingled with those around them.[30] Meredith's heroes often seem flimsy because they are unattached and therefore undefined ciphers, open because recently released (from an ill-fated attachment) and between relationships.

Clara's fixation, however, means that she tries to read Vernon in terms of egoism, a label adopted from Willoughby. This comes close to ruining their potential union at the end, for she refuses to think that he could accept her, knowing her flaws. Yet this blindness is also a more positive one, allowing the quality of their relationship to emerge. Vernon is freer to develop in Clara's mind, which has restrained itself from imposing an epithet, even one plucked from the cherry tree, on him. Yet she must also surrender this image, for it is too one-sided and idealistic.

Meredith thus provides another clue to his own sense of the nature of good imagery. The paradoxical, ironic quality of images such as "rogue in porcelain" or the "haggard Venus" of *The Amazing Marriage* preserves them from one-sided exaggeration. The gift is that which Emma Dunstane attributes to Shakespeare: "The bravest and best of us at bay in the world need an eye like his, to read deep and not be baffled by inconsistencies" (*DC*, VIII:89–90). An ironic mind captures the simultaneity of opposites and the potentiality in character, where the egoist seeks an unambiguous signification. Willoughby is haunted by the "rogue in porcelain" image, which seems a logical contradiction to his either-or mentality. "Women of mixed essences shading off the divine to the considerably lower, were outside his vision of woman. His mind could as little admit an angel in pottery as a rogue in porcelain" (*E*, XI:130).

Unable to combine both, he concludes with the misapprehension that Clara is porcelain. She contributes to his misreading by refusing to speak out fully in asking for her release and leaving an interpretive space too large for him to fill as he pleases—with her apparent conformity. "He, a fairly intelligent man, and very sensitive, was blinded to what was going on within her visibly enough, by her production of the article he demanded of her sex [i.e., purity]." (*E*, XI:132). The word *jealousy*, his private revelatory explanation, thus comes to govern and distort her entire first plea for freedom, in yet another case of linguistic self-deception.

What Meredith has demonstrated, then, in the case of the "Egoist" epithet, is the ability of language to fortify the self behind a bulwark made of the egoism of single vision. Clara's revelation of Willoughby's character inaugurates her own egoistic isolation. The irony of ironies is that her knowledge has led only to blindness. By clinging to private vision and refusing the exploration of the mystery of her own conduct, she slips into a blindness like that of Lord Fleetwood. "Men uninstructed in analysis of motives arrive at this dangerous conclusion [that one's own character is a mystery], which spares their pride and caresses their indolence, while it flatters the sense of internal vastness, and invites to headlong intoxication" (*AM*, XXXV:366). Intoxicated indeed is just how Clara seems to behave, drunk on her personal vision of human behavior.

It nonetheless remains true that Clara in her blindness can still enlighten others, both as to others and as to herself. As she anatomizes Willoughby for other minds, she reveals more about herself than him, but that is still sufficient to establish the current of interpretation that can flow back and energize her. Her sense of vision gives her the courage to seek to reinterpret reality, in which process she begins to emerge as subject. It is Laetitia who most accurately perceives this change, who emerges as the most skilled reader as the text advances, and who is most successful in restoring a measure of hermeneutic integrity to the situation.

She proves able to read not only Clara but the other characters as well, without taking her insights for perfect vision. More significantly, she makes effective use of her knowledge by reflecting it back to those to whom it applies. She has been a reflector all along, at first only of Willoughby's self-image, but increasingly bending the rays to fit them to the contours of her own mind, a more active and promising role. Laetitia aids Vernon in recognizing his love and its nature, "revealing to him at the same instant as to herself, that she swung suspended on a scarce credible guess" (*E*, XXXIII:109). Later, she comes closer than anyone to closing the interpretive chain by returning the epithet "egoist" to its source, Willoughby.[31]

For Meredith, this indirection in the process of knowing self is essential, because the self's knowledge of itself is always incomplete. Personal significations are elided from articulated truth that seems smooth to the subject, so that even self-revelation is deceptive, already bound up in a system of values that justify whatever is revealed. To see that one is an egoist is not at all the same as to see where and how one is an egoist, and perhaps even less so than before, for the satisfaction with an abstract term, with the mere act of naming, disposes of the issue. Only when that self-revelation is articulated back to the subject and thus defined in a more precise way does it become effective self-knowledge. Clara's vision serves everyone but her, for she cannot envision herself.

The truth about the subject emerges from interrogation, from without.[32] External vision, in its divergences from self-image, forces the reassessment and revision of the subject. Clara's honesty is already increased when "the pressure of Vernon's mind was on her" (E, XXVIII:37), but the full force of her self-recognition emerges only from direct questioning by another person. Her submission to such probing shows her awareness of her ignorance of herself and is her most striking difference from Willoughby. Even in her egoism she retains an ironic sense of the incompleteness of herself.

It is Mrs. Mountstuart who begins the process, leading Clara to see and confess her egoism in using DeCraye to seek to manipulate Willoughby and then drawing her toward recognition of her love for Vernon. Mrs. Mountstuart forces Clara toward the brink of those self-evasions born of her private vision. Asked if there is any man she would wish to marry, "Clara sat back with bated breath, mentally taking the leap into the abyss, realizing it, and the cold prudence of abstention, and the delirium of the confession" (E, XXXV:142). She perceives how her mind leaps to Vernon, though she fails to speak his name here. Yet the advance is clear. "She had spoken out more than she had ever spoken to herself: and in doing so she had cast herself a step beyond the line she dared to contemplate" (E, XXXV:144). As we have seen to be typical in such cases, the heightened vision of one person is offset by increased blindness elsewhere, here for Mrs. Mountstuart. She is so certain of her intuition that the man in question is DeCraye that she remains deluded and prolongs the misunderstandings. Wholly intent on guessing correctly, she fails to wait for the truth to emerge from Clara's mind and on her lips.

So it is left for Laetitia to finish enlightening Clara. Convinced of her love for Vernon, Clara still feels that he cannot love anyone so flawed as he knows her to be and takes this as the reason for his hesitation in declaring himself. Laetitia's gently prodding questions lead Clara first to see how her own behavior, flirting with DeCraye, misled Vernon and then to perceive that fuller relationship that surpasses egoistic interactions, that is, love. For Clara here, truth is love, but of a peculiarly ironic kind. "To be loved, I see, is to feel our littleness, hollowness—feel shame" (E, XLVIII:312). Love is where one first sees the self in the other's eyes as partial in a positive, potential sense; it is the basis of and itself based upon completed intersubjectivity. Clara and Vernon are moving toward this earlier defined standard by accepting their not fully ideal status and their consequent need for ironic completion, for mutual self-revelation.[33]

At these moments of interrogatory revelation, language strives toward a precision of understanding that must finally dispense with figurative language like the epithet, for its heuristic function has been accomplished. Now is a time for full explication, and both Mrs. Mountstuart and Laetitia cut off Clara's evasive recourse to simile. " 'Defer the simile,' Mrs. Mountstuart interposed. 'If you hit on a clever one, you will never get the better of it' " (E, XXXV:141)—which is as accurate an assessment of Clara's predicament since the epithet scene as one could desire. It is the recognition, on the other hand, of one's obligation to make oneself understood, of one's hermeneutic responsibility to others, that signals Clara's truer vision of this situation. She conquers the linguistic egoism that has plagued her when Laetitia finally corrects her: "Similes have the merit of satisfying the finder of them, and cheating the hearer" (E, XLVIII:310).

Yet the close of the novel is not all vision and light. Its slip back into blindness has the ominous quality of much of Meredith's work, intently focused on the difficulty of sustaining context-bound vision as one moves on. What we receive at the end is a dose of narrative blindness—to Willoughby's last contortions in begging Laetitia's hand, from which the narrator considerately withdraws. Hence we again lose sight of Willoughby's mind and cannot know the degree to which he may be changing. This is risky, for as we have seen, self-imposed blindness allows one not to alter one's vision of others, to reside in old truths. The text enacts Clara's residual blindness; she has escaped from Willoughby, but not envisaged him.

Laetitia's acceptance of Willoughby's hand is also problematic, for she has proven capable of reflecting others, but who will now reflect her? She is in some ways still posing, no longer the romantic, but rather the disillusioned realist, yet hardly quite so worn out at thirty. Nor is she the egoist she claims to be, marrying for material advantage, when she is clearly giving up herself and her dreams to the needs of others—of her father, of Clara and Vernon, even of Willoughby.

This persistence of blindness is repeated in many other Meredith novels, for the intersubjective vision Clara seems to acquire can be just as fitful as subjective vision. Characters elsewhere often fall short of even the partial vision attained here, owing to their insistent prevision of the revelations before their eyes. To see the full measure of ironic vision in *The Egoist*, it is helpful to look at alternative explorations of the idea of vision. *Richard Feverel* provides an early study of natural revelation and the reliance on preverbal self-knowledge. *One of Our Conquerors*, at the other end of Meredith's career, brings us to the opposite extreme of revelation that is repressed, where the epithet becomes a taboo. These novels suggest how fragile vision is for Meredith and point out how an ironic vision is necessarily an endless revision.

### *The Ordeal of Richard Feverel:* Self-limiting Vision, or the Hermit's Blindness

*He quitted London to take refuge among the mountains; living there in solitary commune with a virgin Note-book.—(ORF, XXXVI:385)*

Unlike *The Egoist's* intersubjective dialectic of vision and blindness born of linguistic evasiveness, *Richard Feverel* seems to hold open the alternative of a more immediate and certain form of self-knowledge. What is offered here is natural vision, immersion of the self in a larger, more stable order.[34] This is opposed to the idea of system, which is in many ways simply the elaboration of the same kind of limited personal vision as the epithet. The embodiment of system is Sir Austin Feverel's program for raising his son to flawless manhood by the exclusion of any lower elements in human nature. To his own mind the logical deduction from his disinterested observations on human nature contained in his anonymously published *Pilgrim's Scrip*, the system is far more a product of his personal bitterness at his wife's infidelity in leaving him for a destitute poet.

Where *The Egoist* depicts a constant pressure toward self-communication, this novel is characterized by an acceptance of hermeneutic isolation; virtually all the characters are self-contentedly monologic. In consequence, language here is a realm of almost unremitting blindness, a place for presumed answers rather than questions. Characters repeatedly attempt to mediate and distill their experiences as private vision, engaging in a dialogue with the self to which only palatable thoughts are admitted. "There is ever in the mind's eye a certain wilfulness. We see and understand; we see and won't understand" (ORF, XL:473). The result of this self-manipulation is the smoothing out of the rough spots of character until one can present a flexible mask to the world. "The Aphorist [Sir Austin] read himself so well, that to juggle with himself was a necessity. As he wished the world to see him, he beheld himself" (ORF, XL:465). When this monologic self-understanding is then used to read the world, interpretation has become an absolutely self-enclosed process. " 'The reason why men and women are mysterious to us, and prove disappointing . . . is, that we will read them from our own book; just as we are perplexed by reading ourselves from theirs' " (ORF, XXIX:288). Interpretations do not intersect, for their function is not to explore, but to conceal the subject.

This is a mode of behavior Sir Austin transmits to Richard along with his System. There is, unfortunately, no Laetitia for Richard,[35] for the relationships in the novel are all one-directional, and the only mirrors are worshipful or lackey-like. This is a novel of narcissism, of self-absorbed self-concern, to a much greater degree than is The Egoist. While Willoughby is an egoist, he is not subject to narcissistic blindness, for he is a social egoist, intent on reading others (though he sometimes errs). In Richard Feverel, however, the characters live on the edge of absolute isolation without sensing their resultant vulnerability.

The final scene is emblematic of this condition. Richard is described by Lady Blandish as unable to imagine his dead wife, whose brain-fever was brought on by his precipitate and self-concerned actions. " 'Have you noticed the expression in the eyes of blind men? That is just how Richard looks, as he lies there silent in his bed—striving to image her on his brain' " (ORF, XLV:542). This has, in fact, been his condition all along, as Richard refused to engage in the hermeneutic dialectic that would force him to see himself in relation to others. He has never had a solid image of Lucy. Hence there is no striving toward shared vision or trust in interrogation. Richard invariably trusts his own eyes; even at the moment when he first hears of being a father from Austin Wentworth, he chooses not to seek knowledge from outside himself, but has recourse to subjective imaginative evocation. "Richard fixed his eyes as if he were trying to make out the lineaments of his child" (ORF, XLII:504).[36] This excessive reliance on personal vision is matched by an equal restraint from intruding on others, which, since no one asks for help, leaves each character in interpretive isolation. Even Austin's role in the above scene, where he seeks to bring Richard back to his wife by telling him of his child, is curiously passive. His role is to provide the facts and then to leave Richard to work it out on his own.

The barrenness of linguistic interaction in the novel means that it is the lyricism of nature and passion that seems to occupy the center of the novel. Lucy Desborough, the spouse whom Richard finds by good fortune despite the System, is a child of nature. Their initial romantic meeting is idyllic in tone, pastoral in setting, and Richard's later recovery of his attachment to her also takes place in nature. The focus of the novel then, seems to be on the effort to define the subject vis-à-vis nature, not in and through other people.[37] There has been a critical tendency to read Romantic principles into this text, yet though the framework is perhaps not yet fully worked out by Meredith, he is already in the process of undermining the egotistical sublime because such vision tends to be hypostasized and kept for private nourishment.

An ironic current develops out of the characters' blindness to parallels for their own situations, which the narrator obligingly provides for the reader.[38] Thus Lucy and Richard first meet under the promising shadow of *The Tempest*, only to have the narrator turn at once to a discrepancy. "If these two were Ferdinand and Miranda, Sir Austin was not Prospero, and was not present, or their fates might have been different" (*ORF*, XV:119). The inability to recognize the metaphors that govern their lives makes the characters subject to them, unable to reassess and correct the patterns they repeat.[39] It is necessary to see the metaphoric texture of life in Meredith's world if one is to position oneself consciously with respect to it.

The alternative is a vision of the egoism of destiny, the sense that one's fate is somehow unique, and hence that one cannot and need not procure advice from others. Both Sir Austin and Richard demonstrate a proud reliance on self, be it intellectual or instinctive. Richard even feels that his own poetry has prophesized Lucy, almost brought her into being.[40] This strengthens an exaggerated sense of the subject as a self-determining agent, not acted upon, and fosters the pride that contributes to Richard's seduction by Bella Mount. Thus the inadequacy of linguistic or intellectual vision revealed in *The Egoist* is already being explored in this earlier novel.

What *Richard Feverel* makes additionally clear, however, is that natural vision provides no better guidance for social life.[41] This becomes evident in the forest scene that is often taken as a sort of natural revelation.

Richard had fled England and his wife out of shame at his own infidelity and because of a recognition of his insensitivity to his cousin Clare, which contributed to her death. Having burned all letters from home, he is unaware that he is a father until Austin seeks him out. Uncertain how to respond, Richard goes on a long forest walk and experiences a storm and a sense of rejuvenation from his encounter with nature. As Jeffers notes, nature acts to restore a sense of humility and proportion to Richard, whose very flight was based on the self-inflation of excessive remorse.[42] Nature is indeed restorative, but as we shall see, also hermeneutically empty.

Richard's walk seems, in fact, strikingly like Sir Austin's hermitic stance, though he is solitary before nature and not a notebook. "Alone there—sole human creature among the grandeurs and mysteries of storm—he felt the representative of his kind, and his spirit rose, and marched, and exulted, let it be glory, let it be ruin!" (ORF, XLII:506). This is hardly ironic humility, even if Meredith may be sharing some of his hero's intoxication here. Active encounter with nature, in fact, leads him away from reflective consideration of his situation. "He sat and eyed them [the glow-worms], thinking not at all. His energies were expended in action" (ORF, XLII:506). As he keeps moving, however, nature does indeed speak through the electrifying touch of a young leveret, which he has found and cradled in his arm. This speech beyond words produces an effect like a conversion or purification and induces Richard to return to his wife and family.

Yet this crucial scene also has overtones that temper its promise. The final element of Richard's vision is not the leveret at all, but an altar of the Virgin holding her Child, which he passes. His implicit identification of them with Lucy and his son, which seems to purify him as well, is a juxtaposition of a kind already seen to be dangerous. What earlier makes Richard vulnerable to Bella Mount is just this sort of loose analogizing, which there leads him to self-abasement. "What had he done in it [his life]? He had burnt a rick and got married! He associated the two acts of his existence. . . . The young man sought amusement" (ORF, XXXVIII:421).[43] The Catholic image is itself problematic, for Catholicism is usually portrayed by Meredith as yet another self-evasion (Countess de Saldar, Lord Fleetwood). In terms of Richard's specific situation, the image is even less satisfying, for the paradigm of the pure virgin-child relationship without a father present is indicative of his own detachment from involvement. He has, essentially, written himself out of the scene to restore its purity, an indication of his mental constraint by egoistic polarities such as good and evil. The restoration itself is equally ominous when examined in detail.[44]

> He looked within, and saw the Virgin holding her Child. He moved by. But not many steps had he gone ere his strength went out of him, and he shuddered. What was it? He asked not. He was in other hands. Vivid as lightning the Spirit of Life illumined him. He felt in his heart the cry of his child, his darling's touch. With shut eyes he saw them both. They drew him from the depths; they led him a blind and tottering man. And as they led him he had a sense of purification so sweet he shuddered again and again. (ORF, XLII:508)

Richard is blind here, too, inevitably and as usual. He is transformed only so long as he is passive, and purified only on the condition that he blot out himself and his past. His confession to Lucy will be too Catholic, too blindly in search of forgiveness rather than the understanding of the factors that led to the sin.

Hence as soon as he returns to action, Richard goes astray again. The same factors of egoism and narcissism turn up when he receives a letter from Bella telling him that she seduced him as the agent of Lord Mountfalcon, who had designs on Lucy. Richard immediately challenges his newfound enemy to the duel that will wound him and lead to Lucy's death. Richard fails to integrate the natural and social vision because he transfers the moral absolutism of nature to human relationships. Like Willoughby, he feels the need to enact an absolute either-or standard of purity or sin. As before with Bella, Richard would reform the whole world at once, imposing his private solution from nature to public problems.[45] What nature provides, however, is only a sense of attachment to others without any specifics on how to establish it. Its very ecstatic quality is conducive to a moral absolutism that would decree the preeminence of the sense of elevation felt with nature. But it is limited vision, effective only if one manages to draw it into an interpretive interaction. Only by seeing the chapter, "Nature Speaks," in isolation can one privilege it as the mode of vision put forward by the novel and feel that the tragic end is anomalous.

How fully Meredith himself sensed the intimate dependence of Richard's vision and blindness on each other may be open to question and may account for the somewhat uneven texture of the text. The opposites are not so much related as juxtaposed, and Meredith often seems to be wholly in whichever alternative he is then presenting, unlike *The Egoist*, where the consequences of vision are more clearly worked out as mental process. *Richard Feverel* is finally only partially ironic, since there is no dialectic between or attempt at hermeneutic resolution of the alternatives.[46] All is played out in the individual mind of the hermit, a losing game of solitaire.

What natural vision leaves out, and the cause of sentimental affinity for it, is the sense of extended responsibility to others for all the ramifications of one's own acts. " 'Sentimentalists,' says *The Pilgrim's Scrip,* 'are they who seek to enjoy without incurring the Immense Debtorship for a thing done' " (*ORF,* XXIV:213). Meredith's famous epigram can be made to apply to everyone in this text, who often evade responsibility simply by refusing to see their involvement. Yet as Beer points out, people in Meredith's world are held accountable even for unintended results of their acts. "The ability to accept the unforeseen consequences of our actions is the basis of his morality."[47] The correlate of this moral premise is that there can be no such thing as individual moral development.[48] This becomes increasingly obvious in Meredith's succeeding novels (*Evan Harrington, Rhoda Fleming, Harry Richmond*), where the moral destinies of numerous characters are all bound up together. One cannot develop alone. With this perspective goes the narrative shift away from character essence and a centering hero, so typical of Meredith's fiction.

Instead of this moral vision, *Richard Feverel's* characters operate in moral abstractions that cut off discourse.[49] The focal instance of moral evasiveness is Richard's parasitic relation to Clare, his cousin. Encouraged by her mother, Clare grew up worshiping Richard and hoping to marry him. Richard failed even to acknowledge her humanity and, once he is married, gets involved only to seek to block the loveless marriage into which she has retreated. Unable to change her mind, he casts her off, contributing to her loss of spirit and death. She leaves behind, however, the record of her pain in a diary, and it is this, not Richard's infidelity, that drives him from England. This communicated vision of himself from beyond the grave is what breaks through his egoism and drives him far from Lucy; it wakens his dormant sense of responsibility. Here is the real sin in need of expiation.

The forest scene, again, makes it evident that Clare's vision and not his adultery haunts Richard. "He was utterly bare to his sin. In his troubled mind it seemed to him that Clare looked down on him—Clare who saw him as he was; and that to her eyes it would be infamy for him to go and print his kiss upon his child" (*ORF*, XLII:505). It is therefore hypocritical on Richard's part to confess only his adultery to Lucy. Even then he cannot face his broader irresponsibility and insensitivity to others, especially since he is in the process of committing exactly parallel omissions. As with Sir Austin, the abstract reverence and concern for purity conceals and displaces the real basis of human relationship and responsibility. Bella's letter can therefore counteract Clare's imperfectly conceived and eagerly evaded vision in Richard, letting him once again externalize responsibility.

With that letter, Richard reinterprets his adultery by putting the blame on others; his lapse was not natural, but socially induced. He sees an "infamous conspiracy" of men and fate, yet another facet of his resemblance to his father, who felt himself more hurt by the deception he saw in Richard's marriage than by the disloyalty.[50] The natural revelation is powerless to check this self-justifying vision, for it never adequately redefined the subject as interaction with an other could have done. Richard emerges from the forest more single-minded than ever, though this is somewhat concealed from us by a characteristic Meredithian ellipsis at the moment of blindness. A portrait of outside factors in one's life permits an inner blindness that remains blind if no outside person speaks.

Richard goes to his duel expecting Lucy, once again, to bear everything by herself. By not confiding in anyone, he conceals his blindness from others and himself from the possible reflection of it back to him. He leaves Ripton, Lucy, and all the others in a mystery, insensitive to their justifiable share in his fate. Lady Blandish condemns his father for just this willful evasion of extended responsibility, though she still favors Richard by not drawing the obvious parallel of his unconcern for Lucy. "But his father eclipsed his wrong in a greater wrong—a crime, or quite as bad; for if he deceived himself in the belief that he was acting righteously in separating husband and wife, and exposing his son as he did, I can only say that there are some who are worse than people who deliberately commit *crimes*" (*ORF*, XLV:539).

Yet Lucy fails Richard as well, and her failure is a measure of the shortcomings of the natural vision she embodies. She forgives Richard too easily, robbing him of the drama he desires, but also obstructing thereby a further, fuller confession of his irresponsibility to her in the whole Mountfalcon affair. Lucy's nonoppositional, yielding nature has just that trait that in *The Egoist* fostered blindness. Her inarticulate inability to do more than sense crimps her influence, much as Lady Blandish's influence has been limited throughout the book by her staying in the terms set out by Sir Austin and her consequent inability to get behind his premises. Lucy is as much as Lady Blandish the "blind angel" of the text, inevitably inefficacious in a world where rectified vision counts for so much.[51]

The repression of speech and inarticulateness are persistent causes of death throughout the novel. Truths are written down and locked up where they can do little or no good, except by chance. Clare's diary, Adrian's letter to Richard at the end, even *The Pilgrim's Scrip*, all fail to enter into the productive dialogue that would come of the acceptance of responsibility for one's own truth in its dissemination. They are the notes of a hermit who must write, but would prefer not to read his own writing, especially as read back by someone else. Private vision refuses interrogation or confession and turns blind. " 'You have nothing to say to me, my son? Tell me Richard! Remember, there is no home for the soul where dwells a shadow of untruth!' 'Nothing at all, sir,' the young man replied, meeting him with the full orbs of his eyes" (*ORF*, XXI:181). At the end, the eyes of his child which might have held Richard back remain, appropriately, closed. Meredith's irony in this novel is harsher than in *The Egoist*, disclosing blindness without locating any vision that can pass beyond it.

### *One of Our Conquerors:* Blindness as Contagion, and Secular Confession

*Ce sont les ténèbres qui tuent*—(*BC*, L:258)

Thus far we have seen vision both as a blindness that becomes revelation for another and as a blindness that turns away from the other. Though Meredith has been probing the interpenetration of identities, motives and blindnesses have still been largely personal in origin. The transmitted blindness arising from excessive affection has been generally confined to minor characters such as Lady Blandish or Rosamund Culling. Other people were more responsible for not correcting blindnesses by means of reflection than for begetting them.

But with the conqueror, Victor Radnor, we get a darker vision of a character intent on imposing what he feels is vision, but which we see as blindness, on others. There is no gap between himself and the world as with Willoughby, nor yet a too-easy narcissistic identification of them as with Richard. Victor attempts instead to conquer through persuasion and seduction of the world to and by his vision of himself. He would find the man he seeks there in everyone's eyes, while his refusal of paradox in his own character is an attempt to confine and master the ironic vision.

In *One of Our Conquerors*, we see blindness as social contagion.[52] Vision is actively manipulated by Victor in order to entrap and subjugate others and finally to justify himself. As he schemes, he makes full use of the power of vagueness and becomes an object lesson on the danger of despair at the limits of language. Such despair is for Meredith only a refusal to confront and seek to change those limits, against which his ironic vision insistently works.

The initial chapter lays out this whole framework for us, as we see Victor endeavoring to replace revealed double vision with the single vision of a consistent image of himself. Most of the main characters and psychic themes are present here, above all Victor's ambivalent guilt about having run off from his older first wife, Mrs. Burman, with her companion, Nataly. This attraction and their unlegalized relationship have survived twenty years, apparently sanctioned by nature (if not by Mrs. Burman or society) and blessed with a daughter, Nesta. Victor, meanwhile, has become a financial conqueror as well and is plotting at present to translate that foundation into social respectability, whether or not the tantalizingly imminent death of Mrs. Burman does indeed take place.

The first chapter, however, is the tale of a fall, a literal one of Victor on London Bridge, which rapidly assumes expanding metaphorical status.[53] This scene is an allegory of the remainder of the novel, which remains invisible to Victor, however, even though it summarizes not only his past but the likely future results of his continued efforts to flee the meaning of that past event. Victor fails to see this, because he tries to reinterpret that fall into his old pattern of ideas, seeing it as a deviation and not a revelation. By smoothing off the rough edges of his truth, he seeks to cover up the spot that appears on his white waistcoat when a workman helps him up. He pleads to himself that the fall has no metaphoric resonance, repressing the whole complex of unarticulated thoughts it focuses, by concentrating instead on an elusive Idea in his mind just before the fall.

Victor veils his potential revelation by his sense of himself as an isolated, self-determining agent, which he progressively reestablishes in the course of the chapter. Unlike the passivity of Sir Austin or Willoughby,

Victor's energy directs itself to bringing the whole world into his realm. He is a secretive manipulator, plotter, orchestrator, so it is altogether appropriate that this introductory chapter take place almost entirely in his mind, where he manipulates the discourse from the start. He seeks to do this throughout the novel, to shape the opinions of others by forcing faits accomplis on them. Nataly, however, becomes increasingly aware of how just this energy blinds him. "She went so far as to think, that Victor was guilty of the schemer's error of counting human creatures arithmetically, in the sum, without the estimate of distinctive qualities and value here and there" (OOC, XXIV:292). Like the egoist, his world is one of sameness.

Yet Victor is much more subtle, devious, and even kind than Willoughby. His mental manipulation springs from a benevolent despotism that makes others feel that they serve him and that he needs them. Even Nataly is convinced that her having committed what she always feels to have been not wholly right is justified because she saved him from despair in his marriage. Victor's success is in directing the sense of reponsibility of others primarily toward himself, to the exclusion of mitigating alternative centers. This device establishes the essential harmony between persons that can veil present difference; it, like music, can be a harmonious, but superficial, evasion. While admitting the counterpoint of diverging opinions in his circle, Victor associates them in one grand vision in his own key and thus defuses them. He is a more dangerous, but also more fascinating, figure than Willoughby, just because of his greater capacity to absorb difference and convert it to his image.

This skill springs from his vanity, his assurance of his control and his invincible rightness. This is the Victor we see immediately after his fall and subsequent uprighting. He "nodded bright beams to right and left . . . making light of the muddy stigmas imprinted by the pavement" (OOC, I:1), both sun-god and Christian martyr at once.[54] His vanity is fostered by surrounding himself with flimsy opponents or dependents, pale satellites that circle his vision. Thus, after a brief verbal altercation where the word *punctilio* is tacked on him, Victor calls on his friends Simeon Fenellan and Colney Durance as he reestablishes his own mental world around himself. "No, but one doesn't like being beaten by anything!" (OOC, I:5). To avoid being beaten, Victor chooses his own antagonists in a continual displacement of confrontation that sustains his preeminence. He sees his friends as servants, coming all too close to the reality of the self-protective relationships he has established, the only kind his insecurity can tolerate. Even Colney, the satirist, is disarmed by him. "As he could not well attack his host Victor Radnor, an irrational man, he selected the abstract entity for the discharge of his honest spite" (OOC, IX:86). We have already seen the ineffectiveness in Meredith's world of dealing with abstractions.

Having disposed of these antagonists and gazing at the London before him, he begins to translate the fall into the terms that in fact govern the whole novel. Self-satisfaction at the scene gives way to fear of a financial or national fall, brought about by the Jew. The fall brings with it an implicit recognition by Victor of the necessity of subjugation as a model for human social relationships, a nonironic union on the basis of rule or be ruled. "But the Law is always, and must ever be, the Law of the stronger" (OOC, I:9). At this point, Victor's Idea, which the fall drove from his head, begins to emerge as he ponders his partner Inchling and Inchling's "dread of the Jews."

The Idea, then, proves to be the flip side of the Fall, the restoration of that imaginative vision of personal integrity that provides Victor's self-justification. They form an either-or complex for him, mutually canceling, hence Victor craves to dispose of the fall and the "punctilio bump" that reminds him of it by fully seeing the Idea, whose clear realization eludes him throughout the novel. Its very vagueness as he tries to recapture it represents the mind's faith in an elusive panacea, an only virtual solution to its dilemmas. As private revelation, it also raises Victor above others, confirming for him his sense of uniqueness, rather like Clara's epithet, but left at the preverbal stage of being simply the "Idea." When at the end of the novel he does finally recover it, it proves to be only a mild program of political reform, so that one wonders if indeed what Victor sees then in the madness into which he has fallen is really his Idea at all.[55]

Though vague, the Idea can also serve as a covering evasion, in its seeming purity, for that full form of it that would embrace both fall and Idea. The idea behind the Idea is the recognition that in Victor's eyes life is seen as a process of subjugation, a variant on the law of the jungle, so that the Idea and the Fall are essentially identical visions of the same fact— only seen from the point of view of conqueror or conquered. The natural vision of Richard Feverel here reaches its demystified expression. Also lurking in the Idea, however, is the further realization that by operating on this principle, Victor enacts the subjugation he fears by subjugating others.

Thus Inchling, afraid of the Jews and hence willing to follow a Victor who can overcome them, will naturally call up the lost Idea. Victor's view of human relations is disconcertingly blatant. "He conquered Nataly and held her subject" (*OOC*, VI:51). But the final irony hiding in the Idea is that Victor himself becomes subject to his own aims, almost sacrificing his daughter to make her respectable.

So the articulation of the Idea would reveal its egoism and rob Victor of the sincerity he needs to press his vision on the world successfully. Its vagueness is a refuge to him, as it was to Sir Austin. "Some indefinite scheme was in his head in this treatment of his son. Had he construed it, it would have looked ugly; and it settled to a vague principle that the young man should be tried and tested" (*ORF*, XXXVI:385–386). Victor both wants and fears to grasp his Idea, continuing to operate in terms of a pattern—conquer or be conquered—whose force his mind seeks to evade. He is, in sum, a "histrionic self-deceiver," who succeeds so much the better by concealing his principles and techniques from himself as well as from others.[56]

The basis for Victor's self-deception, and an illustration of Meredith's subtle mingling of good and questionable motives, is the conviction of his own sincerity in love, seen by him as a harmony of two. That is, the inviolate aspect of the most basic human relation, and his sense of living in harmony with nature, confirm for Victor his social beneficence as well. He takes marriage as a model for society, though the novel will progressively strip away this romantic version of the marriage relation. Victor is therefore willfully blind to Nataly's progressive illness because it seems to him a violation of the natural integrity on which he relies. Nor is his love wholly false; he is less an egoist than Willoughby and relies on Nataly to reflect him. Love, however, begets a blindness of two by conforming to the principle of harmony, and concealing dissension.

> Two that live together in union are supposed to be intimate on every leaf. Particularly when they love one another and the cause they have at heart is common to them in equal measure, the uses of a cordial familiarity forbid reserves upon important matters between them, as we think; not thinking of an imposed secretiveness, beneath the false external of submissiveness, which comes of an experience of repeated inefficiency to maintain a case in opposition, on the part of the loquently weaker of the pair. (*OOC*, XII:122)

Inarticulateness undermines relationship, corrodes ironic sensibility, and contributes to the mutual blindness of Victor and Nataly as they trade roles throughout the novel, taking turns at allowing mock openness to give way to plot and deception.

Love is Victor's constant recourse as the Idea fades, replacing in more palatable form the repressed content of the Idea. "After his ineffectual catching at the volatile idea, Mr. Radnor found repose in thoughts of his daughter and her dear mother" (OOC, II:11).[57] Yet the Idea is not wholly bad, for there is in it a sense of the necessary interconnection with others. Victor is aware that subject and world are reciprocally defined; for this reason he is so intent on harmonizing the public and personal opinions of himself. His compulsion for prominence is in part due to a healthy sense for the need of self-revelation, though he rather too carefully sets the stage before every appearance. This attitude contrasts with Nataly's secretiveness, which is an implicit confession of guilt and a refusal to confront it that allows it to fester even more.

Given this atmosphere of willful evasiveness, it is Nesta who emerges as the problem and focus of the text. How can this clear-sighted heroine come from such misty regions of mind? How can she conquer just those phantoms her parents refuse to face? She resists the contagious blindness around her by virtue of some trait Meredith seems only to attribute to nature. "Natures resonant as that which animated this girl, are quick at the wells of understanding" (OOC, XXXIV:413). Is this strictly a natural gift, or an acquired one as well?

Nesta's growth to vision is a consequence of her encounter with Judith Marsett. This friendship is Nesta's first independent act, when she is for the first time separated from her parents. They fear her discovery of her illegitimate birth as Victor embarks on his scheme for social acceptance. They send her therefore to visit Victor's relatives, the Duvidney ladies, heretofore estranged from the Radnors owing to their violation of social convention. This attempt to keep Nesta blind, however, succeeds in opening her eyes, for she meets and befriends Mrs. Marsett.

This woman is the non formalized spouse of Captain Marsett, attached to him and willing to defer to his disdain for marriage. Her isolation because of this makes her especially receptive to Nesta's friendship, for Nesta knows nothing of the situation and does not prejudge Judith. After hints begin to fall on Nesta, Judith confesses her case and expects, even asks, that Nesta drop her. Nesta, however, relying on her sympathetic and imaginative affinity for Judith's nature, stands by her. This example and Nesta's general behavior lead Mrs. Marsett to thanks and remorse, and a real change of nature. She develops a sense of herself as more than an appendage of Captain Marsett. Nesta's correctness of judgment and her elevation of her friend are made possible because she perceives the individuality of the case, avoiding pinning any label on Judith. She maintains this sense for specifics in her ability to refrain from taking this incident as a crusade and forcing Mrs. Marsett on society. "Promise of a steady balance of her nature, too, was shown in the absence of any irritable urgency to be doing, when her bosom bled to help" (OOC, XXX:355). Her wise passivity is made possible in part because she encounters this situation first in a neutral setting, where she can more easily remain dispassionate.

Yet Nesta does not only give, she also takes from Judith an awakened vision of her own potential. She concedes the validity of Judith's self-defense, and the forceful redefinition of "love" it imposes on her inexperienced and excessively virginal mind. What her parents have concealed from her is just that factor of passion that could justify their case. Having seen it, she is more prepared to understand her parents when she discovers their situation and her own.

Unlike Nesta, both Victor and Nataly fail to recognize the individual case, seeing instead in terms of patterns and generic distinctions, abstractions and epithets. Precisely in their own case are they most insensitive to distinctions and unwilling to confront their extended responsibility for Nesta, not just to find her a respectable spouse to cover her blemish, but to initiate her to the truth of her own identity and to let her act on that. They fear her blaming them and treat her with the same conqueror's nonchalance Victor brings to all his relationships. For if she were to see, they would be forced to look at themselves and assess their magic vision of instinctive, self-justifying love.

Nataly, above all, cannot bear to see herself as she imagines a Judith to be, nor can she resist the parallel. She insists on breaking the friendship and marrying Nesta to the noble nonentity, Dudley Sowerby, whom Victor has been pushing from the first as Nesta's spouse. Dartrey Fenellan, whom Nesta will eventually marry, diagnoses the mother's trouble when Nesta returns, enlightened, to throw light into Nataly's life. "Your way of taking this affair disappointed me. Now I understand. It's the disease of a trouble, to fly at comparisons" (OOC, XXXVIII:454). Nataly instead desires the same compensating purity in all around her that she has always sought as veil for her shame. Nesta's vision drives Nataly into an ever blinder conformity to social conventions, destroying her sensibility to other persons.

The climactic scene between Nesta, Dartrey, and Nataly brings out this juxtaposition of vision and blindness. The first encounter is between Nesta and Dartrey, who in discussing Judith come to perceive a shared understanding that goes far beyond this particular case. They share a revelation of each other that is beyond words, using the language of the eyes. "The sight was keener than touch and the run of blood with blood to quicken slumbering seeds of passion . . . . The quivering intense of the moment of his eyes and grasp was lord of her, lord of the day and of all days coming. That is how Love slays Death" (OOC, XXXVIII:459). But this confirmation of Nesta's private vision of Judith and the associated perspective on human relationships are incomplete; she seeks to prod her mother into speech when she arrives, to turn private vision into shared understanding.[58] This is how she cured Mrs. Marsett, by a form of secular confession, and she seeks to apply the same rite to her mother, who, however, refuses.[59] Reading on her own, Nataly projects her self-defensive viciousness into Dartrey, heretofore a favorite of hers. "These are moments when the faces we are observing drop their charm, showing us our perversion internal, if we could but reflect, to see it" (OOC, XXXVIII:461). But Nataly keeps her vision to herself, and its distortion of both him and herself goes uncorrected.

Nataly is paradigmatic in her mounting to and falling from vision without an ironic acceptance of both extremes or an ironic openness to the other. She tells Dudley the truth about Nesta while Victor is seeking to trap him in a marriage, but she later reverts to becoming his strongest proponent when she feels that contact with Mrs. Marsett has soiled Nesta. Nataly characteristically allows Victor and others to speak for her, surrendering her interpretive responsibility and right to differ. She is willing to be managed, to let others act for her, which may be the worst evasion of responsibility of all. She is therefore as guilty as Victor, in her complicity in abetting his self-image. Like Victor, she justifies the madness of her submission as love. "But, say not the mad, say the enamoured woman. Love is a madness, having heaven's wisdom in it—a spark" (OOC, VI:51). But it is submission that allows the conqueror to conquer and to continue to infect others with his blindness.[60]

What is finally most troubling in Nataly's blindness is its similarity to Willoughby's, its incorrigibility despite her much greater moral and human sensibility. It is only Nataly's confrontation with death that releases her, when she and Victor grant Mrs. Burman's request for a final interview in the old woman's last days. This expiation, Nataly's encounter with her unresolved guilt for Mrs. Burman, transforms Nataly and lets her rejoin Nesta, though the restored harmony remains inarticulate. But this same scene makes us painfully aware of the near impossibility of transferring vision from one person to another, of ever really communicating, with language or any alternative mode of expression. For we are given this scene only through Victor's eyes, still bound up in his private vision, which takes on a grotesquely comic tone inappropriate to Nataly's transfiguration. As they pray, "He beheld his prayer dancing across the furniture; a diminutive thin black figure, elvish, irreverent, appallingly unlike his proper emotion." We finally get a sob from him, but one no more profound or long-lasting than Willoughby's whimper. He throws the whole scene back on incomprehensible human nature. "We are such creatures" (*OOC*, XL:489), and reveals above all his near total estrangement from Nataly. It is this division between them, the slide of their love into silence, and not Nataly's death or Victor's madness, that forms the real tragedy of the novel. For with their vanishing love disappears the one thing that could justify their egoistic irresponsibility to Mrs. Burman.

The pessimism of *One of Our Conquerors* lies not so much in its tragic end as in its insistence on the impossibility of sustaining communication, and thus correcting and interpreting vision. Yet only thus are ironists created. But neither Nataly nor Victor can confess their sins; they can only expiate them. Like Mrs. Burman, their final reckonings are only with themselves, a momentary vision before the fall into death. Even Nesta, the hopeful note with which the text concludes, cannot cure her parents of their shared blindness. And the novel itself slips from its concern, through Victor, with community, into a more restricted vision of the couple, Nesta and Dartrey.

And so Meredith leaves us with a residual blindness, an uncertainty about how to envisage the transmission and sharing of vision that is essential for its definition and correction. Ironic intersubjectivity in his novels is more of a hinted possibility or an imagined ideal, constantly threatened by the vagueness and blindness around it, than an effective possibility. In part, this may result from Meredith's fidelity to the communicative realities around him, where misapprehension rather than understanding is the rule. But the only way to envision a sustained and expanding ironic consensus is to formulate in a more rigorously theoretical fashion the linguistic and psychological problems with which he dealt.

# ‹§ 4

## The Irony of Double Vision: Lacan's Liquidation of the Subject

### Lacan and Ironic Discourse

The works of George Meredith provided us with a model of misinterpretation, a narrative diagnosis of the ways in which the subject could go astray in its pursuit of self-definition. Although Meredith's characters come to be through their language, their limited awareness of its workings in them inhibited their full assumption of hermeneutic responsibility. Against the potential rigidity of vision then, we need to pursue a more positive model of the way in which interpretation can successfully occur, and of what the effort to understand needs to take into account. Such a model, in turn, requires a more complete theory of how and where the subject emerges than Meredith provides for us. Jacques Lacan's writings are useful here because they integrate a diversity of intellectual currents defining the subject in terms of an ironic intersubjectivity that is cognizant of the pressures brought to bear on any communicative act.

Yet Lacan's own writings are themselves elusive for interpretation and resistant to comprehension. So one could perhaps best begin with Lacan by turning to his own pronouncements on interpretation. Lacan does indeed suggest guidelines for such an interpretive act, the mode of which must resemble the analytic practice to which he devoted much of his attention. The first and most crucial rule is the refusal to comprehend. "Begin by not believing that you understand. Start from the idea of a fundamental misunderstanding. That is the first disposition, lacking which there is truly no reason why you would not understand everything and anything whatsoever."[1] The risk of understanding Lacan may not seem excessive, given the complex and involuted nature of his writings, yet that very impenetrability can be the pretext that permits the reader to glide too quickly from explication to application, too fully into a system completed rather than emergent and toward a satisfaction with the repetition of terminology instead of its exploration. Interpretation should resist any easy comprehension. "To do commentary on a text is like doing an analysis. . . . To interpret is not at all the same thing as to imagine one understands. It is exactly the contrary" (I:87). To interpret, then, is to focus on exactly those elements of a text that refuse coherence and synthesis, that resist the too easy assimilation to a system.

The interpretive act for Lacan centers on the indirection of language, on explaining the reasons for the detours taken by the speaking subject on the path to communication. "That in which one must be interested is the point of knowing why she wished precisely that the other person understand that, and why she did not say it to him clearly, but by allusion. . . . If you understand, you are wrong. That which it is precisely a question of understanding is why there is something which one gives to be understood" (III:60). The connection with the indirection of irony is obvious and brings us back to the most interesting question about irony. To concede that one can decipher most ironies does not explain why the speaker should choose (if he or she does indeed choose) to be ironic rather than metaphoric. What is involved in the manner of ironic dialogue that makes it preferable to other styles of communication? Lacan's analysis of the indirection of language is useful in explaining irony by showing how all language really points in the same direction, toward the question of self-identity. Yet Lacan's use of linguistics is not my primary focus here,[2] except insofar as it points to a theory of the subject that lies behind and informs that investigation of language, and that serves to explain the necessity for and the utility of linguistic indirection.[3]

This theory of the subject should be the point where one chooses to take or leave Lacan, rather than at less central questions of terminology or schematization. For Lacan's aim is the liquidation of the traditional subject whose origin he traces to the Cartesian cogito, a liquidation in the full resonance of the term, implying an abolition of that subject that will nonetheless permit its reconstitution elsewhere. The place where the subject is to be recovered will be the scene of an encounter with the other marking the radical provisionality of the subject, the dissolution of either innate or existential essence.[4] The presence of the subject is thus flickering and impermanent, as evanescent as the analytical intervention, where what matters is not so much what one says, as the necessity to speak neither too soon nor too late (I:9).

Lacan's redefinition of the subject is an essentially intersubjective and ethical one. "The statute of the unconscious, which I indicate to you [to be] so fragile on the ontic plane, is ethical" (XI:34). There is no such entity as a subject, except by and with other subjects. This is a subject whose definition is finally impossible, for it is fully osmotic, a radical in the chemical sense—a compound one does not find unattached in nature. The subject for Lacan is dependent on others for its status at any point in time. Insofar as it has any content, it is the sum of its interrupted encounters with all its significant others, which serve as moments of entry, however provisional, into death, which alone can definitively identify the subject.

From Lacan's psychoanalytic perspective, one can envisage the risks of a metaphor such as that of vision and blindness. The image does articulate an intersubjective rapport, but it implies mutually exclusive alternatives and even worse, evokes the possibility of full blindness or vision in an individual subject, that is, the possibility for a single self to be completely in one position or the other, even though this integrity might only be situational. The metaphor clearly valorizes vision as the ideal place for the subject, who can in fact see its own blindness only in the past, insofar as overcome. Vision and blindness imply in their alternation a moment of fully acquired illumination. They thus risk hypostasizing an individual subject as a potential locus of the ultimate idealist synthesis.

One can see, then the flaw in Laetitia's vision as she seeks to be a neutral observer of Clara's behavior. She errs, first, in missing the centrality of Clara's own language (the discourse of egoism) in Laetitia's own passage into vision, forgetting the earlier encounter where Clara passed on to her the truth she now is handing back. Laetitia also leaves out her own dialectical involvement in the questions of identity she tries to help resolve. She refuses to be seen herself, even hiding in her room to escape the gaze of others that would implicate her interrelationship with them. She emerges only to pronounce her own monologue on egoism, and even the advice she gives Clara, which permits the happy outcome, is potentially objectifying in its absorption of Clara's own speech and critical capacities. Laetitia's mistake, then, is a failure to see her own discourse as situational and historically determined, and to see her encounter with Clara as an interaction. The discourse of Lacan, to which we now turn, may not be so strikingly original or radical as has been claimed. But it is invaluable for the rigor with which it explores the intersubjective basis of just such scenes as this, where positive resolution depends upon the refraction of vision into speech in the moment before it slips into blindness.

The primary problem for ironic discourse is to keep open the space created between the subject and the other in the interrogative moment of an intersubjective encounter. Insofar as the other is itself a subject, that distance seems impossible to maintain; one inevitably returns from an encounter to the partial, conscious self, with no fundamental alteration in its structure. It is here that the radical novelty of the psychoanalytic perspective comes into play, for the risk of reducing otherness is solved by Freud by internalizing the other in its irreducible alterity within the subject itself. The unconscious is an other that is ubiquitous for the subject, without ever being wholly accessible to it. The role of the other, as subject, is then not itself to be just another subject, but with the subject to enact a dialectic in which that otherness is brought into being as third term in their interlocution.

The Freudian unconscious provides the subject with a preexistent and simultaneous fullness that counteracts its experience of partialness, without ever being reducible to a partial subject. The subject both contains and is exceeded by the unconscious; it is in a fundamental condition of disproportion to it. "That in the subject, which is of the subject and is not of the subject, is the unconscious" (II:191). The unconscious is always present for the subject, since it exists in and through speech, but it remains inaccessible insofar as the signification of that speech can remain concealed, censured by the ego. "It is there a question of an instance that divides the symbolic world of the subject, cuts it in two, into an accessible and recognized part and an inaccessible, interdicted part" (I:220).

Lacan's revision of Freud privileges the verbal nature of the unconscious, which Lacan insistently repeats is structured like a language, not groundable in any physiological instincts or drives. The resistance of the unconscious to the ego is based, however, on its divergence from conscious language. Unlike ordinary language use, the speech of the id is characterized by the principles of nonorganization, the lack of negation, and the dominance of the death drive (E, pp. 657–658). Its most telling trait, however, is that the unconscious permits the internalization of something that remains resolutely outside of the subject—the symbolic function of language. "This exteriority of the symbolic in relation to man is the very notion of the unconscious. And Freud proved constantly that he held to it as the very principle of his experience" (*E*, p. 469). This exteriority of the symbolic order that structures the unconscious, imprinted from the outside on the individual subject, is replicated at the other end of the circuit, for the subject's embodiment of it will also necessarily be outside itself: "The unconscious, which I represent to you as what at the same time is of the interior of the subject, but which only realizes itself outside, that is to say, in that place of the Other where alone it can take on its statute" (XI:134).

Although not an outside, objectifying other, the unconscious still serves as a link between subjects, the only genuine link in Lacan's terms. It is the subject alone who can articulate it, but its articulation exceeds his accidental and ephemeral self. "The unconscious is that part of the concrete discourse insofar as [it is] transindividual, that which is not at the disposal of the subject for re-establishing the continuity of his conscious discourse" (*E*, p. 258).[5] This means that the unconscious is not itself a subject and hence that interchange with it will not collapse into the narcissistic absorption that continually removes otherness from the ken of the subject. Nor is the unconscious unapproachably transcendent, for it is constituted by human language and action and has no meaning, or even existence, apart from them. The relation of the subject to it is not characterized by the adequation, even progressive, of one to the other, as in a theory of perception or of dialectical sublimation. For the motive and driving force of the unconscious is desire, an unending tension of absolute contraries. "It is in a completely other register of relations [than that of adequation between subject and object] that the field of the Freudian experience establishes itself. Desire is a relation of being to lack. This lack is lack of being, to speak properly. It is not lack of this or that, but that lack of being [or lack of that being] by which being exists" (II:261).

What this redefinition of the subject by insertion of the unconscious into its structure does is to decenter the subject with respect to its own consciousness of itself. This act undermines the pretensions of consciousness to abolish its own particularity in theoretical syntheses, to absorb its situational and interrelational character. "But the Freudian discovery was to demonstrate that this verifying process only authentically attains the subject by decentering it from self-consciousness, in the axis of which the Hegelian reconstruction of the phenomenology of spirit maintained it:

that is to say, Freud's discovery renders even more decrepit every search for the coming to consciousness which, beyond its psychological phenomenon, would not inscribe itself in the conjuncture of the particular moment which alone embodies the universal, and lacking which it dissipates itself in generality" (E, p. 292). This decentering of the subject does not render it partial, however, but rather "excentric" from itself. The subject is that which is in two places at once—no more equivalent to the unconscious than it is to the consciousness through which that resonates.

The reason for this excentricity of the subject is the entry by any individual into the symbolic order, that is, into language, in Lacan's special sense of that term. "I explain to you that it is insofar as he is engaged in a game of symbols, in a symbolic world, that man is a decentered subject" (II:63). The integrity of the subject is therefore not so much denied as displaced into the symbolic structure where its identity is realized. The essence of Lacan's liquidation of the subject lies in this reconstitution elsewhere; his fundamental premise is that that which is the subject is in no way coextensive with the individual human being. "I teach you that Freud discovered in man the weight and the axis of a subjectivity exceeding the individual organization considered as a sum of individual experiences, and even considered as a line of individual development" (II:56).

Subjectivity is therefore not a given, but something to be brought into being. "The subject goes far beyond what the individual experiences 'subjectively,' exactly as far as the truth he can attain, and which perhaps will exit from that mouth that you have just already closed again" (E, p. 265). To define that truth and the process of its emergence is my aim in this chapter, but for the moment it will suffice to sketch its nature. Its quintessential moment, already explored by Freud, is the joke or witticism, the emergence of truth from the mouth of a subject who feels it has come upon rather than created it and senses at that moment the excess of itself as subject beyond its mere individuality. "Nowhere is the intention of the individual in effect more manifestly exceeded by the serendipitous discovery [trouvaille] of the subject—nowhere does the distinction that we make between one and the other make itself better felt—since not only is it necessary that something have been alien to me in my serendipitous discovery for me to take pleasure in it, but it is necessary that it remain so in order for it to bear [pleasure]" (E, p. 271).[6] The very sense of surprise that a wit feels in his own joke is an index of the presence of his own subjectivity, which exceeds his conscious intentionality.

For Lacan, the joke typifies all speech of the individual, where what emerges is a mystery, the problem of that unconscious he somehow contains, however uneasily. The subject in the individual is always diffuse and undetermined or about to be determined, always, that is, ironically incomplete. Lacan's concept of the subject hovers between the subject of the discourse and the subject of the signification, between the speaking subject and a subject-matter that far exceeds the former. Yet it does announce its presence in the *parole*, for subjectivity is in the words of an individual and not in the words of anyone else. Though decentered, the subject embodies its radical unity in all the words and interpreted deeds of any particular person.

This integrity is acquired through the total dependence of the subject on an acquired language, the full truth of which the subject can indeed speak, though not recognize. "This *parole*, that constitutes the subject in his truth, is however forever interdicted to him, outside of the rare moments of his existence when he endeavors, however confusedly, to seize it in sworn faith, and interdicted in that the intermediary discourse destines him to misapprehend it. It speaks, however, everywhere that it can read itself in his being, that is, at all the levels where it has formed him" (*E*, p. 353). Always present yet never there, such is the status of the signification of the discourse of the subject and of the subject itself. The subject is cut off from its own discourse, because it cannot recognize its own place in that flow of words. "The subject does not know what he says, and for the best reasons, because he does not know what he is" (II:286).

Where the subject vanishes is into the apparent solidity of its own language. The very success of that discourse in becoming tangible is the cause of the subject's disappearance from it. "The subject is this surge which, just before, as subject, was nothing, but which, hardly appeared, congeals itself into a signifier" (XI:181). Here lies the difficulty of Lacan's conception of the subject, for it is an entity at once always present and still never realized. It is the subject who speaks, as individual and as existential being, yet insofar as that subject assumes conscious control of its discourse, the subject becomes that which is spoken between the lines. The subject both exceeds the individual and yet is only to be found in the particularity of the individual parole. The being who speaks and the one who hears himself speak are not the same being, but both can be, and are, denominated subject by Lacan. This displacement of the subject is caused by its entrance into the system of the signifier, which forces the subject to withdraw from any particular signifier. "In any case, man cannot aim to be complete . . . once the game of displacement and condensation, to which he is destined in the exercise of his functions, marks his relation of subject to the signifier" (E, p. 692). Freud's discovery that the unconscious speaks in dreams is generalized by Lacan to cover all discourse,[7] so that the subject is always simultaneously, in the same words, both partial and full.

Yet its fullness is not absolute, and Lacan is therefore justified in describing what he terms a "fading" of the subject from its own parole. But the truth of discourse is recoverable because that parole constitutes a form of address to another person; it contains therefore the potential for a dialectical transformation of the rigid shapes into which the subject is repeatedly poured. The fading of a subject into determinate speech can be compensated by its entrance into an interlocution where its fluid identity can reemerge and be reconfirmed. "But if this parole is accessible, however, it is because no true parole is only parole of the subject, since it always operates by founding it in the mediation of another subject, and since by that it is opened to the chain without end . . . of paroles where the dialectic of recognition realizes itself concretely in the human community" (E, p. 353). It is only insofar as parole is interlocution that it can permit the recovery by any subject of its own unconscious structures present in that parole.[8]

This definition of parole as an address to an other is fundamental for the constitution of the Lacanian subject. It is an element latent in all speech, the operation of which one must understand if one wishes to account for the nature of thought and the effects of speech. Not even self-interrogation can occur without the implicit inclusion of the other one implicitly addresses. The essence of the dialogue, then, is not in a reflection of the speaker, but in an echoing of his words that reveals them as being spoken from the outside and across a temporal gap. The role of the interlocutor is even more profoundly mediating, however, for he not only echoes the speech of the subject, but inverts it and thereby demonstrates his own complicity in the dialogue. "For us, the structure of the parole . . . is that the subject receives his message from the other in an inverted form" (III:47).[9]

These two traits define the uniqueness of human language—that it is a message, not only to some other person, but also from the subject to itself, and that that message is recoverable by the subject only in an inverted form. Instead of beginning with the transparency of any discourse,

Lacan insists on the nature of all parole as message and demands that we make the shift to see our own words as messages that require interpretation. "It is first of all for the subject that his *parole* is a message, because it produces itself in [the] place of the Other" (*E*, p. 634). Even the subject's own words are not transparent for it, but subject to a hermeneutic imperative. Language is always a revelation of self rather than an expression of it, before which the subject can only endeavor to catch the overflow of its own meaning. So one must always begin with the parole, since the subject can be defined only out of those bits of its own discourse that implicate it in the act of communication. Yet at the same time, the distinction between subjects is obliterated, along with any sense of the integrity of corporeal or spiritual essences. The subject's own truth is no more in its own words than in those of its interlocutor, so that any self-knowledge will be strictly dependent on the sustaining of a successful interchange.[10]

Unlike in the Hegelian model, progress in the Lacanian dialectic is possible only in and through parole, that is, cooperatively. *Parole alone,* as the concrete instantiation of the possibilities of the system of language, can contain truth and define the subject by constituting it. "That means very simply all that there is to say of truth, of the only [truth], that is, that there is no metalanguage . . . that no language could say the true of the true, since truth founds itself in that it speaks, and that it has no other means for doing this" (*E*, pp. 867–868). Synthesis, as the culmination of dialectical movement, could then only be a regression, a reduction of the tension constitutive of intersubjectivity and truth.

The alternative to sublimation, for Lacan, is the appearance of a third term that can act to restore mobility to a stagnated dialectic, freeing the subjects in, not from, their interaction, by making them aware of their being poised in terms of something their relationship creates without exhausting. "It is our own *Aufhebung,* which transforms that of Hegel, his own lure, into an occasion to raise up, in place and in the place of the leaps of an ideal progress, the avatars of a lack" (*E*, p. 837). The dialectic rapport between subjects can only circle around these avatars of a lack, enacting a truth whose validity remains inexorably bound to its particularity. The subject is thus transformed from *being* a part, only partial, to *playing* a part.[11] There is no need to close one's eyes and blind oneself to hear the truth; one need only open one's mouth.

Open one's mouth, that is, in the presence of an other, for Lacan relocates the subject in an intersubjective paradigm to which individual consciousness is in no way prior. Intersubjectivity is not a secondary phenomenon developed out of the gropings of individual subjects, but their predecessor and the condition of possibility for any individual as subject. There is a kind of integration at work here, but not in terms of the acquisition of knowledge. What occurs instead is a disintegration of the barriers to full intersubjective mobility and the development of a capacity for interknowledge. This perspective forces one to "make objection to defining this society as a collection of individuals, when the immixtion of subjects makes it a group of a quite different structure" (E, p. 415). The definition of any subject, its self-definition, depends upon interlocking with the web of fellow self-defining beings, both in their particularity and as a group. This is what Lacan terms entry into the Symbolic Order. "It is subsequently realized by our relation with others in their totality—the symbolic relation" (I:161). All this is equally true for the other who confronts the subject, if the full intersubjectivity that permits active manipulation of the symbolic order is to emerge. His interjections must establish the injection of his own intersubjective identity into the encounter. This process might well be termed a restoration of irony to the Hegelian dialectic, the circumscribing of the subject—at every phenomenological stage up to and including any absolute spirit—by the mode and operation of its intersubjective rapports. It is to the emergence and shaping of those rapports that we need shortly to shift our attention.

This preliminary dip into Lacan already permits the clarification of ironic intersubjectivity as a particular kind of intersubjective encounter. Ironic utterances are, for my purposes here, partial utterances requiring completion, which make evident the partialness of the utterer as subject. Unable to play all the parts at once, the ironic subject is forced to proceed to an enactment that must be an interaction as well. His parole seeks to call attention to the fact that self-consciousness is both mediated through and maintained in discourse, a discourse that is not just any language or even a metalanguage, but that language concretely present and available. Such ironic discourse is characterized by incompatibilities, the resolution of which depends on the entrance of the interlocutor into an intersubjective dialectic of mutual definition, his reciprocal investment in the subject's discourse.

These utterances are thus appeals for a response that would implicate the other in the dialogue, rather than a response that might directly envisage and reveal the subject. The dependence of the ironic subject on the other is fundamental, for by virtue of his reply the subject comes to be defined or extinguished. Hence the responsibility of a dialogue is mutual; nothing less than the existence of the subject is in question. "Henceforth appears the decisive function of my own response and which is not only, as one generally says, for it to be received by the subject as approbation or rejection of his discourse, but truly to recognize him or to abolish him as subject. Such is the *responsibility* of the analyst each time he intervenes by the *parole*" (E, p. 300). The radicalness of Lacan is here evident; his argument implies that only in speech are we fully existent as human beings, only there does the subjectivity latent in our minds take on any reality, only there can the process of communalization be further extended.

Yet the nature of a dialogue is to be at any moment constitutively asymmetrical and nonreciprocal, always in imbalance of one kind or another. The roles adopted by subject and other can be at best complementary, never identical, for that would imply the integration in each of them of the totality of their relationship. The appeal for completion, of course, is characteristic of all tropes, since they all require an interpretive act. But this should not imply that all tropes are ironic; the difference peculiar to irony is that it deals explicitly with and forces confrontation with the values of the subject—necessarily bound up with the question of self-identity—which are often only implicit in other verbal acts. Irony directly implicates the subject as the originator of the enunciation, while confessing its ignorance of its own meaning.[12] It arises at a split in the subject, where its fractured identity is displayed as an emergent self-inconsistency, a split that only the participation of the other can make fully accessible to the subject. One can, of course, resolve the irony by glossing over that split, but to do so is to ignore the fragmentation characteristic of the subject that is its most effective tie to others.

Through this process of ironic interplay emerges the recognition that the aim of dialogue is primarily the definition of the relation within which the two subjects are acting as constitutive of their identities. "Finally, it is by the intersubjectivity of the 'we' that it assumes that the value of *parole* in a language is measured" (E, p. 299). This mutual emplacement by means of dialogue establishes the subjects in roles that are correlative to, as balancings of, one another, and in terms of some intersubjective ideal of balance which they cannot fully articulate. It is this third term, the relationship itself, and its inclusion in the process of mutual definition, that prevents its degeneration into narcissism. It is the possibilities and prescriptions of relationship that are effectively Other for the subject, and at the source of its dependence on another subject.

Parole, then, is finally split off from discourse, as the place of a particularly human kind of truth. "The true *parole* opposes itself thus paradoxically to the true discourse, their truth being distinguished by this, that the first constitutes the recognition by the subjects of their beings in that they are there inter-ested, while the second is constituted by knowledge of the real, insofar as it is aimed at by the subject in objects" (*E*, p. 351). This stance does not abolish the partial subject of Romantic irony, but neither does it privilege it, for the ironic encounter with another subject can fulfill the full measure of language's function—"the pure function of language, which is to assure us that we are, and nothing more" (I:180). The linguistic slippage this might seem to entail is arrested by the status of being as a question—the question of mutual social definition and consensus.

Intersubjective encounters will necessarily reveal ironic patterns (as in Meredith's novels), where one can perceive the seams of individual identity.[13] For the primary function of language is to found and confirm the human relationships about which it insistently speaks. "It is a question of the value of *parole*, no longer this time insofar as it creates the fundamental ambiguity, but insofar as it is a function of the symbolic, of the pact tying subjects one to the other in an action" (I:255). Irony is that trope that centers not on the ambiguity common to all tropes, but on the pact their operation serves to engender. The question, then, is whether one chooses to make use of that potential for irony in all language, to seek to be consciously and not just unwittingly ironic. Irony will actually be fully operative only to the extent that both speaker and hearer (not necessarily the addressee) are aware of it and feel implicated by it.

To make the paths of intersubjective dialogue clearer, we need to enter more deeply into the intricacies of the Lacanian system, and thereby into the process out of which the subject emerges. Entrance into both the Imaginary and Symbolic orders is essential if the subject is to pass on to a realm of fully realized discourse. I propose to examine the essential transitions in Lacan's theory of the subject, the turns and returns that indicate its resistance to systematization. My focus, then, will be on Lacan's work as a whole, and will perhaps provide an inadequate sense of the dialectical development in that work. But his own seminar on "The Purloined Letter" suggests the utility of privileging certain central scenes as indicative of the structure of the whole. This approach can even be deemed advisable as a counter to the centrifugal force Lacan's writings create, as they spin off allusions to crucial terms in a dizzying succession that resists the fuller explication to which an analysis of Lacan must remain committed.

## The Imaginary and the Split of the Subject
*Introduction*

Lacan's theory of the Imaginary can be seen as an answer to the questions posed by Meredith's novels—whence the blindness into which the individual subject repeatedly falls? Why cannot vision be sustained? The error characteristic of the Imaginary is that omission of self from one's own discourse that led Freud to remind Dora that her tale was finally essentially about herself.[14] This self-omission is narcissistic, for it takes place only through a projection of herself into her discourse that is so complete that she need not appear there as an agent. Her story takes the place of a direct self-interrogation as to her own identity, seeming to describe a real situation structured by those people around her. The Imaginary self, the ego, is blind because it thinks that in this story it has the answers, that it can neutralize the impact of its own desire on the events it relates.

The Imaginary order brings about the first occurrence and first recuperation of alienation for the subject. The nonintegrity of self and other, of child and mother, defines the child as separate, but its physiological dependence guarantees that the very basis of the child's self-image will be intersubjective. The source of that image in perception, and especially in the visual, means that its modulations will be biologic, its knowledge corporeal in mode. The entrance into the Imaginary is triggered, like all movement in Lacan, by the question of identity. Its essential moment is what Lacan calls the mirror stage, the period between six and eighteen months when the child acquires its first sense of integrity through the jubilatory assumption of an alienating, reflected image of itself. Though often described by Lacan as a single moment, the complexity of the relations involved in the mirror stage makes it worthwhile to break down the temptingly unitary structure of that event into three aspects in which we can examine sequentially the various factors that make up the Imaginary. These three facets or stages can be termed those of the *Je Spéculaire*, the *Je Social*, and the *Je Semblable*.[15]

*The Je Spéculaire*

The specular nature of the ego is an element that pervades the whole of the Imaginary for Lacan. Yet at the same time it finds its purest moment in the initial response of the child before a mirror. At the age of six months or so, the primary experience of the human infant has been of its own fragmentation. Self-identity is in abeyance, for the baby is both imperfectly differentiated from its environment and fragmented, differentiated from itself. Lacan describes this period as an "intraorganic and relational discordance of the human infant, during the first six months, where it bears the signs, neurological and humoral, of a physiological natal prematuration" (*E*, p. 113).

Born before its time, before it is able to function as an entity, the first step of development for the infant will be its psychic maturation, its initial cognizance of its own image, held by its mother before a mirror that can reflect it. Lacking any internal sense of coherence, the precocious development of its mental apparatus nonetheless allows the child to anticipate a future integrity at the moment when it recognizes that lump in the mirror as itself, or *assumes* its image, as Lacan puts it. "It suffices to understand the mirror stage *as an identification* in the full sense that analysis gives to this term: namely, the transformation produced in a subject when he assumes an image" (*E*, p. 94).

The primary effect of the infant's assumption of its own image is a positive one; it provides a sense of self as whole, as a Gestalt that can deflect the prior sense of fragmentation. But the experience is an essentially imaginary one, a psychic prematuration that precedes the child's real control over its body. "It is on this that I insist in my theory of the mirror stage—the mere view of the total form of the human body gives to the subject an imaginary mastery over his body, premature in comparison to the real mastery" (I:93). Hence the mirror experience lays the foundation for a whole series of mental constructs of one's own self-image that can only be described as hallucinatory. "It is the original adventure by which man encounters for the first time the experience that he sees himself, reflects himself, and conceives himself other than he is (not)—essential dimension of the human, which structures all his fantasmatic life" (I:94).

Other than he is (not)—this phrase brings out the fundamental self-alienation also present in the mirror stage, despite its positive aspect of providing a sense of self as a whole, a Gestalt. The infant, as subject, is already split in identifying with an image outside of itself. "The human being sees his realized, total form, the mirage of himself, only outside himself" (I:160). As soon as it acquires its first integral awareness of itself, the infant finds itself alienated from itself, eyeing an image that is and will always remain out there. This image is necessarily other in that it contradicts the primary experience of the child, which involves a lack of control, to be sure, but also a freedom of movement the imago inevitably arrests. "The fact is that the total form of the body, by which the subject anticipates in a mirage the maturation of his power, is only given to him as *Gestalt*, that is to say, in an exteriority where certainly this form is more constituting than constituted, but where above all it appears to him in a bas-relief of stature which congeals it, and as a symmetry that inverts it, in opposition to the turbulence of movements by which he feels himself animated" (*E*, pp. 94–95). The image assumed by the infant is thus referred to by Lacan as an "armure," a rigid shell that integrates the self only by denying certain portions of that self. Integrity is acquired through the loss of mobility.

This Je Spéculaire leaves behind an initial gap, or *béance* in the subject, a gap that will have profound consequences for its whole development. It permits the two distinctively human experiences to arise—the awareness of death and the manipulation of symbols. "It is in effect by the gap [*béance*], which this prematuration opens in the imaginary and where the effects of the mirror stage abound, that the human animal is *capable* of imagining itself mortal, not that one could say that he could do it without his symbiosis with the symbolic, but rather that without this gap which alienates him in his own image, this symbiosis with the symbolic could not have produced itself, where he constitutes himself as subject to death" (*E*, p. 552).

The death perception is made possible by the duality the gap creates *within* the subject, which allows the superimposition of the differential symbolic order onto the subject and its assumption of its own death. "But the human being has a special relation with the image that is his own—relation of *béance*, of alienating tension. It is there that the possibility of the order of presence and absence inserts itself, that is to say, [the possibility] of the symbolic order" (II:371).[16] The Imaginary appears, then, tied to the apparition of death and the possibility of the subject to be "existent," to be, outside itself. This is a possibility, however, which will be immediately closed up; the Imaginary could be defined as the evasion of the insight of one's own death as absence from oneself, a forgetting of the very insight from which it springs, which only accession to the Symbolic can restore for the subject.

For the self in the mirror stage loses itself in its image, taking that appearance for its being, and overlooking the gap over which it looks at itself. This imago is the Ego in Lacanian terms, an initial representation that becomes a psychic defense mechanism by resisting the amorphous openness of the subject. It corresponds not to reality but to the primitive psychic mechanisms of affirmation and expulsion by which the infant first structures its environment in its own image. Yet the Ego here, as Je Spéculaire, is essentially without content, not yet objectified. The assumption of its image by the child is not the self-contained process it might here seem to be, for this step acquires its significance only in the subsequent forms into which it immediately passes.

### The Je Social and Identification

What characterizes the mirror stage is not just the infant's recognition of its image, nor even its assumption of that image, but its jubilation at that assumption, an act that is constitutively relational and intersubjective. Immediately upon its assumption of its own image, the child turns to the other, the mother holding it, in a ludic call for confirmation of its discovery. This obviously involves its losing sight of itself, a replacement of itself as object of its vision by the other to whom it turns in hopes of seeing that first image reflected there. I see the other when I disappear; this totalizing either-or rapport will characterize all the instances of the Imaginary. As the béance of the original image anticipated the emergence of the Symbolic, so does the secondary image (image because subjected to the same constraint of integrity that governs the whole mirror scene) anticipate the intersubjective relations through which the Symbolic comes to be. But this is a form of intersubjectivity that denies the difference between subjects and its attendant alienation by restoration of a narcissistic unity.

This transferred gaze is captivated by the other because of its irresistible superiority in terms of the physiological maturation toward which the infant yearns. The other embodies just that integrity the infant wishes to possess, but realizes, at least in part, that it does not. The acquisition of identity thus immediately becomes a process of identification with what seems to be an ideal image of the self. "If the game is valorized for the child, it is because it constitutes the plane of reflection on which he sees manifest itself in the other an activity which anticipates his own, in that it is the tiniest bit more perfect, more mastered, than his own, his ideal form" (I:199). The confirmation the other provides thus turns out to be the evidence of its own greater integrity and control over its own movements (and eventually behavior in the larger sense).

This identification, made for the sake of the integrity it provides, can only be total and hence bring about a loss of difference, an absorption by the other that causes a further alienation of the self. "Thus, essential point, the first effect of the *imago* which appears in the human being is an effect of *alienation* of the subject. It is in the other that the subject identifies himself and even senses himself first" (*E*, p. 181).[17] Lacan's term for this immersion in the other is *fascination*, an absolute forgetting of the gap that permitted the Imaginary to emerge at all. "Fascination is absolutely essential to the phenomenon of the constitution of the ego. It is insofar as fascinated that the uncoordinated, incoherent diversity of the primitive fragmentation takes on its unity" (II:67). Released from its own image, the child is immediately recaptured by another image in a displacement that seeks to conceal the inaugural gap within the subject by relocating its integrity elsewhere. "The total captation of desire, of attention, already presupposes lack. The lack is already there when I speak of the desire of the human subject in relation to his image, of this extremely general imaginary relation that one calls narcissism" (II:371). Lacan's example for this total loss of self in the other is the psychoanalytical category of transitivism, where uncertainty of identity marks the child's entrance into language. It can impute its own actions to another or similarly appropriate the words or deeds of that other as its own (*E*, p. 180). The ego, given content during this phase, remains marked by the transitive lack of difference. Thus the acquisition of the possibility of subjectivity by the infant passes inevitably through the loss of its discrete subjectness. Its identity is in no way equivalent to or deducible from its own lived experience.

The identification with the other, in the first instance with the mother, is not to be seen as the adoption of personality traits or behavioral characteristics. What the child sees when it looks at the mother is not only, if ever, an answering gaze but the blind regard that symbolizes her desire, which is the first and determinative answer to the question implied by its glance.[18] The child wishes, by looking, not only self-confirmation but also the reestablishment of the rapport its discovery has undermined. Its jubilation is a resistance to the separation implied by its newly acquired identity. This wish of the child is properly termed *demand* in the Lacanian system and is characterized by its severance from all physical needs, its totalizing pressure. "Demand in itself bears on something other than the satisfactions it calls for. It is demand of a presence or of an absence" (*E*, pp. 690–691). The demand is a demand for love, but one that can encounter that love through the mediation of the mother's desire, which can never provide the reciprocal self-sufficiency the infant demands.

The jubilatory turn for confirmation, and the identification with the body of the other, will thus serve as the means by which the child is drawn into the world of desire. The emptiness in the desire of the mother will prolong the child's exploration of its own self-identity as it seeks to ascertain the reason it is inadequate to that desire. Hardly formed, the child's ego is already transformed into an object of exchange with which it hopes to seduce the desire of the other. "Desire is, in the human subject, realized in the other, by the other—*in the place of* the other, as you say. That is the second time, the specular time, the moment when the subject has integrated the form of the ego. But he was only able to integrate it after a first game of balancing [*bascule*] where he has precisely exchanged his ego for this desire that he sees in the other" (I:200–201).

What this means is that the child accepts, is forced to accept, the external determination of its ego and its desire. Its identification with the other involves the exteriorization of its desire, its location in the other. "Before desire learns to recognize itself—let us now say the word—by the symbol, it is only seen in the other" (I:193). Even when the child has acceded to language and ostensibly has the power to name its own desire, that desire will remain retroactively marked by the adoption of language from the other and with it the desire of the other. The other, already in speech and hence possessing an additional mastery, has the power to define the child and its desire. "In effect, as you see, the desires of the child pass first via the specular other. It is there that they are approved or reproved, accepted or refused. And it is by that, that the infant does its apprenticeship of the symbolic order and accedes to its foundation, which is the law" (I:202).

I reserve a fuller discussion of desire and its law for my consideration of the Symbolic. But I would emphasize that this model of Lacan's serves to shift the entire problem of irony, conceived as the dilemma of a partial self. That partialness, and the illusory wholeness it brings with it as imago, are both lifted from the outside, from the other, and are not constitutive elements of the subject. "If you have followed what I said just now before, you ought to see that it is always from the outside that what one here calls the internal process comes. It is first by the intermediary of the outside that it is recognized" (I:177). That is to say, the subject is from its origin dialectical and intersubjective, even in its imaginary wanderings. "[The imaginary relation] has taught us that the *ego* is never only the subject, that it is essentially relation with the other, that it takes its point of departure and of support in the other" (II:209). To take this imaginary self, with its dialectic of partialness and integrity, for the essence of the subject, is to ignore the process by which it comes to be and to foreclose the possibility of its transformation. "Lacan's *moi* corresponds to the internalization of the other through identification; we are conscious of this self, but unconscious of its origins."[19] Unless we take into account the Imaginary and its play of identifications, we are likely to fall into the trap of substantializing it and taking it as something real and unalterable.

The importance of imaginary identifications goes even beyond the dualistic intersubjectivity they foster. For through its passage into an other the child is initiated into desire and thus inserted into the whole social drama. Identification for Lacan is never just a one-to-one relationship, an assumption by one person of the character of another, but instead an assumption of the whole framework of intersubjective and social relations within which the object of one's identification exists, and of the history by which those came to be, hence an entrance into the Symbolic order. "[Freud] demonstrated this function of the image in discovering in experience the process of *identification:* quite different from that of *imitation*, distinguished by its partial and groping form of approximation, *identification* opposes itself to that not only as *global* assimilation of a structure, but as the *virtual* assimilation *of the development* implied by this structure at a still undifferentiated state" (E, pp. 88–89). The subject, as an infant or ego, is in the Symbolic without being of it, subject to its determinations without yet being able to articulate them, caught in its alignments without the possibility of shifting place to redefine that structure. Before it can move into the Symbolic, however, the subject must pass through a third stage of the Imaginary, where the Je Social is further defined as a Je Semblable. The twin narcissisms of self-reference and mother-fixation need to be further supplemented by the additional alternative of an object relation.

*The Je Semblable and Aggressive Rivalry*

The stage of the Je Semblable still needs to be considered a prelinguistic one, however far its effects may stretch into the experience of the speaking subject. Its essential structure is that of a reprojection of a desire internalized from the other back into the other, where the narcissistic relation becomes further intensified by its maintenance at a point where the other is perceived to be separate, no longer the mother, but the rival. This implies a further diversion of the child's gaze, first focused on itself and then seeking confirmation of itself in the mother, but forced by the nonpresence of her desire to look beyond her and recognize its own desire, for her or for whatever else, in a secondary identification with some other ideal-ego.[20] "I was able to make you grasp that desire, alienated, is perpetually reintegrated anew, reprojecting the ideal-I into the exterior. It is thus that desire verbalizes itself. There is there a game of balance between two inverted relations. The specular relation of the ego, which the subject assumes and realizes, and the projection, always ready to be renewed, in the ideal-I" (I:197). Externalized in some particular other, the relation with the ideal-ego is one of competition, an intense struggle for the now emergent object of their mutual desire. Its only possible resolution, as long as one remains on the level of the Imaginary, is a struggle to the death. "At the origin, before language, desire only exists on the single plane of the imaginary relation of the specular stage, projected, alienated in the other. The tension that it provokes is then deprived of outlet. That is to say that it has no other outlet . . . than the destruction of the other" (I:193).[21] The first rival, of course, is the father, as the child moves from the position of demand (and the desire to be the phallus for the mother) to the stage where it wishes to have the phallus, where it gradually detaches that desire from its focusing on the mother.

The Je Semblable is Lacan's version of Hegel's master-slave dialectic and like it is structured around a new element, the object to which desire becomes attached. The relation of rivalry is not centered on the demand for love, but on the hate engendered by the struggle for that first object, which rapidly becomes insignificant as the mere symbol of a relationship that exceeds it. This level of the Imaginary brings with it a recognition of the other lacking in primary identification, but without the interaction that would allow some sort of acknowledgment of that other as another subject. The identification is too complete for such distance to be possible.

The object of this mutual desire is illusory, since the real struggle is for recognition. The intrusion of the object into the intersubjective relationship serves only to divert it from its structural similarity to the jubilatory call for confirmation of the infant's identity. "In sum, nowhere does it appear more clearly that the desire of man finds its meaning in the desire of the other, not so much because the other holds the keys to the desired object, than because its first object is to be recognized by the other" (E, p. 268). The difference between this desire of the Je Semblable and the earlier Je Social is that the passage through the latter phase, with its exposure to the desire of the mother, has brought the self to conceive its identity not in any delusion of integrity but in its desire. Like the work of Hegel's slave, however, the object does make possible the recuperation of the primal béance, its realization by the subject in a form less threatening to its identity.

This explains the persistence of desire, for no attained object, nor any momentary recognition, can satisfy it. It requires the continued affirmation by another subject of the subject's own identity, and shows itself therein radically dependent upon that other. "The repetitive insistence of these desires . . . and their permanent recollection . . . find their necessary and sufficient reason, if one admits that the desire for recognition dominates in these determinations the desire which is to be recognized, by conserving it as such until it should be recognized" (E, p. 431). Desire is mediated through the other, which makes possible the substitution of objects that frees desire from the fixity of demand.[22] Its signification is not in the object itself but in the role one gives to one's adversary, that is, the particular kind of imaginary structure one seeks to enact. "To put it differently, the meaning of a defensive or an offensive action is not to be sought in the object over which it apparently disputes with the adversary, but rather in the design in which the action participates, and which defines the adversary by its strategy" (E, p. 376).

The process of imposition of this strategy on the other, by which he can be made to play the role assigned him, is the point where the ego, the Moi, emerges. "Demystifying the meaning of what the theory calls 'primary identifications,' let us say that the subject always imposes on the other, in the radical diversity of the modes of relation . . . an imaginary form that bears the seal, indeed the superimposed seals, of the experiences of powerlessness where this form has molded itself in the subject: and this form is none other than the ego" (E, p. 346). The first experience of impotence, the child's inability to draw to itself the desire of its mother, inaugurates a series of such encounters in which that failure marks the self by its absorption of the traces of the desire of that other for which it has exchanged its ego.

The ego is the sum of these imaginary identifications, the record of their passage across its surface. "For the ego is made of the series of identifications that have represented for the subject an essential reference mark, at every historical moment of his life, and in a fashion dependent upon circumstances" (II:197). From another angle, it is the conscious knowledge that the ego assumes exhausts those encounters, its own personal resolution of their significance, in which the element of desire, as unfulfilled, is erased. The ego's primary trait is its opacity for interpretation, its resistance to explication by the individual alone. "In short, we designate in the *ego* that kernel given to consciousness, but opaque to reflection, marked by all the ambiguities which, from good will to bad faith, structure the experience of the passions in the human subject" (*E*, p.109).

The Imaginary, at this ultimate level of its operation, may be defined as a freezing of the Symbolic, a stagnation of the movement by which the Symbolic is characterized.[23] The Symbolic order may be what necessitates repetition, but the Imaginary is how it repeats, the particular forms in which it is expressed. The symptom is the characteristic way in which the Imaginary appears, insistently repeating past situations and identifications that persist because of their nonresolution. Lacan defines the constituent condition of the symptom thus: "[The constitutive condition of the symptom] is that a mnemic element of a privileged anterior situation is taken up again in order to articulate the current situation, that is to say, that it is employed there unconsciously as a signifying element with the effect of molding the indeterminacy of experience into a tendacious signification" (*E*, p. 447). Being tendacious, the symptom will always have as its effect the reinstitution of the relationship of rivalry characteristic of identification, but will further mean that the struggle for recognition will always reenact the battles of the past, different for each participant, who thus despite their mutual identification can only engage in a form of psychic shadowboxing.

Lying behind the symptom and the identifications it conceals is the original question of identity, asked by the child through its mother's deflected desire, a desire that is evaded in the subsequent series of identifications. All subjects enact the process described by Lacan as typical of the neurotic, using the ego to pose the question of identity at such a level that it avoids the real confrontation with the provisionality of that identity. "The Freudian topic of the ego shows us how a female or male hysteric, how an obsessive, employs his ego in order to pose the question, that is to say, in order not to pose it" (III:196). Thus the Imaginary is permitted to govern the actions of the subject without its being able to recognize that patterning. Despite the primacy of the Symbolic, Lacan can still assert that "the fundamental, central structure of our experience is properly of the imaginary order" (II:50). Its effect is to distort the structuring of the Symbolic and the patterns of intersubjectivity on which the latter is based.

But absolutely essential is the Lacanian claim that the Imaginary is not to be dismantled on its own terrain nor to be attacked in its own terms. Only by means of a revisioning through the Symbolic are the confusions and errors of the Imaginary to be erased. We need to reject the idea of the representing subject, to replace it with that subject that is, from its origin, both represented and representing, caught in a dialectic of intersubjectivity. "But the important point is that this form situates the instance of the *ego*, from before its social determination, in a line of fiction forever irreducible for the single individual—or rather, which will only rejoin asymptotically the becoming of the subject, whatever might be the success of the dialectical syntheses by which he must resolve, insofar as *I*, his discordance with his own reality" (*E*, p. 94). Any resolution can occur only through the interpretive analytic intervention of another subject.

*Analytic Interpretation*

The analytic experience that takes for its task the unearthing of the Imaginary in the subject is therefore marked from its origin by the engagement of the imaginary process in an unraveling dialogue between analysé and analyst. Unlike everyday, imaginary-laden discourse, the analytic interpretation seeks to force the emergence of the Imaginary in order to allow its subsequent neutralization. The role of the analyst, in his silence, is to serve in an overt way as a repository for the Other, taken for the moment as the process by which the subject has been constituted from the outside. "Distinguishing the Other—as a category of Otherness, or as related to the 'significant other'—from the other (or present counterpart) is methodologically useful. The analyst may be viewed as the (neutral) other who is constituted as the Other by the subject (who is not talking to *him*) on the basis of the original or primordial constitution of the subject by Otherness."[24] By neutralizing the possibility of any new imaginary structures, the analyst induces the analysé to articulate more clearly the ones he retains from his past and to move toward revelation of their origins. Thus the goal for the analysis should not be a further identification, that of the analysé with the analyst, but rather the transference onto the analyst of the succession of past identifications of the analysé. Their incongruity with the current situation can then serve as clue to their discovery.

It is essential, then, that the analyst adopt insofar as possible an initially unresponsive stance. "Again, let us repeat it, this *imago* only reveals itself inasmuch as our attitude offers to the subject the pure mirror of a surface without accidents" (*E*, p. 109). The recurrence of the mirror motif should not imply that what is occurring here is another specular identification, for the analysé is confronted with a fogged mirror that resists his reprojection outward of his identificatory desires. Rather than permitting the Imaginary fixation on some partial goal, the analysis seeks to undermine the conscious self-direction that allows the subject to evade itself. "The rule proposed to the patient in the analysis lets him advance in an intentionality blind to every other end than his liberation from an ill or an ignorance of which he does not even know the limits" (*E*, p. 106).

What results from this blind speaking is not, however, an undirected monologue, because the nature of parole is always to address some other. Confronted with the silent analyst, the analysé addresses instead an imaginary figure drawn from his own mental past, in what Lacan calls an "orthodramatization" of his own repetitive script which pins a role on the analyst. "Put differently, transference is nothing real in the subject, if not the appearance, in a moment of stagnation of the analytical dialectic, of the permanent modes according to which he constitutes his objects" (*E*, p. 225). The subject in analysis thus vacillates between a dialogic relationship with the analyst and moments when the Imaginary of his own ego supersedes that rapport, when the dialogue breaks down and the relationship becomes totally one-sided. This dialogue is not necessarily any less imaginary than the process of transference or regression, but its greater congruence with the current situation makes its imaginary character much more resistant to recognition by the subject.

The reversion to past imaginary structures brings out for the first time the basic structure of the subject, its historically determined status. "The center of gravity of the subject is this present synthesis of the past that one calls history" (I:46). History is not something accessible to the conscious subject, however, because of the imaginary process in which we have seen that it comes to be. Each identification supersedes prior ones; each new synthesis by the ego erases anterior ones. Yet at the same time the mode and structure of the synthesizing ego, both agent and product of repeated identifications, incorporates the entirety of its past in invisible patterns and repetitions. It is this hidden structure of history, its origin in desire and its intersubjective tangles, that analysis pursues by shattering the present encounter. "For the subject, the disinsertion of his relation to the other makes the image of his ego vary, shimmer, oscillate, completes and decompletes it. It is a question of him perceiving it in its completeness, to which he never had access, in order that he can recognize all the steps of his desire, all the objects which have come to bring to this image its consistency, its nourishment, its incarnation" (I:205). Regression then reactualizes the separate identifications from the subject's past, to divide them in a way that makes them for the first time individually accessible, hence comparable with one another for the subject.

Rather than providing another opportunity for imaginary interaction, the analysis throws the subject back on its own Imaginary, taking its ego as the subject of the analysis and making it significative. The discourse of the subject shifts when confronted by its own ego, assuming its own history in its entirety, and as a process rather than a product. The ultimate significance of that history is in the way it has been assumed, adopted from the outside in the register of the Imaginary. "But whatever the fundamental destiny, the biological destiny, what the analysis reveals to the subject is its signification. This signification is the function of a certain *parole*, which is and which is not *parole* of the subject—he receives this *parole* already entirely made, he is its point of passage" (II:374).

The recovery of its own past by the subject can occur only in the dialogue, where the presence of the other permits a simultaneous immersion in and distance from Imaginary stages in its past. It is a path closed to the individual, always bound in a reflexive imaginary structure, and open to him only if the other resists the further elaboration of that structure. "It is opened only by verbalization, that is to say, by the mediation of the other, that is, the analyst. It is by the spoken assumption of his history that the subject engages himself in the path of realization of his truncated imaginary" (I:312). The recovery of the Imaginary is a rediscovery of the alienation characteristic of the structure of identification and of the ego. The attempt to define oneself verbally, to use one's own terms, shows instead how one can only have recourse to the words of others, even in the most private moment of self-definition. "He finishes by recognizing that this being was never anything but his construct in the imaginary and that this construct disappoints all certitude in him. For in this work that he performs to reconstruct it *for an other*, he rediscovers the fundamental alienation that made him construct it *as an other*, and which always destined it to be taken from him *by an other*" (*E*, p. 249).

The assumption by the subject of its own history is dependent finally on its awareness of and reentry into the Symbolic order that can mediate its desire. The reconstruction of one's own past is obviously dependent on a prior access to linguistic capacities, but involves as well a fuller assumption of the Symbolic, a recognition of its determinative role in the modulations of the Imaginary. The subject needs not only to assume its own past but in so doing to become cognizant of the process of history-making in which it has been engaged. If the analyst-interlocutor chooses merely to provide interpretations and suggest explanations, the subject will never pass beyond an imaginary understanding of its own past. The recovery of history must comprise an understanding of the process of signification by which it has come to possess meaning. This understanding provides an awareness of the real nature of history, its suprapersonal dimension, and of the presence in the individual of a subjectivity that far exceeds him. "The interest, the essence, the foundation, the proper dimension of analysis, is the reintegration by the subject of his history up to its last apprehensible limits, that is to say, up to a dimension that exceeds by far the individual limits" (I:18–19).

The interpretation of the analyst needs to be seen in this light, as an attempt to restore a broader dimension to the subject's imaginative restriction of its identity to this encounter or these particular events, to demonstrate instead the radical intersubjectivity of the subject in its innumerable ties stretching it beyond the limits of its own experience. The validity of interpretations is thus largely irrelevant; their role instead is to restore a symbolic mobility frozen by imaginary restrictions and repressions. "What is it then to interpret transference? Nothing other than to fill with a lure the void of that dead point [of dialectic stagnation]. But this lure is useful, for even [if] deceptive it relaunches the process" (*E*, p. 225). The utility of incorrect interpretations, of course, exists only insofar as they draw the subject closer to awareness of the process of signification and interpretation itself, only insofar as they turn the analysé himself into an analyst.

The analyst thus undermines his own authority as respondent to and guarantor of the analysé's imaginary identifications. He refuses the role of master interpreter, holder of the keys to the subject's identity. "And the non-activity of the analyst resembles strongly a definitive renunciation of all power."[25] Instead, the analyst seeks to initiate the analysé into the process of analytic dialogue, finally leaving him free to make his own way toward a *parole pleine*. With this implicit freedom, we rejoin the track of irony, which finds its place in the Symbolic rather than the Imaginary, as the reopening of the question of identity rather than its provisional slamming shut. The parallel between irony and the action of the analyst, himself in the place of the Symbolic, is sharply drawn by Shoshana Felman. "Since irony precisely consists in dragging authority as such into a scene which it cannot master, of which it is *not aware* and which, for that very reason is the scene of its self-destruction, literature, by virtue of its ironic force, fundamentally deconstructs the fantasy of authority in the same way, and for the same reasons, that psychoanalysis deconstructs the authority of the fantasy."[26] Yet irony operates, as I hope to show, not so much toward a rejection of authority, toward some kind of interpretive anarchy, as toward a reconstitution of authority, as a continual reminder of the possibility of redefinition. What it deconstructs is the idea of authority as being in a particular place or a particular person, for authority can emanate only from the entirety of the positions and persons in an intersubjective structure.[27] Authority will not cease to exist, as the pressure of Lacan's own authority should remind us; there is no poststructuralist utopia of perfect freedom beyond the unveiling of the Imaginary.

## The Symbolic Order and the Subject of Irony
*Introduction*

With the emergence of the Symbolic order, it becomes possible to pose the question of identity without having to close it off immediately by an imaginary response. The Symbolic permits the problem of self-identification to pass from endless imaginary reflections into speech, where identity can be brought into activity instead of described retroactively. "What I look for in *parole* is the response of the other. What constitutes me as subject is my question" (E, p. 269). That the question, in language, can be asked of an other, opens new possibilities for flexibility in response. Lacan's chosen inheritance from Freud is the inexhaustibly interrogative pressure of his interpretations. "[Freud] knew, and he gave us this knowledge in terms that one could call indestructible, inasmuch as since they were emitted, they sustain an interrogation that, up to the present, has never been exhausted" (XI:211).[28] The aim of interrogation is to replace the struggle for prestige, for imposition of one's desire, by the mutual exploration for it in language. "But this desire itself, in order to be satisfied in man, insists on being recognized, by the consensus of *parole* or by the struggle for prestige, in the symbol or in the imaginary" (*E*, p. 279). Barred from an outlet in the Symbolic order, desire can only have recourse to the divisive path of imaginary gratification.

Hence the possibility of agreement and consensus is the defining trait of language. "This effort to find a consensus constitutes the communication proper to language. This *you* is so fundamental that it intervenes before consciousness" (I:9).[29] Intersubjectivity, that is, in its essentially linguistic character, is prior to any consciousness and orders its functioning. The pact toward which language strives is one whose essence will be the mutual definition of two subjects in the act of interlocution.

This accord can only take place, however, through the introduction of a third term, and with it the possibility of mediation, into what has heretofore been a dual relationship. The duality of identification with the other is structurally destined to degenerate into some variant of narcissism. Only because the other subject brings with it a latent third term, the Other of Lacan's system, is this degeneration avoidable. "The ambiguity, the gap of the imaginary relation requires something that could maintain relation, function and distance. . . . In order that the human being can establish the most natural relation, that of male to female, it is necessary that a third [term] intervene, which would be the image of something successful, the model of a harmony" (III:111). What releases the two subjects from an identificatory fixation on each other is their reinsertion in a relation that exceeds them in its general character, its universal human signification. The liberating power of the signifying term lies in its capacity to redefine the two original subjects in terms of a third factor, in terms of the system within which their particular relationship exists.[30] This third element, though, is not a transcendent perspective, but the *je* with which speech enters the world. This is the missing third term that makes it possible to conceptualize the Imaginary at all, to recognize the processes by which it comes to be, to envisage, in sum, the possibility that it might not be, or be other than it is. "The imaginary economy has meaning, we have a hold on it, only inasmuch as it inscribes itself in a symbolic order that imposes a ternary relation" (II:296). The Symbolic makes it possible for the subject to change places, without thereby losing its sense of place.

The Symbolic order plays on multiple registers for Lacan; its constituents can be most clearly seen if broken down and treated separately, however artificial such an operation may be. It finds its original moment, its correlate to the mirror stage, in the *fort-da* game where the child enters into the Symbolic field of language. But the Symbolic order also represents the desire by which this access to language is governed, the law that determines its operation, and the social order for which and in which it functions. By examining each of these in turn, I hope to demonstrate the ironic character of Lacan's Symbolic order, the irresistible pressure of language toward the intersubjective examination of the process of self-definition that takes place in language.

### The Symbolic Order as Language

If the central Freudian discovery is of an unconscious rooted in desire, the key Lacanian step is his premise that the unconscious is structured like a language. This claim stops short of the assertion that the unconscious is a language in order to emphasize that the essence of language lies in its structure. Lacan's interpretation of this term can be found in his treatment of the fort-da game described by Freud in *Beyond the Pleasure Principle*, at the very outer limits of the psychoanalytic system. "This game by which the child exerts itself to make an object disappear from its view, in order then to bring it back, then to obliterate it anew, an object furthermore indifferent in nature, even while it modulates this alternation of distinctive syllables,—this game, let us say, manifests in its radical traits the determination that the human animal receives from the symbolic order" (E, p. 46). Given its central importance for Lacan, one would wish to define its exact role as a transitional event for the child, the sum of the individual aspects highlighted at various points by Lacan.

The fort-da game marks the child's initial entry into an object world and the creation of a maintainable difference (in contrast notably to the ever-collapsing imaginary dualities). The scene is often read as an effort at mastery by the child, whose words are taken as imperatives that precede and foreshadow its own actions of retrieving or throwing away the object. By so doing, the child would be seeking to overcome, via representation, the traumatic absence of its mother, over which it can assert no comparably absolute control, while also totalizing the poles of presence and absence within a diachronically complete verbal opposition. From Lacan's perspective, this interpretation errs in its optimistic erasure of the subject's constant incapacity to recreate any full presence. "To say that it is simply a question for the subject of instituting himself in a function of mastery is foolishness. In the two phonemes, the mechanisms characteristic of alienation embody themselves—which express themselves, however paradoxical that may seem to you, at the level of the *fort*" (XI:216). Language does not reestablish or inaugurate any lost sufficiency for the child, but rather inscribes its alienation in inescapable terms.[31]

The fort-da game permits the child to destroy the object so central in the Imaginary and to reappropriate thereby its own alienated integrity. By making the object vanish, the child absorbs within itself the dialectic of presence and absence, of integrity and fragmentation, and makes itself the locus of both the available possibilities. The child takes its own action, its own desire as present and absent, as the real object of its activity. "For his action destroys the object, which it makes appear and disappear in an anticipatory *provocation* of its absence and its presence. It thus renders negative the field of forces of desire in order to become to itself its own object" (E, p. 319). The subject here provokes the alternation of the object as a means of negating the dominance of the object over its own response.

The emptiness of absence, the terrifying void of the departed mother, can thus be alleviated by being drawn into a system where even absence has a content, a name. "By the word that is already a presence made of absence, absence itself comes to name itself in an originary moment whose perpetual recreation the genius of Freud seized in the game of the child" (E, p. 276). The absence that means solitude for the child can thus be relocated in a structure where a reciprocal presence, a possibility of return, is always reassuringly contained. This act is not the mimetic reproduction of an experience, but its reinscription in a *code signifiant* characteristic of all language, where each term implicitly contains its negation.

The fort-da game thus marks a liberation from the object—be it mother or toy—that is the definitive trait of the human world. The playful entrance into language makes possible all the subsequent substitutions of objects that will characterize the structure of both subject and human society. In a way, the game is only an assumption of the possibilities inherent in the imaginary alienation from the object, which is always the object of the other, the object of his desire.

But the fort-da experience is not just a liberation from the real or even the imaginary object. Its centrality stems from the fact that the subject is structured into the relation, that it is its *own* presence and absence that are in play here. The mother is here only as an absence, as a representation whose involvement is peripheral, since the child in no sense aims at provoking her return by its game. But the child is dramatically and dynamically present, itself the entity behind the words it expresses, and entered into an oppositional structure with the object, where both can adopt either phonemic pole indifferently. The child in fact completes the mother's or object's absence by coming into being as the presence that confirms relationship, albeit only by reconfirming the split within the subject. Relation displaces and masks the emptiness of separation, but cannot abolish it. "It is the repetition of the departure of the mother as cause of a *Spaltung* in the subject—surmounted by the alternating game, *fort-da*, which is a *here or there*, and which in its alternation aims only to be *fort* of a *da*, and *da* of a *fort*" (XI:61).

The words *fort* and *da*, then, refer to the subject itself and describe not a recovery of a presence, but a synchronic simultaneity of presence and absence, where even the da-ness of the subject cannot abolish its institution against a ground of absence. The primordial phonemic opposition establishes the interdependence of alternatives, without thereby reestablishing an integrity between them that would only be imaginary. This alienation of the subject is thus also a founding, at once an objectification of its own action and assertion of the primacy of that action in its self-constitution.

So the essential acquisition of the child in the fort-da game is a recognition of the synchronic integrity of oppositional terms. The signifier for Lacan is that which unites presence and absence; each signifier enacts the process by which signification comes to be. The signifier thereby overcomes the mutual exclusiveness of presence and absence at an imaginative level, the insistence on either-or. "[The sign] connotes presence *or* absence, by bringing in essentially the *and* that connects them, since to connote presence or absence, it institutes presence upon a fund of absence, just as it constitutes absence in presence" (*E*, p. 594). Even existence comes to have significance only insofar as the possibility of nonexistence gives it a differential character. This nature of the signifier makes it uniquely suited for posing the question of identity, for the subject both is and is not, or has not always been. The nonexistent is finally only that which has not been spoken, which, though perhaps not speakable, still insists on being spoken. "The fundamental relation of man to this symbolic order is very precisely that which founds the symbolic order itself—the relation of non-being to being. . . . The end of the symbolic process is that non-being come (in)to being, that it be because it has spoken" (II:354). An impossible aim, perhaps, but one to which language is nonetheless bound.

The form in which this constitutive structure of presence and absence emerges in language use is a *renvoi de signification*. Each sign sustains itself only through the regress of signification through the entire system of language, via the implications it conveys. Invoked to fill the absence of a prior signifier, each new signifier in turn reveals itself as incomplete, as necessarily calling up yet another signifier to supplement its own absence. The essence of language is its multivalency and combinatorial multireferentiality. "*Parole* never has a single meaning, the word a single usage. Every *parole* has always a beyond, supports several functions, envelops several meanings. Behind what a discourse says, there is what it means to say, and behind what it means to say, there is yet another mean-to-say, and none of it will ever be exhausted" (I:267). External referentiality to things is secondary to this multiple internal referentiality of language. "The word is not a sign, but a knot of signification" (*E*, p. 166).

Though based on Saussure's theory of the strictly differential nature of the linguistic sign and its separation into signifier and signified, Lacan's theory of language stresses the lack of a one-to-one rapport between the two halves of the sign, the incommensurability of signifier and signified. The bar put between them by Saussure becomes the symbol of their constant separation from one another. "The *S* and the *s* of the Saussurian algorithm are not in the same plane, and man would deceive himself to believe himself placed at their common axis, which is nowhere" (*E*, p. 518). Their relationship is rather a holistic one, of totality to totality, of system to system.

The same relation holds between the symbolic system and reality, so that the nature of signification is that it be totalizing and omnireferential. "In order to conceive what occurs in the proper domain which is of the human order, it is necessary that we start from the idea that this order constitutes totality. . . . The symbolic order is given first in its universal character" (II:41–42). The integrity of the symbolic system is not, however, accessible for consciousness, which will lead Lacan in the following seminar to replace *totality* by *ensemble* (III:207). Though its ultimate pattern may thus remain opaque to consciousness, however, the covariance of the elements in the Symbolic order allows us to follow its functioning. Significance will be a function of position within the system, of the joints each element makes with those around it. "But these significations themselves, [the analyst] will take them as being able to be grasped with certitude only in their context, that is, in the sequence that is constituted for each of them by the signification that refers back to it and by the [signification] to which it refers back in the analytic discourse" (*E*, p. 418).

The power of the word lies in the positional coherence and metaphoric openness that make it representative of and signal to the whole system of language. Signification is therefore subject to a constant process of *glissement*, of slippage of meaning through reinterpretations.[32] For my purposes, however, the key aspect of the signifier is its definition as "that which represents the subject for another signifier [*pour un autre signifiant*]" (*E*, p. 819). The first half of the definition, the fact that the subject is represented by the signifier, is clear enough. But what does Lacan mean by the statement that this representation is "pour un autre signifiant"? The resonance of the *pour* here implies first that the subject represents itself "in terms of" another signifier, that is, within a differential system of language, whose entire structure is brought to bear on that single signifier. Yet there is an additional implication here as well. "But this subject is what the signifier represents, and it could not represent anything except for another signifier: to which henceforth the subject who listens is reduced" (*E*, p. 835). The other signifier, then, is the interlocutor as well, the one for whom the utterance is made and through whose presence the latent presence of the whole Symbolic system can be made evident. The child of the fort-da game is already speaking itself for the other, locating itself as *da* when the object is *fort, fort* when it is *da*, so that the other can see where it is.

What the other subject adds is the possibility of duplicity characteristic of the system of human language. "What this structure of the signifying chain uncovers is the possibility that I have, precisely to the degree that its language is common to me and to other subjects, that is to say [to the degree] that that language exists, for me to make use of it for signifying *something quite other* than what it says" (*E*, p. 505). That potential in language is tied to the self-objectification of the fort-da game, and the potential therein of using language to deflect the overwhelming presence of the other, insofar as that other comes to represent the absolute Other-

ness of a language that would define and annul the self. "[The radical fil-
ing past of *parole*] is reproduced each time that the subject addresses the
Other as absolute, that is to say, as the Other who can himself annul him,
in the same way that he can behave with the Other, that is to say, in making himself an object to deceive the Other" (*E*, p. 53). The subject here assumes its own splitting, itself performing the self-alienation to which it
has always been subject, and in so doing opens up the possibility of a
nonfixed identity.[33] But language's primary function is to establish a rapport between subjects; its referentiality is back to the relationship it creates. "The word *reference* in this case can only situate itself in regard to
what discourse constitutes as a bond" (XX:32).

So the slippage of signifier and subject is not an absolute free play. It
is arrested by the question of being, by the direction in which language
moves of seeking to articulate the subject who articulates it. This term
*being* has a precise sense for Lacan; it is delimitable as what he terms *universal discourse*. To pursue one's being is to seek to locate oneself in relation to
language. "It is by rapport with that [the universal discourse] that the subject situates himself insofar as subject, he is inscribed there, it is by that
that he is already determined. . . . His function, inasmuch as he continues
the discourse, is to rediscover himself at his place there, not simply insofar
as orator, but insofar as henceforth entirely determined by it" (II:326).

This imperative limits the subject according to the places at which it
has entered into language, that is, according to the intersubjective relations through which its entrance was mediated. "It is for that reason that it
is false to say that the signifier in the unconscious is open to all meanings.
It constitutes the subject in his liberty in regard to all meanings, but that
does not mean that it is not there determined" (XI:227). The subject is further determined by a final element that confines its identity, which is the
confrontation, at the limits of its inquiry, with its own death. The split between presence and absence on which the signifier was made to rest will
inevitably provide a space where the imaginary béance can reemerge in a
way more fully integrated with the subject's identity. Language brings into
being the possibility of desire, which is the second aspect of the Symbolic
order.

### The Symbolic Order as Desire

Desire is, for Lacan, the fundamental and defining trait of human
existence. It is the element that renders inadequate any strictly perceptual

or cognitive model of a subject, which is from its origin intersubjective and unconscious. As the mirror stage makes evident, desire appears as a generalization of lack from the child's particular situation to a shared human state, seen and acquired through the mother's desire. The alienation realized by the child in the mirror stage provokes its "unconditional" demand, not for satisfaction of needs but for love. The remainder of demand after the provisional satisfaction of a need is where desire can come to locate itself. "Desire sketches itself in the margin where demand is torn apart from need: this margin being that which demand, the appeal of which can only be unconditional in the place of the Other, opens in the form of the possible defect which need can bring to it, of not having universal satisfaction (what one calls: anguish)" (E, p. 814). The recurrence of needs continually ruptures and defers the unconditionality of demand by making evident the child's dependence on an other for its satisfaction.

The imaginary belief in the other as all-powerful leads the child to see the response to its needs as willfully inadequate; it perceives that its mother's gaze is directed elsewhere than at it alone. With its needs and demands defined from the outside and in language, the child finds itself subjected to the displacements that dependence entails. "They are first of all from a deviation of the needs of man [arising] from the fact that he speaks, in this sense that as far as his needs are subjected to demand, they return to him alienated. This is not the effect of his real dependence . . . but indeed of the putting into signifying form as such, and of the fact that it is from the place of the Other that his message is emitted" (E, p. 690). The child's demand thus leads it to recognize in the desire of the mother, directed elsewhere, the barrier to the full satisfaction it wishes. From an idealization of the other—as self-sufficient and able to satisfy its needs—the child passes to the inevitable recognition that this other is itself incomplete, "if the Other, place of the *parole* is also the place of this lack" (E, p. 627).

The ability to elicit a full response is thus dependent on the ability to ascertain and fulfill the other's desire, a desire that is never partial, but always absolute. It is in this sense that "the desire of man is the desire of/for the Other" (XI:213). Lacan's oft-repeated aphorism contains the double meaning that the desire of another subject, via identification, is made mine, and also that the other is the object of my desire. This latter desire is not a desire to possess that other, but rather a desire for his recognition of my desire, by which my own desire can be made tangible. This

Other is ultimately not just the specific other, the mother for the child, but the whole web of social relationships to which her own desire links her.

The entrance into a world of desire thus serves to draw the child beyond an essentially narcissistic relationship, as it begins to look through the mother into the structuring intersubjectivity that defines her. "For it is not a question of the assumption by the subject of the insignia of the other, but this condition, that the subject has to find the constituting structure of his desire in the same gap opened up by the effect of the signifier in those who come to represent for him the Other, insofar as his demand is subjected to them" (E, p. 628). Desire is therefore much more complex than the identification with another; it entails the absorption of a whole range of intersubjective relations, by which and in which the subject can be defined.

The child's accession to desire, implicitly the desire of the mother, in the fort-da game substitutes for the unconditionality of demand the absoluteness of desire, an equally infinite longing based on the subject's dependence on others. The central consequence of the lack in the subject is an endless recourse to intersubjectivity. "Desire situates itself in the dependence of the demand—which, by articulating itself in signifiers, leaves a metonymic remainder that runs beneath it, element which is not indeterminate, which is a condition at once absolute and unseizable, element necessarily in impasse, unsatisfied, impossible, misapprehended, element that is called desire" (XI:141). Although equally insatiable, desire still represents a radical transformation of demand, because it frees the subject from subjection to a particular other. "[Desire] reverses the unconditionality of the demand for love, where the subject remains in the subjection of the Other, in order to raise it to the power of the absolute condition (where the absolute also means detachment)" (E, p. 814). Lacan's formulation of this absolute state, if quite compatible with the Absolute of Schlegel, is still more precise in its depiction of how it comes to be and how it affects the subject. It is a state of detachment, the form of which is not defined by the total and irrecoverable inequalities of the Hegelian dialectic. Once the Other has been seen to be only a mediator of desire, the subject is freed from fixation on a single love-object and hence becomes able to enter into a variety of relations.[34]

Just this freedom, however, renders desire insatiable, for no particular object can ever be the ultimate object of desire, which partakes of a hallucinatory plenitude in the mind of the self. Instead, the object of desire is transformed by the ego in an endless series of displacements, each attained object vanishing into a chain of substitutions. Any specification of the absolute object of desire brings the ego and its fragmentary structure into play. "But it is indeed of the subject, of a subject primitively out of tune, fundamentally fragmented by the *ego,* that all objects are desired. The subject cannot desire without himself dissolving himself, and without seeing, from this very fact, the object escape him, in a series of infinite displacements" (II:209–210). What this series of displacements can conceal is the fundamental structure of desire, which has its focus in no particular object (as does need), nor any particular person (as does demand). It is instead the opening out of the subject into the full range of possible human relations, and the corresponding loss of determinate identity that Lacan terms a *manque à être.* For the desiring subject enters fully into the void where its identity is in abeyance, subject to the response of the object toward which it strives. "Desire, a function central to every human experience, is desire of nothing namable. . . . Being comes to exist precisely in function of this lack. It is in function of this lack, in the experience of desire, that being comes to a sense of self in relation to being" (II:261–262).

The characteristics that make up the conventional view of identity take on significance only against a background of absence, the possibility that they might have been different. The subject, for Lacan, is absolutely bound up in the provisionality of its identity and the potentiality of its metamorphoses. "For the experience of desire . . . is that itself of the lack of being by which any being could not be or be other, or put differently, is created as existent" (*E,* p. 667). This is the reason the encounter with the other can have such far-reaching effects on the subject, the reason it is subject to the dialectic of intersubjectivity in which it is engaged. The peculiar embedding of desire in the search for identity makes any form of individual response to that question impossible.[35]

Desire is finally the desire to know the nature of one's own desire, to understand the process by which one assumes the network of intersubjective bonds that comes to replace a direct response from the mother. Unlike demand, desire pursues recognition rather than satisfaction. Its transformation into language enacts the creation of bonds on which identity depends. "*Parole* is this dimension where the desire of the subject is authentically integrated on the symbolic plane. It is only when it formulates itself, names itself before the other, that desire, whatever it may be, is recognized in the full sense of the term" (I:207). Though insatiable, desire can be recognized, at the moment when a particular encounter comes to resonate with the behavioral and linguistic patterns of the individuals located in it. This expansion of the individual dialogue into a more universal discourse is the moment when the Symbolic order emerges as the Law.

*The Symbolic Order as Law*

The structure the child perceives by entering into the mother's desire is that Law embodied by the father. Her gaze, turned toward the father, first reveals to the child its subjection to patterns beyond their limited, narcissistic encounter. The Law converts the absence felt by the child, both that of the mother and its own absence from itself, into a socially determined lack, a prohibition. The self-absence that was so playfully entered into by the child becomes concretized as the threat of castration, which regulates the paths through which desire can flow. "It is therefore rather the assumption of castration that creates the lack by which desire is instituted. Desire is desire of desire, desire of the Other . . . that is, subject to the Law" (*E*, p. 852). The pattern of relationships seen through the mother's absent gaze is not a random or freely manipulable one, but one already fixed and determined.

The father therefore replaces the blind or absent mother for the child as the significant other, for he serves as the focus of her desire.[36] This secondary identification is quite different from the initial one; it is not simply a rechanneling of narcissistic drives toward the father, because the child's relation to him is mediated by and through the mother. Nor does the father seem unable to satisfy the child's demands, but instead refuses to allow their fulfillment. What the father centrally prohibits is incest, the effect of which is to make the child's desire *autonomous*. Forcefully turned away from the mother, it is led to perform the first substitution in an unending chain whenever it seeks any alternative gratification. "Freud reveals to us that it is thanks to the Name-of-the-Father that man does not remain attached to the sexual service of the mother, that the aggression against the Father is at the principle of the Law, and that the Law is at the service of the desire that it institutes by the interdiction of incest" (*E*, p. 852). If entry into the mother's desire made possible the shifting of objects of desire, the father's presence makes that movement necessary. The law's prohibition cuts the world in two, performing an irretrievable act of differentiation for the child, a splitting that no narcissistic reflex can recuperate. A failure to recognize or to encounter the Law results in a permanent suspension of the emerging subject in the mother's desire.[37]

This shift is articulated by the Oedipal complex, which converts the impossibility of desire into the language of myth. The central application of the law is to sexuality, which is thus transformed from a biological force into a symbolic one, whereby the identity of the subject is drawn into the broader reaches of a totalized symbolic system. "The subject finds his place in a preformed symbolic apparatus that establishes the law in sexuality" (III:191).[38] As a limitation on sexuality, law forms the reverse of desire, an opposite inseparable from it through which desire comes to be significant. The Law structures human relations according to the degrees of permissible access, thus subjecting appetites to an independent Symbolic order. Only via entry into this order can a subject begin to replace its imaginary self-image with a recognition of its fully provisional status, an indeterminacy that is counterbalanced by the network of defined social relations. "But it is still necessary that the order of the signifier be acquired, be conquered by the subject, that he be put in his place in a relationship of implication that touches his being, which culminates in the formation of what we call in our language the super-ego" (III:214).

The key to this step is the recognition of the father, and indeed of all roles, as pure signifiers, as positions rather than essences. Hence Lacan comes to speak of the Name of the Father, rather than the actual or imagined father, as the operative element in the Oedipal complex. "It is indeed what demonstrates that the attribution of procreation to the father can only be the effect of a pure signifier, of a recognition, not of the real father, but of what religion taught us to invoke as the Name-of-the Father" (E, p. 556). This awareness of the possibility of positional shifts, which is central to the "Purloined Letter" essay, also permits the subject to become mobile itself. The potential then to change roles, to identify with a succession of different persons rather than any single one or single type, is the characteristic of a subject at the level of the Symbolic. The real significance of the Oedipal complex is that it frees the subject from being in any one place, allowing it to enact differences without being trapped by them. "However, we can articulate this complex, its triangular crystallization, its diverse modalities and consequences, its terminal crisis, called a decline, sanctioned by the introduction of the subject into a new dimension, only to the degree that *the subject is at once himself and the two other partners*. This is what the term of 'identification' that you are always employing signifies. There is therefore *intersubjectivity, and dialectical organization, there"* (III:224; italics here are mine).

This process of engagement with other subjects and mutual partition of diverse roles is the point where the only possible fullness of the subject can emerge. Lacan, like Schlegel, insists on the partialness of the subject, while focusing as well on the completing enactment, for that partialness is made evident only through the presence of a structure comprising the subject's parts. The fundamental split of the subject, that between male and female, is only resolvable in a dramatic form. "Only this division [into male and female] . . . renders necessary what was brought to light first by the analytical experience, that the paths of what it is necessary to do as man or as woman are entirely abandoned to drama, to scenario, which places itself in the field of the Other—what is properly the Oedipal complex" (XI:186). The categories of male and female, once recognized in a pattern that draws them together and illustrates their interdependence, provide the subject with a maintainable difference to resist its narcissistic pressures. This expansion of the partial self takes place in another dimension as well, that of history. "Sexual desire is in effect what is used by man to historicize himself, inasmuch as it is at this level that the law is introduced for the first time" (III:177).

The consequence of the symbolized mobility of the subject is, as Jameson acutely notes, not submission to the Law but a radical alienation and sense of self as separate and incomplete. The Law promotes this ironic incompletion by institutionalizing rather than healing the subject's splitting. "If we recall that for Lacan, 'submission to the Law' designates, not repression, but rather something quite different, namely alienation . . . then the more tragic character of Lacan's thought, and the dialectical possibilities inherent in it, become evident."[39] Desire and the Law, unlike demand, are dependent upon the radical alterity of the Other, the irreducibility of the structure of that Other to the mere sum of the subjects it envelops. The Other is not equal to an actual interlocutor any more than it is identifiable with the real father. Rather than being itself a subject or a person, the Other is rather more akin to the conditions of possibility for any dialogue, the place where intersubjectivity can come to be and to bring individual subjects into being. *"The Other is therefore the place where the I who speaks constitutes itself with the one who hears"* (III:309).[40] The Other is the cause of the subject and therefore beyond it, a possibility no individ-

ual subject can reach nor any metalanguage circumscribe. "Which we formulate by saying that there is no metalanguage that could be spoken,
more aphoristically: that there is no Other of the Other" (*E,* p. 813). Like
Schlegel's Absolute, however, this Other should not be considered to have
an independent existence apart from the individual subjects and interlo-
cutions to which it is dialectically bound.[41]

How then is the Other present? As an initial answer, one could say
that the Other is enacted by the other subject or with the other subject. It
appears in the response, between the two subjects as the place of a response that exceeds the intentionality of the respondent and the interpretation of the original subject. This fluidity of the response is what permits
all the elements of ruse and deception that Lacan finds characteristic of
language. The dialogue brings into play what Lacan terms an *entre-je*
(III:218), which serves as a sliding third term, the place of which is determined by the modulations of an interaction. The invocation of this Other
is finally a duty, for one enters into the world of the Law only through the
assumption of a symbolic debt, an ethical debt owed to all other subjects.
To be in the Law, as is any subject in the Symbolic order, is already to be
guilty of its violation, whence the need for it arose. "How can this attachment be established, how does man enter into that law, which is alien to
him, with which he as animal has nothing to do? . . . It is necessary that
man make himself into participant as guilty" (III:275). The source of the
Law and its possibility of ordered human relations is the murder of the father, his transmutation from a real to a symbolic figure.

*The Symbolic Order as the Social Order*

The problem of ironic intersubjectivity is articulated in a precise way
by Lacan's treatment of the Symbolic as a structuring of the social order.
The role of language, the force of desire, and the effect of the Law are to
permit the subject to pose and to answer the question of self-identity on
the symbolic level where intersubjectivity becomes possible. There can be
no full intersubjectivity, no interpenetration in mutual definition, until
desire is expressed in the language of the Law. This occurs only in dialogue, where the content of the other's response is the location of the subject within a social reality.[42] "This discourse of the other is not the
discourse of the abstract other, of the other in the dyad, of my correspon-
dent, nor simply of my slave; it is the discourse of the circuit in which I am
integrated" (II:112). The signifiers the subject receives serve to identify

and explain it, but in terms of the symbolic circuit, not in terms of its character or essence. These latter elements are finally inessential in determining the being of the subject. "The founding *paroles*, which envelop the
subject, are all that constituted him, his relations, his neighbors, all the
structure of the community, and not only constituted him as symbol, but
constituted him in his being" (II:30). This system is necessarily exterior to
the individual subject, who is nonetheless in a sense the focus of all its
members.

For Lacan, the subject is always subject to the Symbolic order. "A
psychoanalyst ought to assure himself in this evidence that man is, from
before his birth and beyond his death, caught in the symbolic
chain . . . break himself to this idea that it is in his very being, in his total
personality . . . that he is in effect caught as a whole, but in the form of a
pawn, in the play of the signifier" (*E*, p. 468). The subject is finally only a
locus of relations, a point of intersection; the symbolic relation is the sum
of these relations, "our relation with others in their totality" (I:161). This
symbolic chain into which the subject is linked has a triple dimension,
comprising its history, its subjection to linguistic overdetermination, and
the "intersubjective game when truth enters into the real" (*E*, p. 438). This
predetermination of identity is alienating for the subject; its omnipresence
in language subjects it to the *ironie propre du langage*. The subject cannot escape the irony of language by which it is continually defining itself with
borrowed terms. Yet that subject is really only fully constituted in the intersubjective play of a parole addressed to an other; its acquisition of a latent subjectivity must pass through intersubjectivity. The assumption of
subjectivity, which means the recognition of its transindividual functioning, is for Lacan the aim of psychoanalysis. "It is indeed this assumption
by the subject of his history, insofar as it is constituted by the *parole* addressed to the other, which constitutes the basis of the new method to
which Freud gives the name of psychoanalysis" (*E*, p.257).

The realization of the Other in discourse therefore depends upon the
success of the address to the other subject. This involves at its most basic
level the use of the *you* that "hooks" the interlocutor into a dialogue. "The
*you* is in the signifier what I call a way of hooking the other, of hooking
him in the discourse, of hanging on him signification" (III:337). Yet this act
must not involve any restriction of the other, any anticipation of his response. "The register of the truth situates itself there where the subject
can seize nothing if not the very subjectivity that an Other in absolute

constitutes" (E, p. 20). This pure subjectivity is one which can, like the first subject, use the signifier for the purpose of deception or feint; its place is a provisional and undetermined one. It is the contrary of the imaginary semblable, recognized without being therefore comprehensible. "Absolute, that is to say that it is recognized, but that it is not known" (III:48). Only under these conditions, by the attribution to the other of an absolute status, can the subject acquire for itself that same absoluteness and freedom from determinate identity.

The replies of this Other are unanticipable, which forces the subject to constitute and reconstitute the image it confronts.[43] It is when the subject endeavors to invoke an other subject in its totality that that other becomes Other, for it succeeds in passing beyond its partial and imaginary determinations of that other. "In this formula, it is therefore not to an ego, insofar as I make him see, that I address myself, but to all the signifiers that make up the subject to whom I am opposed" (III:343). This total address restores to that other subject the indeterminacy, the excess beyond conscious intentionality, that the subject pursues for itself. "The Other, with a large O, it is indeed necessary that it be recognized beyond this relation, even reciprocal, of exclusion; it is necessary that, in this vanishing relation, it be recognized as just as unseizable as myself. In other words, it is necessary that it be invoked as what, of himself, he does not know" (III:342). The entrance into the Symbolic order must be a mutual one, a mutual recognition of one's likeness to another subject in the oscillation between subject and ego. "It is necessary for him to get out of his subjection to the Other, to get himself out of it, and in the getting-himself-out, in the end, he will know that the real Other has, just as much as himself, to get itself out of it, to pull itself free. It is indeed there that the necessity of good faith imposes itself, founded on the certitude that the same implication of the difficulty in relation to the paths of desire is also in the Other" (XI:172). The likeness between subjects and the basis of their recognition is the likeness of the task before them and the recognition of their dependence on one another for its completion. The address to and ethical reliance on the other reiterates the dependent nature of the subject, for it opens itself in this address to the possibility of refusal. Its identity depends on the other's willingness to interject itself and its identity into the dialogue.

The central role of language for Lacan is communication; its significative focus is on the current intersubjective rapport and the attempt to include its dynamic qualities in the process of self-definition. Subjects, as individuals, do not precede their communicative encounter except as imaginary constructs. Parole is above all an enactment of a dynamic human interaction, and the prime task of parole is to define the intersubjective rapport it establishes and confirms. "Even if it communicates nothing, the discourse represents the existence of communication; even if it denies the evidence, it affirms that the *parole* constitutes truth; even if it is destined to deceive, it speculates on the faith in testimony" (E, pp. 251–252). This rapport provides the concrete basis of the entirety of the community. When the subject restores to the other its full complement of indeterminacy, it invokes at the same time the network of social relations that alone can sustain such lack of definition. "There is there an extension, and which implies in truth the present assembly of all those who, united or not in a community, are supposed to make up its body, to be the support of the discourse in which ostension inscribes itself" (III:340). Yet in this totality which parole makes present, the subject remains only a part, a limited character. Parole retains its more limited function as an expression of self-identity, the purpose of which is "to indicate the place of this subject in the search for the true" (E, p. 505). Though it can invoke the Other, the subject never becomes it.

The recognition of the Other is therefore identical with the subject's recognition of its difference from and its ignorance of that Other, its alienation from itself. Language does not just establish a bond, but also reveals the fundamental inadequacy of the subject to its own truth, its incapacity to realize the complete resonance of the symbolic and social systems within which it moves. "The *parole* is mediation, doubtless, mediation between the subject and the other, and it implies the realization of the other in the mediation itself. . . . But there is another facet of *parole*, which is revelation" (I:59). What is revealed to the subject, in dialogue, is the unconscious, which is really just another word for its own ignorance of itself, a process Felman describes as a new form of reflexivity. "A reflexivity, whereby ignorance itself becomes structurally informative, in an asymmetrically reflexive dialogue in which the interlocutors—through language—inform each other of what they do not know."[44] For every entrance into language brings with it a fading of the subject that reveals its internal split from itself.

The overcoming of any partial ignorance does not imply the resolution of the basic ironic dilemma of ignorance. The solidity of the intersubjective rapport is balanced by heightened elusiveness of the individual subjects for themselves. "The *parole* transforms them, in giving them a certain just relation, but—and it is this on which I wish to insist—a distance which is not symmetrical, a relation which is not reciprocal. In effect, the *I* is never there where it appears in the form of a particular signifier. The *I* is always there by right of a presence sustaining the totality of the discourse" (III:310). The acquisition of the intersubjective dialogue thus seems a very tenuous one, providing no knowledge with which one can depart from that encounter, no long-term retention of the identity experienced there.

The dialogue does indeed provoke the vanishing of subjects' identities into the tie between them, a tie that exceeds them as individuals and thus provides only an evanescent sort of knowledge, dependent on their presence with each other. "Knowledge, in other words, is not a *substance* but a structural dynamic: it is not *contained* by an individual but comes about out of the mutual apprenticeship between two partially unconscious speeches which both say more than they know."[45] Felman's description of the Lacanian dialogue is very close to my definition of ironic intersubjectivity, an interaction where the recognition of ignorance serves as a springboard to ethical involvement with another subject.

Yet there is a knowledge the subject can bear away from the dialogue with another subject, which is the reaffirmed knowledge of its unceasing dependence on other subjects. Relationship, and not knowledge, is really the focus for Lacan, for the inescapability of ignorance has as its correlate the effects of that ignorance in redefining the question of identity in properly intersubjective terms, where personal knowledge ceases to have privileged status. "Each time that a person speaks to another in an authentic and full fashion, there is, in the literal sense, transference, symbolic transference—something occurs which changes the nature of the two beings there present" (I:127). Language does this because of its communicative aspect, the necessary bond of understanding it involves between separate subjects. "For in its symbolizing function, it [the *parole*] aims at nothing less than transforming the subject to whom it is addressed by the tie it establishes with the one who emits it" (E, p. 296).

Language *unites* subjects in their ignorance and in so doing prepares the way for a recognition of the primacy of intersubjectivity over all individual subjects. It creates a reality not there before, of relationship, where the core of the subject will be found to exist. "It is [the *parole*] which is the founding medium of the intersubjective relation, and which modifies retroactively the two subjects. It is the *parole* which, literally, creates what establishes them in that dimension of being that I try to make you dimly apprehend" (I:302–303). The subject is constituted as subject only through intersubjectivity; to see this is to accept the necessity for a complementary and interdependent definition of personal identity. Such a definition of intersubjective selfhood rearticulates the radical provisionality of the subject and reopens the béance of the Imaginary. The radical lack of definition of the subject is what enables its dialectic attachment to any aspect of the community of subjects. "The possibility at every instant of again putting in question desire, attachment, indeed the most persistent signification of human activity, the perpetual possibility of a reversal of sign in fuction of the dialectic totality of the position of the individual, is of such common experience that one is stupefied to see this dimension forgotten as soon as one has to do with one's likeness, whom one wishes to objectify" (III:32). Only insofar as the other is not my semblable, can that other be a subject.

What Lacan's work provides, then, is a negative ethic of leaving space for the other. The analytic ethic, he says, is a stoic one, which recognizes the subjection of one's own desire to the Other (XI:229). Yet it is not just passive, for it entails as well an acceptance of responsibility for one's effects on the particular others whom one encounters, effects that stretch far beyond any personal actions, since for that other the subject may be in the position of the Other. It involves further an acceptance of the transformation and distortions that mark one's language as seen in its impact on other subjects, for it accepts identity as something not wholly personal, as much in others as in oneself.[46]

The intersubjective dynamics of Lacan's system revolve around the interminable question of personal identity. The parole pleine of which he speaks is a question rather than a statement, an attempt by desire to fulfill its desire to name itself, and to understand the reason for its persistence. "We teach, following Freud, that the Other is the place of that memory that he discovered under the name of the unconscious, memory that he considers as the object of a question that remained open insofar as it conditions the indestructibility of certain desires" (*E*, p. 575). This question is finally the question of the significance of the subject's own history, since that history is marked by the continual reviviscence of desire. "The question of the subject does not refer at all to what can result from a certain weaning, abandonment, vital lack of love or of affection; it concerns his history insofar as he misapprehends it, and it is that which he expresses quite despite himself through all his conduct, inasmuch as he searches obscurely to recognize it" (II:58). The recognition of that history does not, however, abolish its force, but turns past contingencies into future necessities, the inevitability of which, in the force of intersubjective identity, the subject has come to comprehend.

Nor is it really possible ever to assume fully the Symbolic order, to comprehend or enact completely the network of intersubjectivity it represents. "It is something quite different from the narcissistic relation with the likeness; it is the relation of the subject with the law in its entirety, insofar as he can never there have any relation to the law in its entirety, since the law is never completely assumed" (II:158). The subject is never in the place of the Other, however aware it may become of how that functions. The persistence of the Imaginary is inescapable, except perhaps on the very edge of death. "There is no reason why the subject would come no longer to have an ego, unless it were in an extreme position such as that of Oedipus at the end of his existence" (II:254). At most, the awareness of the Symbolic order permits the subject to smooth the point of their intersection, to know where it is in regard to both registers.

The role of the Symbolic order in this regard is to regulate and render visible the paths of the Imaginary ego, not to abolish it. Like the analytic act, any fully interactive dialogue can reveal the symptoms of the Imaginary that block the full emergence of the multiplicity of connections that make up the Symbolic. The characteristic of the Symbolic order, and of the human relations it governs, is a full mediation between all elements of the structure, the possibility for any element to enter into any other position. It is this sort of tentative subject, not far from the decrepitude of Oedipus at Colonus, that we find defining itself in the writings of Samuel Beckett.

## ◈§ 5

# Beginning with Beckett

*It was he told me I'd begun all wrong, that I should have begun differently. He must be right. I began at the beginning, like an old ballocks, can you imagine that? . . . Here's my beginning. It must mean something or they wouldn't keep it. Here it is.*
—Molloy, p. 8

*The danger is in the neatness of identifications.*
—Our Exagmination, p. 3

## Irony and the Reading of Beckett

Before beginning with Beckett, we should perhaps pause to assess what irony, pursued over many pages, has presently become. Any definition of irony would have to begin with its operation as the negation of determinate meanings, a way of saying one thing while meaning another. As I have argued, however, ironic negation goes further and puts in question the very possibility of determinate meaning, for it hints at the awareness that all local meanings must finally depend on an inexpressible global signification, an elusive unity of discourse. To confine oneself to local ironies is to leave out a large part of this ironic import, which enables us to make the transition from irony as a rhetorical device to irony as a philosophical or aesthetic stance.

Irony is further characterized by an impulse toward self-reflexiveness. The urge to know, which lies behind any ironic mind, leads inevitably to reflection upon the conditions of possibility of knowledge and eventually to consideration of the nature of the subject itself. Irony moves toward the negation of that individual subject as either totalized or totalizing, stressing the partial nature of all individual consciousness. For the self-reflexive quality of the mind subjects it to a paradoxical self-limitation, unable to know how it can know without assuming that act of knowledge it seeks to define. Yet at the same time the falling-short that summarizes ironic insight can be taken as proof of a sense for something beyond ironic incapacity, or else the ironist could not realize how or even that he has failed. My examination of German and English Romantic figures sought to focus on their respective abilities to maintain a tension between these contrary aspects of the subject.

172

Irony is not simply equivalent to skepticism, for it starts with the recognition that ignorance is much harder to maintain than certitude. Irony adds to skepticism a doubt of one's own ability to doubt, because it recognizes the incurable positivity of the mind and of language. We can use, but not really effectively think, negation, as the repeated slips into blindness on the part of Meredith's characters demonstrated. The limitations on the subject seem to arise from its tendency always to be present in one place at one time. Nor can negation exhaust what is excluded by any such positional consciousness.

So irony can be more fully defined as a skeptical enactment of one's own position of ignorance, which submits the adequacy of one's skepticism to another subject for further evaluation. Irony establishes an intersubjective bond based on an awareness of the *partial identity* of the subject—at once part of the dialogue and only part of itself. At the minimal level, irony thus creates at least a shared attitude toward a common predicament. Yet it does more, too, since the characteristically incomplete ironic utterance invites the other to a larger exploration of the subject of discourse. The ironist requests the involvement of the other as a way to supplement his own perspectives, opening up the possibility of a historical recovery of the subject.[1]

At the same time, irony reveals the dependence of the subject on this concrete speech situation, its *occasional identity*. Irony is a response to and not just an expression of the fragmentation of the human world it accepts as inevitable. Rather than trying to define or fix identity, it opens out into the dialogue, the response where identity can come into being. Irony provokes a movement toward intersubjective coherence by exposing the unacknowledged seams of personal identity. It is a testing for rather than an assumption of shared values, hence it necessarily oscillates back to the here and now, grounding the transcendental moment of doubt in the real encounter. In its fullest operation, irony is the expression of the mind in search of what will suffice.

The subject discovers in irony the degree to which it is dependent upon an alien language, speaking with the voice of the other. Yet Lacan illustrates for us how the apparent alienness of language stems from a false premise of individual subjectivity, one that fails to acknowledge the real source and structure of subjectivity. The notion of a subject is dialectically dependent on an idea of community, more an "it" than a "they." The recovery of the subject from its apparent fragmentation requires then a recognition of that subject as product and member of its community.[2] The subject is not defined by its attributes or even its actions, but by how it defines itself in using an inherited language.

These themes of ironic subjectivity are brought to explicitness in the work of Beckett, perhaps the last and most ironic Romantic ironist.[3] In reading Beckett, it becomes clear that the meaning of irony needs again to be subtly shifted, even from the sense we could give it in the theorizing of Beckett's contemporary, Jacques Lacan. Beckett gives to the tension between conflicting aspects of subjectivity its full experiential and emotional resonance. In so doing, he returns us to the Romantic roots of irony in the nature and limits of the idea of the subject.

I intend, then, to explore the work of Beckett within this framework of irony, to investigate it as an examination of the myth of an essential self and the consequences of that for the subject. My concern with Beckett is twofold: with what he teaches us about the subject in or as language and with what he teaches us about how to read and about the role of the critic. There has been too little discussion of this latter question, with a few exceptions such as Martin Esslin's fine introduction to his early collection of essays on Beckett.[4] Esslin outlines three methods of approach to Beckett's work that remain viable despite the apparent insistence of that work on the impossibility of "secure" meanings. He advocates first the elucidation of the allusions in a Beckett text, which in my terms would involve the recovery of the communal aspect of the discourse of the subject. This would presumably include literary-historical and biographical work on Beckett's texts. A second possibility is the uncovering of the structural principles, the "main design" of Beckett's work, by which the integrity of the oeuvre, its organic unity, and behind it that of the subject itself, might be ascertained. Both thematic and structural criticism could loosely be joined in this category. A third alternative is to establish the critical response, to define the place of Beckett in the literary canon, what one might now refer to as a reader response approach. Rather than examining the historical basis for an integration of subject and community, at its best such criticism would focus more precisely on defining the present sense of community that governs our reading.

The very affinity of Esslin's proposed models of interpretation with current schools of criticism provokes a lingering suspicion that we perhaps have persisted in reading Beckett in a largely pre-Beckettian fashion, that we continue to insist as critics on the very verities and unity he undermines, while resisting the implications of his discourse for our own acts of interpretation. Beckett's works can thus be enclosed within some linear, teleological framework,[5] an originary one relying on biographical data or manuscript facts, or a mimetic one seeing there a representation of the human condition. What results then is the idea of the oeuvre of Beckett, the unifying vision behind discrete works. The very fragmentation of Beckett's works produced an early, now somewhat abated, tendency to go the further step of unearthing an archetypal Beckett figure, and to speak of *the* mind, *the* consciousness, *the* narrator of any individual Beckett text, or even of the work as a whole.[6] In sum, we arrive at the organic unity of Beckett's work and works, as they pass through various phases or stages on their way to preordained ends. Beyond all the local contradictions and retractions, we discover "an *oeuvre* . . . singleminded and ruthlessly consistent with itself."[7] The easy acceptance of such Romantic survivals keeps one from even approaching the question of whether it is possible to do otherwise. Can one read Beckett without reimporting a notion of personal identity?

A tentative answer might be that one cannot do without it entirely, but also that excessive reliance on such unifying notions unduly restricts the impact of Beckett. It is as though his fiction told us only of its distinctive qualities and not about the nature of all discourse, when surely he tells us the reverse, that all language is subject to the breakdown of discourse and of identity which he envisages. One should perhaps establish as a first premise the incapacity of the critical act, rendered hesitant and reflexive by the confrontation with Beckett. Clues for such a mode of reading do exist in the criticism and can be found already in the conclusion to Esslin's essay. "It is not the content of the work, not *what* is said, that matters in a writer of Beckett's stamp, but the *quality of the experience that is communicated*."[8] If it is indeed the quality of the experience that counts, we need then to look more closely at the experience of reading Beckett, and not simply at the interpretive residue that is left behind.

The best theory on how to begin with Beckett is that of H. Porter Abbott, who uses Yvor Winters's idea of "imitative form" to interpret the content of Beckett's texts as the experience in which they engage the reader. "Thus, when we speak of 'imitation' we refer not so much to a notion of reflection or representation as we do to a generation in the reader of experiences that are at the same time the subject of the work."[9] If indeed the "mess" of which Beckett speaks has already invaded our experience and also his literature, can we hope to keep it any longer out of our criticism?[10] What does Beckett teach us about how it is to reread literature?

## Beckett in Search of Proust

To begin with the critical work of Beckett himself is almost requisite in any study of Beckett, even though this foists on Beckett a role he has repeatedly declined to perform for his own work.[11] The dominant premise in such studies or evocations of Beckett the critic, naturally enough, is the unity of the critic and artist Beckett. Without overemphasizing the point, one should recognize that this assumption resurrects the unified identity that Beckett has consistently sought to problematize. As a consequence of this premise, however, Beckett's own aesthetic formulations, though rarely directed at his own work or even at literature of any kind, have acquired near-doctrinal status. Beckett's brief pronouncements, whether intentionally or not, have succeeded in circumscribing the critical act and in creating a severely delimited literary-philosophical tradition behind him. Joyce himself, the master of self-exegesis, would have to envy the degree of control Beckett seems to exercise in this regard.

To assume, however, that Beckett has indeed told us how to read his own work is to run the risk of too often going back to the same Beckett. This is a Beckett structured, for instance, by the dichotomy hallowed by Israel Shenker between Joyce, the capable synthesizer, and Beckett, the artist of impotence and disruption.[12] The opposition is an interesting one, but one wonders about the neatness of the identification. Such aids drawn from Beckett's criticism may indeed help us to notice more in Beckett, but what we notice is likely to be more of the same thing.

Above all, reliance on Beckett's own exquisitely worded formulas may allow us not to confront the possibility that we still do not know how to read Beckett, how to articulate in a sufficiently complex way our responses to his writing. First of all, then, we need to get some distance from Beckett's criticism, to see how little his own pronouncements and systems may fit his own work.

As an illustration of this, one could hardly do better than to begin with the beginning, with Beckett's own first-published prose, his study of Proust.[13] This work, Beckett's only foray into the hazards of academic interpretation, is structured by its dualist premises—a dualism of subject and object, to be sure, but even more profoundly a dualism of the mental faculties themselves.[14] There is a split between voluntary and involuntary memory, between habit and imagination, between temporality and eternity. These opposites are provided with a corresponding valorization, the former conditions exhibiting only a false or partial being, the latter ones a true being of both the self and the world. This division will serve as the basis for Beckett's later denunciation of the fabrications of the mind, where fiction is equated with the habits of a lazy or fearful mind. Behind these evasions, however, will be the search for a truer, lost self-identity, recovered here through the processes of involuntary memory, that moment of attentive silence so elusive in Beckett's own fiction.

What lies behind this schema is a totalizing critical mentality, reducing human experience to a set of either-or distinctions.[15] The moments of involuntary memory are privileged as an experience of full presence, an escape from a dualism that is due to the double presence of the self as both real and ideal, both physically and imaginatively active. "But if this mystical experience communicates an extratemporal essence, it follows that the communicant is for the moment an extratemporal being. Consequently the Proustian solution consists . . . in the negation of Time and Death."[16] Involved here is a dual recovery of the past, doubly distanced by the never adequately experienced object and the desiring subject who interfered with any possibility of pure perception. Involuntary memory permits a revisioning of the past because the subject now can separate from its experiences its own distorting activity of that period. The experience ostensibly provides negative access to a real self, which emerges out of the canceling of a false past identity. By subtracting its own desires from the equation, the subject can reach the essence of its own past.

This possibility is based on Beckett's neat divorce of mental faculties, a separation between the habit-inducing will and an alertly passive perception. His solution, then, is to work toward evacuation of the will and a courting of suitable "favorable circumstances"—a "relaxation of the subject's habit of thought and a reduction of the radius of his memory, a generally diminished tension of consciousness following upon a phase of extreme discouragement" (*Proust*, p. 54).[17] Beckett describes this state as that of a "pure subject," whose identity is confirmed by the assurance that the resurgent memories that survive the subtraction of self are indeed those of that subject.

Beckett thus privileges a single, synthesizing mental faculty. There is a double process at work here, based on the analogy of unified perception and involuntary memory. For the same technique, the same moment, reaches both the integrity of the object and the elusive totality of the subject. Beckett repeatedly stresses their interdependence. "The source and point of departure of this 'sacred action,' the elements of communion, are provided by the physical world, by some immediate and fortuitous act of perception" (*Proust*, p. 23; see also p. 55). The reduplication of a stimulus that elicits involuntary memory is an exact analogy here for the metaphoric imagination that Beckett sees as the ultimate solution in the Proustian matrix. Both the poetic imagination and involuntary memory destroy habit, reinforcing the relativism and impressionism that define Proust's art for Beckett. This process necessarily rests on a belief that the oneness of being guarantees that once beyond the strain of trying for local and habitual connections, broader and more essential ones will emerge.

A problem arises, however, in that this aesthetic optimism is neither congenial to Beckett nor deducible from his (as contrasted with Proust's) theoretical framework. We need to recognize how irrelevant in many respects the model erected here is to Beckett's own concerns and solutions. The doctrine of involuntary memory is based upon a notion of personal identity that the rest of Beckett's essay refuses to support. Its authority stems from the forcible yoking together of a model of perception to a model of memory, that assumes their objects are in some fundamental way similar.

The neatness of the identification is upset by another pair of terms left out or behind at the moment of resolution, the opposition between habit and the suffering of being. Here is the other side of the equation, the subject's focus not on the object it recovers but on itself at that moment. Its anxiety is the remainder resistant to the neat division of being performed by Proust's aesthetic passiveness. For the attained awareness of being is first coupled by Beckett with the correlative experience of loss. At the moment of Marcel's awakening, being is seen as novelty, as change, as flux (directionless change), and ultimately as a sense of the dying self. Habit can die or simply sleep, but Beckett insists that "the first and major mode is inseparable from suffering and anxiety—the suffering of the dying and the jealous anxiety of the ousted. The old ego dies hard" (*Proust*, p. 10).[18] The subject resists such change because it, the "mortal microcosm," recognizes in the attained awareness of time its own potential and, even worse, actual dissolution.

The recovery of self that seemingly occurs in involuntary memory is actually only partial and incomplete. There is no full presence of self analogous to an immaculate perception. "At any given moment our total soul, in spite of its rich balance-sheet, has only a fictitious value. Its assets are never completely realisable" (*Proust,* p. 27).[19] As Beckett says further, one's life can be represented by a series of parallel tracks, different segments of the whole, on only one of which one can be at any one time. It is inadequate to argue that only a nonessential part of the subject, the habitual, vanishes during these switches, since we will see that the very concept of identity is eroding from Beckett's text, undermining his own later resolution.

For what the subject recovers in involuntary memory is only an absence, a self-absence not recuperable in the way a concrete sensation is. Beckett's analysis of "Les Intermittences du Coeur" indicates this, showing how Marcel's fundamental experience of the past is associated with his grandmother, before whom he is always present only in his own absence. This section of Proust's novel is the one selected by Beckett from a list of eleven to illustrate the mechanisms of involuntary memory, which it does all too well. Marcel's cognizance of his grandmother's death is marked by the real loss of the object of his perception and the parallel loss of his prior subjectivity and its conditions of possibility. His own past sensibility becomes inaccessible to him, so that he does not so much reexperience the past as measure the distance between his past and now-altered self.[20] The loss of self is, in fact, a double one—of the Marcel with his grandmother, who could not see her, and of the later Marcel, on whom her death had no impact.

The measure of the self-alienation involved becomes clearer in the movement of Beckett's own text. The evocation of the mystical moment of release from temporal contingencies is immediately succeeded by the longest and most charged section of the study, a sixteen-page segment on Marcel's relationship with Albertine. Here we get the message that the neat equation of perception, memory, and imagination will not really work for Beckett. His loyalty both to Proust and to his own doctrine produces unreconciled tensions in the text, where a rhetoric of salvation coexists uneasily with a reality of damnation.[21]

The Albertine section echoes and reinforces the themes of "Les Intermittences du Coeur."[22] The transition between them is made by the element of suffering common to both episodes. For the consequence of the subject's encounter with the ideal-real is not an obliteration of time, but a heightened awareness of it. What the involuntary recall of his grand-mother's death produces in Marcel is a heightened sense of guilt and a re-gret at lost opportunities. The discussion of love in the person of Albertine reveals the source of suffering to be the endlessness of possible reinter-pretation, not so much the loss of the loved one as the emergence of an infinite succession of personal, interpretive selves, the inexorable frag-mentation of the subject. For the subject can have no final memory, no correct revision of Albertine. As Beckett notes, the poet's true tribute would be not the crown of bay but the "ideal core of the onion" (*Proust*, pp. 16–17). The excavator uncovers therein not just the richness of the past, but the paucity of his own identity, his inability to expropriate and exploit that past to confirm his own identity. Involuntary memory must fi-nally be seen to have a zero content, because its essence is negation, that is, an awareness of the flux of time and the subject's subjection to that. What results in the section is the mutual contamination of one another by those faculties so carefully separated by Beckett. Suffering becomes a habit, and the habit of suffering extends without limit into all the recesses of subjectivity.

Marcel's life with Albertine is thus both a prevision and a perversion of the poetic grace Beckett will evoke at the end of his work. Marcel the lover "searches for a relation, a common factor, substrata" to explain Al-bertine, just as Marcel the poet does before reality. The reduplication that signals an involuntary memory is not so far from the repetition of habit, and just as Marcel is enabled to relive his life from the whiff of a made-leine, so is he condemned to relive endlessly the stages of his life with Al-bertine (*Proust*, pp. 63 and 44). Beckett recognizes in Albertine the "Goddess of Time" before whom the subject is forced to bow. The central question, then, is whether the library scene can cancel the implications of the section on Albertine, whether the poetic sensibility can free itself from the desiring subject, whether finally the uncertainty about the other can be abated by the heightened self-certainty of the imaginative recovery of one's own past. To conclude from the temporal positioning of Marcel's discovery of vocation its logical priority over the life with Albertine would be, from Beckett's point of view, a fictitious extension of our feeble human reason.

Yet such privileging of the poetic imagination does seem to be im-plied in the concluding pages of this section. After the intermittences of the heart, after Albertine, comes a typically Beckettian assessment of the virtues of friendship, as contrasted with the suffering love brings. Friendship is ridiculed as an impossible goal, one that inevitably degenerates into incomprehension or mimicry, in any case a loss of identity in the process of its expression. "Either we speak and act for ourselves—in which case speech and action are distorted and emptied of their meaning by an intelligence that is not ours, or else we speak and act for others—in which case we speak and act a lie" (*Proust*, p. 47). The correct response to the suffering of being encountered in love and the futility of friendship seems to be a retreat into the self, a choice signaled on the next page by Beckett's first evocation of the artistic mission, a withdrawal from the world that restores both the integrity of that world and the assurance of personal identity. In a statement often cited as the germ of his own prose, Beckett says, "The only fertile research is excavatory, immersive, a contraction of the spirit, a descent. The artist is active, but negative. . . . He cannot practice friendship, because friendship is the centrifugal force of self-fear, self-negation" (*Proust*, p. 48).

The alternative open to the artist, presumably, is self-affirmation through cultivation of unbiased perception and involuntary memory. Yet this is in no sense a recovery of a personal past, according to Beckett's theory. The lesson of "Les Intermittences" is that the integrity of the subject is already in doubt, so that to surrender the other person is a futile and unnecessary defensive gesture. The suffering of being reminds us that the subject is as divorced from its own past, that spirit it would excavate, as it is from other human beings. Both self and other are subject to identical conditions of inaccessibility, so that to fill up the content of that internal research with the shards of involuntary memory is at best a form of archaeological fraud. Beckett's pure subject is an absent subject, one not part of Proust's world at all, one that evacuates any meaningful notion of personal identity, hence also the relevance of involuntary memory as confirmation of an essential, atemporal self. As an individual subject, as a repository of memories, one never gets beyond the suffering of being.[23] The privileging of personal memory as relevant to the artistic mission will never be part of Beckett's own practice; the neat dichotomies that define *Proust* are already vanishing.

Like its identity in memory, the subject's identity in perception also disappears. The pure object evoked early in *Proust* (p. 11), particular and unique, recoverable by a disengaged intellect, is finally subjected to the reduplication of memory. There is no first time when it could be perceived as it really is, before the second time of its recovery, when it becomes nothing more than an occasion for involuntary memory (p. 56).

There is nothing like the mechanism of involuntary memory in Beckett's own prose, either as agony or as enchantment, no similar linking of perception and recollection.[24] Images act not to confirm identity but instead to fragment the subject even further. They cannot be claimed as the subject's own, and memory as a discrete mental faculty blurs into invention and even overhearing. Hence retraction and revision become the characteristic mode of Beckett's work, the technique par excellence of Marcel in his life with Albertine. Hence one needs to be hesitant about the relevance to Beckett's own work of phrases such as "diver" into the "gouffre" of self or "excavation" of an internal realm (*Proust*, pp. 18 and 48), when the notions of self and its investigation are both put into question.

*Proust*, then, besides providing entry into the Beckettian suspicion of personal identity, should also serve as a warning against imposing too great an expectation of coherence on Beckett's own work. Its tensions and richness come in large part from its inconsistency with itself, from privileging a model of mental activity that its own strictures undermine. No single trend, even a minimalist one, seems adequate to account for Beckett. Any theory of the organic wholeness of his work seems especially suspect, for to fit it together one would have to leave out too much.[25] Such suspicions should be part of the critical act, too, since interpretation is as prone to restore unity as is the notion of involuntary memory. Beckett's works, even his individual narrators, are not self-consistent or even subject to a higher coherence, but are made up of multiple and discrete mental operations. His attack on the integrity of the subject is so radical that one should ask how and why one can continue to speak of *a* narrator at all. As a premise true to Beckett, however, one might better assume that oeuvre, text, narrator form no coherent wholes, however firmly the fiction of personality may haunt the texts and however necessary it may be to a critical vocabulary.

## Beckett's Dogma of Failure

With these strictures in mind, we can perhaps turn toward outlining a critical approach for the reading of Beckett. While guarding the proper

caution, we can turn to a central critical tenet of the later Beckett, his fidelity to incapacity and failure. Beckett summarized this attitude in his dialogues of 1949 with Georges Duthuit, as an alternative aesthetic he saw in
Bram Van Velde: "The expression that there is nothing to express, nothing
with which to express, nothing from which to express, no power to
express, no desire to express, together with the obligation to express."
Hence Van Velde is seen as "the first to admit that to be an artist is to fail,
as no other dare fail, that failure is his world and the shrink from it des-
ertion, art and craft, good housekeeping, living."[26]

Critics have pointed out, in ways almost as various as the critics
themselves, how admirably Beckett succeeds at failing, how satisfactorily
he succeeds in expressing the circumstances and conditions of his failure.[27] Yet this is a stance Beckett explicitly rejects in the dialogues. "I
know that all that is required now, in order to bring even this horrible
matter to an acceptable conclusion, is to make of this submission, this admission, this fidelity to failure, a new occasion, a new term of relation, and
of the act which, unable to act, obliged to act, he makes, an expressive act,
even if only of itself, of its impossibility, of its obligation. I know that my
inability to do so places myself, and perhaps an innocent, in what I think
is still called an unenviable situation; familiar to psychiatrists" (p. 21).
How consistently Beckett himself avoided this alternative of expressing
one's incapacity to express may be questionable, since it sounds much like
a summary of *The Unnamable*. Yet at the same time, we should perhaps see
if, without overindulging in wordplay, we can ascertain what is at stake in
this claim.

The necessity of failure is based on Beckett's assessment of the impossibility of human knowledge—the nature of consciousness necessarily
cuts it off from the full penetration of its object that would make knowledge of that which it would know possible. The recurrent desire of Beckett's narrators, then, is to attain a state of non-being where this dilemma
would be exorcised and where self-knowledge might be possible in an
objectless world. In terms of the artwork, success would have to be the
creation of an adequate experience of this incapacity; the artist can share
his confusion, not enclose or define it. Such a work would be marked by
the refusal to impose an order or even to insist on the absence of order.[28]
At the extreme, this would be a refusal to formulate, as does indeed occur
at the end of the dialogue on Tal Coat, but that is not terribly compatible

with the continuation of art. More recently, Beckett reformulated the task as one of presenting a problem without a solution.[29]

Yet the success critics attribute to Beckett lies on the other side of the equation, not in the artwork as an adequate expression of the chaos but in the success of the artist's "accommodation" of that chaos. This typically resonant and ambiguous term, Beckett's own, to be sure, provides much leeway for the critic. Most frequently, it is taken as a measure of the artist's ability to maintain distinctively human attitudes and values before the chaos. The potential stances include aggressive confrontation with chaos (existential revolt) or reconciliation of the self to the unalterability of that (stoicism), by which a part of the subject is separated from the chaos by its refusal to be implicated in it.[30] A stability of mental attitude, a residue of humanism, rests opposed to external flux. Alternatively, one can stress the comedy of Beckett's prose, whereby the subject maintains a distance from its own relapses into an illusion of order and coherence.[31] Or again, one can emphasize the imaginative negation of external chaos, the self-sufficient repose of the mind within its own bounds.[32] Finally, one can reimport the reader as the repository of meaning and give credit to Beckett's largesse; the act of imagination thus gives birth not only to itself but to a communion of author and reader.[33]

All these choices, however effectively sustained, seem to me to minimize the risk of reading Beckett. They confront Beckett as his characters confront their own incapacity, as Janvier puts it, "pour s'en rendre maîtresse" (p. 9).[34] They all succeed in mastering the anxiety rustling throughout Beckett's works, in reducing the tensions and incoherencies scattered among the leaves of his texts.

Yet this effort of critical authority is just what Beckett fails to peform himself and refuses to allow us. It elides or subordinates the anxiety of reading Beckett, the sense of relief that is as much a part of ending a novel, fragment, or play as the aesthetic "exhilaration" of which Esslin speaks. Rosen captures some of this feeling, as does Dieter Wellershoff in a superb essay on Beckett. "The strength of this *oeuvre* lies in the way in which the paradox is kept up. It keeps the reader in its grip, compels him to pass through all the dialectical turns. There is no direction in which he might leave this *oeuvre* with the consciousness of having been confirmed in his own being by the author."[35] Or to choose from among Beckett's own words, "And what I saw was more like a crumbling, a frenzied collapsing of all that had always protected me from all I was always condemned to be."[36]

This anxiety is not really parallel to the suffering of being in *Proust*, but rather the exponential anxiety of not being able even to attain that unmediated presence before self or world that Marcel achieves in his half-sleep. In Beckett's world, one is *always* too much awake. Instead, Beckett's reader confronts the failure of language to understand, to explain, or to communicate either that suffering or any other mode of being. The problem is not that there is nothing but language, but that there is not even that. Beckett's works are a punctuated reiteration of his/our inability to make a truce with chaos, an inability marked by the refusal of his texts to cohere, except in the most deceptive and traditional ways. The experience of reading Beckett has to confront the fear that the flow of words may finally itself shatter from the pressure of the local contradictions and nonrelations it contains, were we not continually to reimport the old ways of making meaning.

What Beckett's works do above all is to show us, and perhaps mock as well, how we continue to rely on traditional ways of interpreting even as we read about their inadequacy. The sense that the end exceeds, defines, contains the meaning of the beginning, or the priority given to final formulations as full with the experience of the preceding ones, or the privileging of repetition as order, all build toward what is here the final refuge of interpretation, the subject whom we cannot do without. All such devices are precisely what Beckett's narrators, beset by constant involuntary forgetting, fail to be able to deploy.

Beckett works out in his fiction the consequences of the liquidation of the subject articulated by Lacan (among others).[37] In so doing, he provides a critique of some of the implications of that process, interrogating us as to the meaning of the equation: subject = consciousness = language. Without the unifying factor of personal identity (*the* voice), a vertiginous failure to understand, to integrate, is forced upon the reader. Why these images, stories, why these questions and nonanswers, why in this order which may not be one?

From the contractions and retractions of the prose arise the isolated images and stories that survive a reading of Beckett. For he is finally a mythmaker, but of what kind of tales and pictures?[38] The power of myths lies not in their correctness but in their ability to bind a situation to an emotional-intellectual response. Yet Beckett's images seem to resist even such binding. They are not, for instance, tragic, a mode in which incomprehensible events can be bound down by a positive excess of meaning, an overdetermination that permits such complexes to pass through consciousness. It is perhaps for this reason that a narrator like the one of *How It Is* remains even more disturbing than Oedipus, who does finally arrive at Colonus.

What we have in Beckett is the inexplicability of dream images, a reflection that should give us pause. For dreams are things that Beckett's own characters fear to confront. "Estragon: 'I dreamt that——' Vladimir: 'DON'T TELL ME!' "[39] Furthermore, we lack the ability to psychoanalyze them effectively, as Freud would remind us, without the active cooperation of the dreamer.

It may be more effective, then, to approach Beckett's oeuvre as fragment, in the German Romantic sense of the term. It partakes of a whole, or seems to, but not as a microcosm nor yet organically. Rather, it exists in incompleteness, without real endings, requiring integration into the literary and personal history of the reader. One's first task should be to ask what is left out and why. This is not a Joycean pursuit of multiple and proliferating connections,[40] for Beckett's preferred technique is not analogy, but paradox, which can stand in for all possible connections by the very radicalness of its juxtapositions. To respond appropriately to the unfinishedness of Beckett's work, one would have to evoke an antithetical body of work, while resisting the apparent integrity its aesthetic atoms seem to preserve.

We should, in sum, pursue its inconsistencies. In the terms of irony and the subject, we need to recognize how the fragmentation of the subject, repeatedly evoked, is held in check by the absorptive monologic quality of the texts.[41] However often expelled, the notion of identity eternally recurs to shape these texts.

My intent, then, is to explore the reading of *How It Is* from an ironic perspective.[42] The approach will necessarily be tentative and retractive, a great deal like the crawling of Pim, in fact. As with Beckett's other works, it is hard to hold the text as a whole in mind, rendering it risky to generalize about the tone or quality of any particular work. Inevitably, I can only begin such an analysis, while retreating before the sense that the complexities of many Beckett texts render their analysis after several pages unmanageably complex.[43] "You explore it as never before and find it possessed of unsuspected delights. In short it becomes infinite" (*Three Novels*, p. 140). As a general procedure, then, I expect to attend to the linear flow of the text, the level where Beckett makes the most severe assault on our synthesizing capacities, our own critical identities. In so doing, I hope to discover the incoherencies beneath the perfectly ordered structure, which can hint at the contradictions of our hero-narrator. Me, to begin.

## In the Beginning: How It Is

*How It Is* is remarkable first for its radical difference from the *Trilogy*, the *Texts for Nothing*, and even the intervening plays. It is doubtful whether anyone could have anticipated the course that Beckett's writing would take in the 1950s, making it that much harder to assimilate *How It Is* into a unified, organic Beckett canon. Two shifts are particularly notable in this text. First, there is the recovery of a self-sustaining myth, one that goes far beyond the aborted fictions of the *Trilogy*. Second, there is the recovery of company, the restoration of interaction between the narrator and his creature, whether the latter be real or created. These elements reinforce the sense that there is an increasing unity of subject matter in this text, which could serve to buttress the coherence of the subject itself.

In considering *How It Is* in regard to its ironic functioning, one should first remark that it is overtly ironic in ways similar to Beckett's other works. The text frequently juxtaposes unmediated contraries without displaying any urgency to decide between them. It also reveals the self-reflexive consciousness characteristic of Romantic irony. As I have repeatedly argued, the prevalence of these ironic mechanisms in a text indicates its concern for the nature of the subject, its sensibility to the fragmentation that threatens subjectivity. How legitimate is it, then, to speak of *the* narrator of Beckett's text?

Closer examination reveals that what we really have here is a triple-selved narrator (to remain for the moment at the level of the most obvious divisions), whose identity could be (and of course is) as fictional as any other element in this narrative of exposition and cancellation. As readers, we fall more easily into the validity of this particular fiction because of the absence of certainties elsewhere in the text. The narrator is our last refuge of meaning. Yet that narrator's narrative reveals an insistent divorce of the mental faculties, of the modes of selfhood, that corrodes the certainty of the synthesizing power of subjective consciousness. The connections that define identity are missing here—on the literal, grammatical level as well as the psychological one. Beckett here shows how the breakdown of the subject is a function of the noncoherence of language, of the multiple, but not interdependent, ways of articulation that constitute language.[44] He leaves out the interplay that would allow a subject to emerge from intersecting thought processes, that would allow one to say with assurance that it is the same mind recounting the entire tale.

To speak of *a* narrator here seems difficult at best, when examined from the logical perspective the text insists upon. Yet the text does convey such an assurance and does seem to justify it. The narrator has the memories of his own mental processes, knows (more or less) where he is, was, and will be. There is also a continuity of tone and of topics across the breadth of the text and a repeated reliance on the same phrases. Yet at the same time, these repetitions seem the most alienated, the least controlled utterances of the narrator. The connections among the parts of the narrative are actually nothing more than verbal ones; the guarantees of identity are nothing more than linguistic ties. The narrator is he who always says the same words, who divides now into before-with-after, who speaks in bursts of phrases separated by empty lines. "I," in fact, is a function of such typographical conventions as much as of linguistic ones. As the Unnamable realized, "the same words recur and they are your memories" (*Three Novels*, p. 395).

Three parts of the narrator (to deal only with three here for the sake of clarity) in *How It Is* are clearly discernible. Although unintegrated, they flow into and even blend with one another at times. In part 1, the narrator exists as something akin to the "pure subject" of *Proust*, a product of memory and perception. He possesses an absent past and a firmly perceived present, with the fragmentary and detached quality of his memories offset by the homogeneous quality of the latter. In part 2, the narrator is presented as a desiring subject, revealed as a character through the proclivities he displays in his encounter with Pim. He moves toward the creation of a unified self through his imaginative encounter with the other, relying for his effort on the traditional techniques of the novel. This shift is visible in the reworking of both life in the mud and life above. The creation of Pim parallels the creation of a narrative self-identity, achieved through the creation of a unified narration, where sequence implies development, explanation via recourse to motive is legitimate, and character or role has consistency. In part 3, the narrator arrives at the status of a social or socia-

lized subjectivity. This condition is connected with his mathematical speculations here, providing us with a structural model of society based on the
permutations of available possibilities. It is no surprise, then, that we even
see the emergence, out of nothing, of a God and a religion.

To begin with the narrator as subject, however, may be a bit precipi-
tous. So let us return to the first paragraph of how it is. To begin yet again,
I quote:

> how it was I quote before Pim with Pim after Pim how it is three
> parts I say it as I hear it[45]

The subject here is a self-assured one, confident in his use of "I." What is
initially striking is the insistent tripartite structure of the paragraph, made
up of six phrases divisible into three categories. Two phrases deal with his
state of being (how it is/was), two others with the question of ordering
that state (three parts/before, with, after Pim), and two more with the
voice or subject itself (I quote/say it as I hear it). The initial phrase itself
consists of three parts—subject, verb, modifier, embedding the threefold
structure in language itself. The narrator will later tell us that there are
three parts, "for the sake of clarity."[46]

The bareness of the text seems to provide little space for interpretation, but it is interesting to observe how this spareness is an acquired trait
of the prose rather than natural to it. The word *part*, for instance, illustrates how any initial uncertainty about its meaning is quickly recaptured
by Beckett before it slides over into allusiveness. The local identification
of *part* with the three parts of the text or of the narrator's life is an easy and
inevitable one. Beckett typically pins down potentially resonant words in
just this way, eliding their alternate significations. Yet *part* is especially
multiple in this text. One thinks of the parts in a play, as the narrator here
will play Pim, himself and Kram. Or of the parts of the subject already
discussed. Or of the verbal sense, *to part*, natural to this text full of leave-
takings and abandonments. In any case, the use of *part* imports with it the
notion of a whole, of a harmony of parts, that works against its sense as a
detached fragment. Both impulses, we shall see, are operative in *How It Is*.

Section 2, I say it as I read it:

> voice once without quaqua on all sides then in me when the panting
> stops tell me again finish telling me invocation

Suddenly we find ourselves in a wholly different place, part of the narrative, kind of discourse, as Beckett confronts us directly with what is

always an enigma in his texts, the problem of the transition. This disorientation is quickly recovered by the realization that this whole section could serve as an elaboration of the concluding phrase of section 1, how he hears it. Nevertheless, this paragraph sets up competing structures, dual and not tripartite, and thus justifies its separation. This occurs on the level of content (inner/outer voice), grammar (you/I structure of the imperative verbs), and form (voice/invocation), a mirroring effect also present in tell/telling. As the tripartite structure fosters a sense of openness and change, so does the dual structure here effect closure: *voice* and *invocation* enclose the voice between them.

This shift of the dominant structure indicates a breakdown of the simple self-identity of the intial segment. The ambiguity (in the English version) of the implication of *tell me* (direct or indirect object) hints at the increasing elusiveness of the subject. The uncertainty of where the voice is, or whose it is, furthers this instability on the level of content, as does the pronounced shift from *I* to *me*, an objectification of the subject even at the level of grammar.

This breakdown of coherence also occurs at the level of the phrase, as the *quaqua* interrupts the smooth flow of the prose. We encounter here as well a problem that will recur with even more ambiguity elsewhere in the text. *When the panting stops* is one of those phrases that an initial reading may well hesitate over whether to attach to the prior or subsequent phrase. The decision here is easier than elsewhere, but still exhibits the ambiguity of internal signification we noticed above in *part*. Beckett uses this device to inhibit recourse to external significations, creating a seamless text where significations close in on themselves.[47] In the face of a potential breakdown of coherence and of the initial tripartite structure, meaning is provisionally recovered via dual oppositions, like that between the voice and panting, like that of the reader who pairs this section with the prior one to squeeze meaning from both of them.

> past moments old dreams back again or fresh like those that pass or things things always and memories I say them as I hear them murmur them in the mud

What is noticeable in this third section is the first appearance of the connectives *and* and *or*. Yet their deployment does not so much promise an emerging order of discourse, a system of connection and subordination, as it opens up further the diversity of linguistic possibilities. We have, in sequence: apposition, adverbial and adjectival modification, comparison and coordination before the voice reverts to an old refrain and locates the first eighteen words as a set of direct objects attached to the final portion. The connectives complicate and render ambiguous the words, joining not strictly parallel lexical items, but instead an adverb and an adjective, a temporal term (*moments*) with a mental category (*dreams*) and then with concrete *things*. A further difficulty is engendered by the inability to determine which connective, if any, governs the others. As in a mathematical equation, one flounders without parentheses to identify the sequence in which the operations that would produce an answer should occur.

This disorganization may arise in part from the proliferation of the discourse, as the *it* of the first section becomes the *them* here. The contraries of the second section are further intensified, approached as paradox in the pairs *past-old/fresh* or *back again/always*. The subject itself is still further objectified, pressed from the direct object into the possessive adjective, its self now become its life.

The analysis threatens to become infinite. So we should perhaps reduce the level of magnification and move on to an overview of the first six sections, which form the "invocation" preceding the beginning proper, and the subsequent nine sections concluding with "recapitulation." Section 4 echoes section 2 and reinforces the dualism established there, while also providing the first direct elision of the subject from its own apparent identity as a voice ("voice in me not mine"). Sections 5 and 6 recover something of the assurance of the first section, speaking of "my life" with a certainty that negates the "not mine" with which section 4 concludes. But this certainty of proprietorship is purchased with a double loss. It is indeed "my life," but the subject will not equal its objectified life, since that is only a "version." Nor is that version itself really how it is, since "all lost nearly all." Both the subject and the pure object have vanished from the narrative. The invocation concludes with a fully realized fragmentation of the subject among its roles, as noting and listening are added to experiencing and perceiving and speaking—all so apparently discrete that they will eventually be attributed to independent personages. We have moved, then, from a full assurance of identity, through memory, to doubt and a splintering of identity. The multiple personae result from the fragmentation of the mental faculties themselves, not from the relative simplicity of a psychologically split personality.

The solution, clearly, is to recommence. Hardly begun, the narrator has to begin again, so lost is he amid inaccuracies and losses. He moves then into a nine-part prelude centered on an assessment of his present situation (as the threes accumulate comfortingly around him), beginning with an introduction that constitutes the longest section thus far. The "I" becomes "we" here, establishing the modality of this shared textual experience, although the referent of that "we" remains imprecise (narrator and Pim? and scribe? and us?). Here, too, he appeals to a "natural order," a sequence that might salvage him from the fragmentation into which he is sliding.

The narrator's subjectivity will then be doubly grounded: first in the temporal "before-with-after" schema, before which there is nothing (or almost nothing), and second in the spatial "above-here below" schema. Yet even these orders contaminate one another, as the narrator insists there is no past and then evokes another life above drawn from some such past. Finally we move into what will be the dominant mode of part 1 and is already the dominant segment here (5 sections), description of the present environment. This indeed seems to be the ultimate certainty here, the final guarantor of identity, the real origin—"it's the beginning of my life present formulation."

Only as we read on do these certainties also become doubtful. With a firmly established identity, the narrator can move on to the earlier evoked moments-dreams-memories, the less real parts of himself. His own language, however, betrays him. "I see me on my face," he begins section 16, as he will later see himself asleep (p. 24), an obviously impossible self-observation. This impossibility reduces the certainties here to the same level as the images above, all images, all fiction. Why then do we, as readers, tend to privilege the priority of the narrator and the mud, describe him as the "one" who has or hears or sees the other images, the other experiences?

For despite the overt disintegration of the narrator, a measure of authority abides, a tendency to privilege a particular level of the text. This becomes clearer when, as in section 14, we encounter for the first time the oft-repeated phrase, "something wrong there." This is a typical Beckettian revisionary reflex, yet also freer than in other texts, harder to pin down to some specific error in the discourse.[48] Having been born into grammar, however, we tend to read it: (1) backward, (2) as having some specific referent, and (3) as relevant to something immediately preceding, as having, in sum, its proper place and direction. Beckett's text operates in this way, too, balancing the breakdown of language and persona with the authoritative linearity of prose and reimporting the subject as the source of that authority. The subject here is, above all, the one who says "something wrong there."

It is curious, nonetheless, that we continue to accept/read/create the narrator as a unified persona. One reason for this may be that failure to do so would lead to the endless regress intimated in *Company*, the deviser devising a deviser who devises a deviser devising. *How It Is* suggests that the individual ego may not yet have found an adequate substitute for or reformulation of itself, either in the text, which reimposes unity in its linearity and repetitions, or in the reader, still inclined to trust the narrator when he asserts that a fourth part would be unnecessary, as a mere duplicate of part 2.[49]

For the problem is that the parts do not come together very well here. As will be the case in *The Lost Ones*, the aesthetic, ethical, mythical, and logical layers of the text, of the self, are not so much inadequate as hopelessly distant from one another, not mutually dependent in their (failed) functioning. The same narrator who knows (more or less) where his narrative is going, that the images will disappear (p. 10), can be surprised when a tin-opener turns up among his tins (p. 9). There is a nonintersection more profound than mere contradiction at work here, one that ferrets beneath all the linguistic balancings and harmonizings we use to create order. What we are finally (finally?) left with (or without) are the incommensurables, the phrases that elicit not words but screams. "WHAT'S MY NAME screams good . . . THAT'S MY LIFE screams good . . . I SHALL DIE screams good" (pp. 146–147).

## A Provisional Punctuation

One might well ask, then, what kind of irony is at play here, skeptical or recuperative? The narrator's end seems a sort of Fichtean nightmare, the self-created "I" lost in an agony of undefinable solitude. Yet critics have been very successful at salvaging a positive message from the novel. Bernal speaks of how it expresses a need for the other who can confirm one's identity, and Janvier goes so far as to term this a fraternal need.[50] The other human being is recognized in *How It Is* as it never was in the immediately prior fictions, as an essential source of the subject's own possibility of meaning and integrity. As Kenner puts it, "Pim, Beckett's generic other person, is the stable and ordering principle. Pim confers, it seems, all the meaning that life before us can aspire to."[51]

The only problem is that *How It Is* points out how even the other cannot do this, how only linguistic ploys can salvage or enforce a measure of self-identity. Even company cannot confirm the vanishing subject. *Company* will be particularly insistent on this, but the theme runs from Murphy's gazing at Endon through the last searcher's pursuit of the blank eyes of the first vanquished in *The Lost Ones*. Hence the evocation of company is a mere respite, another way of wishfully speculating how one might be. "Need for company not continuous" (*Company*, p. 31). The "you" of *Company* is an empty term, as empty as the "I" of *How It Is* or the "she/he" of *The Lost Ones*, all versions of a ubiquitous "it," the final refuge of the subject.

Beckett's fiction tells us all too little about how it is, or even about how we are, except perhaps how we too often confuse that with fiction. "How it is" is an empty phrase until it is filled up with a concrete "it," at which point it loses at least part of its generalizing power. Wellershoff argues that Beckett finally forces us to turn from his fiction, to recognize that it cannot in any way allay the anxiety it arouses. "The paradoxical involvement can only be broken by an evidential experience which Beckett provokes precisely by denying it."[52] Reality, excluded from Beckett's resolutely nonmimetic texts, is a possible answer to our earlier question of what one needs to add to Beckett's fragments. Yet his assistance here is minimal, for he closes off the allegorical path back to experience and provides no wisdom at all except a reinforced sense of our own ignorance, with perhaps a heightened sense of how much time we may actually spend dealing with nonessentials. Which, if not a conclusion, is perhaps not a wholly undesirable place from which to begin.

# Notes

*Introduction*

1 Cleanth Brooks, "Irony as a Principle of Structure," in *Critical Theory Since Plato*, ed. Hazard Adams (New York: Harcourt Brace Jovanovich, 1971), pp. 1041–1048. Brooks here defines *irony* as "the acknowledgment of the pressures of context."

2 See, for instance, D. C. Muecke, *The Compass of Irony* (London: Methuen & Co., 1969), pp. 23–29. Wayne Booth refers to this characteristic of irony as its "subtractive" nature, in contrast to the additive traits of other tropes such as metaphor (Wayne Booth, *A Rhetoric of Irony* [Chicago: University of Chicago Press, 1971], pp. 22–24; page numbers hereafter cited in text).

3 Fragments of such a work do, however, exist. Notable here is the work of G. G. Sedgwick on the classical origins of irony and its place in drama, of Norman Knox on the rise of irony in England from 1500 to 1755, and of Ernst Behler on the German appropriation of the concept of irony (G. G. Sedgwick, *Of Irony, Especially in Drama* [Toronto: University of Toronto Press, 1935]; Norman Knox, *The Word Irony and Its Context, 1500–1755* [Durham: Duke University Press, 1961]; Ernst Behler, *Klassische Ironie, Romantische Ironie, Tragische Ironie: Zum Ursprung dieser Begriffe* [Darmstadt: Wissenschaftliche Buchgesellschaft, 1972]).

4 One could, in fact, easily categorize kinds of irony according to what the implied source of this incompatibility is taken to be—for instance, rhetorical, existential, linguistic, and so on.

5 I should make it clear that for me virtually all instances of discourse can be seen as posing in some form this question of the identity of the subject. Hence unintentional and unconscious meanings constitute a great deal of the subject matter of ethical irony, and most language can indeed be seen as potentially ironic, open to the generation of incompatibilities provoked by the irresolution of subjective identity.

6 This should not be taken as implying that the ironist envisages a perfect coherence at the level of society but simply that the shifting of focus to another level of analysis can make many apparent paradoxes within the subject less resistant to resolution.

7 This movement from verbal incompatibility to suspended judgment to assessment of the basis of judgment is the cause of the self-reflexiveness typical of

irony, which also finds its model in the Platonic dialogue. It is evident in the *Republic*, for instance, where a philosophical inquiry into the nature of justice becomes an inquiry into the conditions of possibility of philosophy itself, a remarkable frank exposure of the potential incompatibility of the philosopher and the state, the ironist and the community.

8 Hence I would prefer to term such irony "progressive" rather than "suspensive," the latter a mode of irony by which Alan Wilde characterizes the postmodern sensibility. Suspensive irony arises from an attitude of acceptance and an ethic of fragmentation, which ethical irony, more epistemologically restless, would resist. See Alan Wilde, *Horizons of Assent: Modernism, Post-Modernism and the Ironic Imagination* (Baltimore: Johns Hopkins University Press, 1981), especially pp. 9, 44–45, and the chapter on Barthelme.

9 A more complete recounting would begin with Socrates and consider the role of dialogue in the Platonic dialogues as a counterargument to Kierkegaard's stress on irony as infinite absolute negativity.

10 Kierkegaard makes the dichotomy evident when he speaks of the incapacity of an aesthetic sensibility to recognize the absolute quality of irony as a "total striving." "But to apprehend irony in this way requires a wholly unique intellectual disposition differing qualitatively from every other. In particular, a rich poetic disposition is poorly endowed to conceive such irony in the eminent sense. Such an intellectual disposition might easily feel itself attracted by the individual expressions of irony without ever comprehending the infinity here concealed, might sport with them without any idea of the enormous daamon that inhabits irony's desolate and empty places" (Soren Kierkegaard, *The Concept of Irony, with Constant Reference to Socrates*, trans. Lee M. Capel [Bloomington: Indiana University Press, 1968], p. 155; page numbers hereafter cited in text). The polarity between philosophy and poetry becomes even more striking when one considers that the poetic sensibility here in question is Plato and the problem, his alleged incomprehension and disarming of Socratic irony.

11 Kierkegaard, p. 292. As Kierkegaard's interpretation of Schlegel shows a closer reading of Hegel than of Schlegel, so do modern interpreters show a more attentive reading of Kierkegaard than of Schlegel. "For Schlegel at least, the metaphysical Ego seems to have become the individual ego and in particular the ego as artist" (Muecke, p. 191). Emphatically not. Such a reductively aesthetic irony is far from doing justice to Schlegel's acute perception of the epistemological and ethical implications of ironic discourse.

12 This is especially true of the German revival of interest in Schlegel signaled by the monumental study of Ingrid Strohschneider-Kohrs, *Die romantische Ironie in Theorie und Gestaltung* (Tübingen: Max Niemeyer Verlag, 1960). Even Behler's much more broadly based and penetrating study tends in the same direction. Behler credits Schlegel with transforming irony from a rhetorical figure within a text to a concern with "the problem of literary communication . . . the constant breaking-through and transcending of one's own poetic creation" (Behler, p. 10). This is not, I would argue, the real center of Schlegel's irony. More original and insightful are Behler's later comments on the dialectical and dialogic character of consciousness, its dramatistic quality (p. 83), although this, too, remains at the level of the isolated artist-subject.

13 Anne Mellor, *English Romantic Irony* (Cambridge, Mass: Harvard University Press, 1980) is the most direct example of this, but relies almost exclusively on

Strohschneider-Kohrs for its view of German Romantic irony, adding a faintly existential tinge. More provocative is David Simpson, *Irony and Authority in Romantic Poetry* (Totowa: Rowman & Littlefield, 1979), where irony is treated as part of the reading process, an authorial technique for the avoidance of closure and prematurely determinate meanings. Simpson thus moves toward the process of intersubjectivity that I would argue is central for the German Romantics.

14 There is nonetheless much in Booth's approach that I find to be extremely useful. His breakdown of the ironic operation into its components and his careful attention to ironic modulations within texts are especially helpful. Yet he consistently downplays the progressive and dynamic aspects of irony; he tends to stop too soon and thus restrains his model from confrontation with the most complex instances of irony. Hence my focus here is on the more rigid overtones of his argument, the places where he seems to me to stop short of the full implications of an ironic stance.

15 Booth does concede that exploratory norms may govern some ironies, but unduly restricts this possibility to a relatively modern period, our era (Booth, p. 169).

16 Thus he characterizes his initial set of examples with a criterion that governs his choice of ironies. "They are all *intended*, deliberately created by human beings to be heard or read and understood with some precision by other human beings" (Booth, p. 5). This claim could be made fully credible only within the framework of a more complex notion of intentionality. The best discussion of such a model in relation to literary study that I have encountered is laid out by Charles Altieri in *Act and Quality: A Theory of Literary Meaning and Humanistic Understanding* (Amherst: University of Massachusetts Press, 1981), especially chapter 3, "The Concept of Action, and the Consequences for Hermeneutic Theory."

17 See, for instance, his retrieval of Beckett's character and values from critical assessments of his work (Booth, pp. 257–267).

18 Booth, of course, is far from giving this term the full Hegelian resonance it has for Kierkegaard and might be reluctant to concede the parallel.

19 Just how deceptive this can be is illustrated by Booth's own analyses of statements by St. Mark and Samuel Johnson. He concludes that "there is a curious further point about this community of those who grasp any irony: it is often a larger community, with fewer outsiders, than would have been built by non-ironic statement" (Booth, p. 29). This very possibility should alert us to the way in which some ironies can blur relevant distinctions. By requiring assent to some minimal point, that is, by collapsing all alternatives on a continuum away from a rejected pole, stable ironies can evade serious consideration of those issues they raise.

20 How far this is from Kierkegaard's ironic "moment" is well illustrated by the following quote: "The disguise and mysteriousness which it entails, the telegraphic communication which it initiates, inasmuch as the ironist must always be understood at a distance, the infinite sympathy it assumes, the elusive and ineffable moment of understanding immediately displaced by the anxiety of misunderstanding—all this captivates with indissoluble bonds" (Kierkegaard, p. 85). Irony for the earlier critic is much more suspect, but also potentially much more powerful.

21 Paul de Man, *Allegories of Reading: Figural Language in Rousseau, Nietzsche, Rilke, and Proust* (New Haven: Yale University Press, 1979), p. 301; hereafter abbreviated as *AR* and cited in text.

22 For a fuller discussion of this process in light of an example drawn from Proust, see *AR*, pp. 62–67. De Man's discussion of Nietzsche and Rousseau further elaborates the way in which metaphoric connection, which still contains a sense of difference, is converted into the universal similarity of the concept, thus completing the full divorce of thought from experience. "The contingent, metonymic link of the sensation *[Empfindung]* becomes the necessary, metaphorical link of the concept" (*AR*, p. 122). See also *AR*, pp. 154–157.

23 Paul de Man, *Blindness and Insight: Essays in the Rhetoric of Contemporary Criticism* (Minneapolis: University of Minnesota Press, 1983), p. 225; hereafter abbreviated as *BI* and cited in text.

24 This is equally true of spatial models, which like temporal ones subsume difference beneath universal, difference-reducing categories. "Spatial models— and the same would have to apply to temporal models—are metaphorical conceptualizations of *differential* structures, which is why they engender such redoubtably effective and misleading powers of unification and categorization" (*AR*, p. 231). Their apparent fidelity to noncoincidence acts as a rhetorical screen to their reinsertion of coincidence on a wider scale.

25 This incongruity is thematized in the essay "Lyric and Modernity" as that between representation and allegory, but numerous alternate thematizations are deployed by de Man elsewhere. "The Mallarmé-Baudelaire relationship is exemplary for all intra-poetic relationships in that it illustrates the impossibility for a representational and an allegorical poetics to engage in a mutually clarifying dialectic. Both are necessarily closed to each other, blind to each other's wisdom" (*BI*, p. 185). De Man's work is itself resolutely nondialectical, refusing the synthesis of difference and removing from itself any intersubjectivity beyond "the systematic undoing of understanding." Whether understanding need be absolute *or* absent, normative *or* impossible, is the final question to which I will turn in this section.

26 Much of the Socratic seductiveness of de Man stems from this capacity always to locate one more turn in the movement of his analysis.

27 De Man notes the contractural basis of such consensus, but is more intent on using this to support his arguments of epistemological indeterminacy than on exploring the dynamics of social consensus. "The innumerable writings that dominate our lives are made intelligible by a preordained agreement as to their referential authority; this agreement however is merely contractual, never constitutive. [Need one give full ontological weight to "constitutive," as de Man does here?] It can be broken at all times and every piece of writing can be questioned as to its rhetorical mode, just as *Julie* is being questioned in the Preface. [Need questioning proscribe consensus?] Whenever this happens, what originally appeared to be a document or an instrument becomes a text and, as a consequence, its readability is put in question" (*AR*, p. 204).

28 Friedrich Schlegel, *Kritische Friedrich-Schlegel-Ausgabe*, ed. Ernst Behler et al. (Munich: Verlag Ferdinand Schöningh, 1958–1980), II, 370; hereafter abbreviated as *KA* followed by volume number, page number, and where applicable, fragment number, and cited in text.

29 The prescience of Schlegel's and Novalis's notion of role-exchange becomes

evident only when we consider how well it suits the model of intersubjectivity worked out in psychoanalysis. An awareness of this blurring of identity in its multiple roles is the major lack in a schema of irony like that of Muecke, where the roles are parceled out in all too neat a fashion.

30 Charles Altieri's book delineates just such a middle ground, developing the notion of qualities of actions to explain the exemplary force literature has in the creation of human values. Romantic irony is given much the same role in a political context in an article by Charles Mosher, "Civic Identity in the Juridical Society: On Hegelianism as Discipline for the Romantic Mind," *Political Theory* 11 (1983):117–132, which uses it to define an alternative between liberal idealization of the individual and Hegelian absorption of the individual into the state.

*Chapter 1*

1 This reassessment of the significance of Schlegel's thought is well developed by the editors of the *Kritische Ausgabe* and further clarified by Werner Hamacher, "Der Satz der Gattung: Friedrich Schlegels poetologische Umsetzung von Fichtes unbedingtem Grundsatz," *Modern Language Notes* (1980): 1155–1180, where Schlegel is located against the background of Fichte's dialectic.

2 Examples include not only the polemical attacks of Hegel and Kierkegaard but also more recent works, which, while doing far more justice to the complexity of Schlegel's philosophy, still focus on the incapacity of self-consciousness to pass beyond its own limits. Among these are Beda Allemann, *Ironie und Dichtung* (Tübingen: Gunther Neske Pfullingen, 1956) and "Ironie als literarisches Prinzip," in *Ironie und Dichtung*, ed. Albert Schaefer (Munich: Verlag C. H. Beck, 1970), as well as what remains the single most insightful study of early German Romanticism's philosophical basis, Manfred Frank, *Das Problem "Zeit" in der deutschen Romantik* (Munich: Winkler Verlag, 1972).

3 Under this rubric can be collected the diverse analyses of Ingrid Strohschneider-Kohrs, Anne Mellor, and Franz Norbert Mennemeier, *Friedrich Schlegels Poesiebegriff* (Munich: Wilhelm Fink Verlag, 1971), and of Jochen Hörisch, *Die fröhliche Wissenschaft der Poesie* (Frankfurt: Suhrkamp Verlag, 1976).

4 Allemann, p. 56, emphasizes the literary antecedents, and Frank, pp. 25–27, the critique of Fichte.

5 Hörisch, pp. 15–20.

6 This operation is most closely described by Strohschneider-Kohrs. See, for instance, pp. 67–68.

7 Hörisch's treatment is more profound here, locating the subject's status within a complex dialectic of intersubjectivity that he sums up as role-exchange; see pp. 110–127. Strohschneider-Kohrs, in contrast, reduces irony in practice to a self-representation that comes very close to aesthetic narcissism in her treatment of Hoffmann; see pp. 49 and 362–419.

8 So that it seems inadequate to consider only the latter, as does Strohschneider-Kohrs, pp. 24ff.

9 Schlegel differentiates himself from Fichte in his effort to unify all three spheres. "Our main difference consists herein, that for me the philosophical,

moral, and aesthetic intuition is only one and the same, while Fichte separates them" (*KA* XVIII:433, frag. 68).

10  This referring of irony and communication in general back to ethics finds a parallel in H.-G. Gadamer's *Wahrheit und Methode* (Tübingen: J. C. B. Mohr, 1975). Gadamer's Husserlian critique of Schleiermacher's excessive subjectivizing of the hermeneutic act (pp. 275–283) precedes his recovery of "the fundamental hermeneutic problem" of a specifically ethical kind of truth, to be found in the questions of practical application and accumulated experience, whose exemplars are the question-answer format of the Platonic dialogues and the Aristotelian separation of ethical from logical knowledge (pp. 295–307). Whether Schlegel aims at the more objective criterion of Gadamerian *Wahrheit* (or would have wanted to do so) is less certain.

11  This term, left evocatively nebulous by Schlegel, is used interchangeably with *das Höchste*, and in its manifestation to the subject in its finitude is referred to as the "Universe" or the "Infinite." It carries connotations both of the revelatory moment of inspiration and of a perfect, all-encompassing order made tangible to individual self-consciousness at that moment.

12  Mennemeier, p. 317.

13  Hörisch refers this question back to Schlegel's critique of Kant's critique of aesthetic judgments; see pp. 42–44, also Mennemeier, p. 403.

14  Grice's theory of meaning rests on a very similar reciprocity of mental processes between speaker and hearer. See Paul Grice, "Meaning," *Philosophical Review* 66 (1957):377–388, and "Logic and Conversation," in *Syntax and Semantics*, vol. 3, ed. Peter Cole and Jerry L. Morgan (New York: Academic Press, 1975), pp. 41–58.

15  All three elements are juxtaposed by Julius in *Lucinde* (*KA* V, 9).

16  As Mellor implies on pp. 4 and 10.

17  Reversal as characteristic of irony and self-consciousness has close affinities with the structure of the unconscious and the often neglected third operation in Freud's dream theory. Besides displacement and condensation, Freud gives great attention to various other *Darstellungsmittel*, whose characterizing trait is their breaking down of the logical categories of mind in the unconscious, via opposition, contradiction, reversal, and transformation into the opposite.

18  Frank, p. 77. Time itself, rather than irony, is the final mediating force for Frank, who points out that the inability to reconcile the relative and the Absolute, to overcome the deficiency of the former and of reflection, is where Fichte's *Wissenschaftslehre* runs aground (p. 25).

19  The parallels between irony as enactment and the effort by Charles Altieri to expand the Gricean model of meaning to cover dramatic implicature suggest that irony may be an archetypal case of such dramatic implicature. See Charles Altieri, "What Grice Offers Literary Theory: A Proposal for 'Expressive Implicature,'" *Centrum* 6 (1978):90–103.

20  In the Gadamerian sense, as opposed to logical truth.

21  The extent to which Schlegel's point was lost can be measured by his assimilation into a Romantic current defined by Schelling, as in M. H. Abrams, *Natural Supernaturalism* (New York: W. W. Norton & Co., 1971).

22  Lacan's analysis of the fort-da game depicts a similar meshing of recollection, self-assertion, and symbolization. See my discussion in chapter 4 under "The Symbolic Order and the Subject of Irony."

23 The contrast with the Hegelian dialectic and its stress on positive appearance of the Absolute Spirit is clear. It should, however, be kept in mind that the Jena Lectures were given in 1800–1801, five years before the publication of the *Phenomenology*, and with Hegel very possibly in attendance.
24 Frank, p. 25.
25 Ibid., p. 84.
26 Mennemeier, p. 65. Mennemeier is the most energetic proponent of the positivity latent in Schlegel's aesthetic theorizing, although his stress on the continuity of objective poetry as an ideal leads him at times to underestimate the metamorphoses of Schlegel's ideas. He does note, however, the tension this causes with Schlegel's growing historical consciousness, against which he sees the clinging to verifiable standards rooted in an Absolute as a doomed rearguard action. See pp. 68 and 116n.
27 The *Wille zur Utopie* is not just the other side of irony, as Allemann notes (p. 191), but an integral aspect of irony itself, already included in the self-awareness that constitutes the ironic act.
28 That this imperative may be the last barrier to a sense of encroaching modern egoism and isolation is certainly possible. It often seems that Schlegel, like Schleiermacher, lacked a full sense of the possibility of incomprehension, of a communicative hiatus.
29 This vacillation is typical of the whole history of conscience as a philosophical term, but especially prominent in German philosophy from Kant on. Joachim Ritter, *Historisches Wörterbuch der Philosophie* (Stuttgart: Schwabe & Co., 1971), provides a useful summary.

*Chapter 2*

1 Ingrid Strohschneider-Kohrs, p. 8. While Strohschneider-Kohrs's treatment of German Romantic irony is an excellent analysis of such aesthetic irony, her perception of the early Romantics takes a very particular slant in viewing them as though they reached their culmination in the work of E. T. A. Hoffmann. Her consideration of irony in Schlegel's later work (pp. 80–88) collapses irony and love, arguing that both serve a similar synthesizing function, a judgment that does little justice to the continued complexity of Schlegel's philosophical thought and his concern for the actual mechanisms of dialectical mediation.
2 The question of how completely the Nature of Schelling or the English Romantics can be equated with an absolute subject (as in the formulation of Schlegel or Novalis) is a complex one and beyond the scope of my concerns here. That the particular term opposed to the finite subject makes a difference to the nature of the relation is obvious and lies behind my preference for seeing irony as intersubjective and not just self-representative. Yet at the same time, insofar as that other term is in some sense absolute, it reduces the subject to dependency and desire, so that its naming is an act of secondary importance in light of the relation itself. Only if the subject attempts to move into the position of the Absolute does the particular terminology acquire full significance.
3 The classic instance of this, of course, being M. H. Abrams, *The Mirror and the Lamp* (New York: Oxford University Press, 1976), especially chapter 4, "The Development of the Expressive Theory of Poetry and Art."
4 Abrams, pp. 290–293. David Simpson (p. 177) puts the point well: "We can

never cognitively receive that universality as a *sharable* fact of communication." Simpson's book is an excellent study of how the experience of poetic ecstasy must immediately go over into the problem of whether and how that insight might be given communal force.

5  Strohschneider-Kohrs, followed later by Mellor, makes this the primary trait of her treatment of irony, salvaging negativity as that which makes continued creation possible and as a necessary response to human finitude; see, for instance, pp. 48–49 and 74. Mellor makes the connection of this duality with the life-death process explicit in her discussion on pp. 7–30. She speaks of "the incredibly difficult but not impossible dual awareness that everything one believes is both true and false" (p. 13), which is fine as a definition of irony, but fails to convey a sense of how this difficulty is to be overcome, unless perhaps as a massive focusing of will. The Romantic solution was perhaps most subtle in its laying out of the precise mechanisms by which this "difficult awareness" might be attained.

6  M. H. Abrams, *Natural Supernaturalism*, pp. 183–187. It should be noted that this focus reduces process to a single cycle, collapsing it on top of the Christian paradigm and treating irony as a single point in an essentially linear movement.

7  Rene Wellek, "The Concept of 'Romanticism' in Literary History," *Comparative Literature* 1 (1949):1–23, 147–172; see especially pp. 147 and 161. Central references in Abrams are *Mirror*, pp. 21–26 and 100–103, and *Natural Supernaturalism*, pp. 172–195.

8  Hans Eichner describes the shift in Schlegel's thought thus: "Always again and in every area, in ethics as in aesthetics, one finds in Schlegel's writings from this time the concept of the individual in the place where, in the Enlightenment, but also in German Classicism, the concept of the species stands" (*KA* V:xxxi). Schlegel himself states, "Precisely individuality is the original and eternal in the human being" (*KA* II:262, frag. 60) and regularly associates individuality with the idea of system (as in *KA* XVIII:89, frag. 715).

9  Immanuel Kant, *Critique of Pure Reason*, trans. Norman Kemp Smith (London: Macmillan Press, 1973), p. 154. "Only in so far as I can grasp the manifold of the representations in one consciousness, do I call them one and all *mine*."

10  Abrams, *Natural Supernaturalism*, p. 174.

11  As in de Man's reading of Romanticism in "The Rhetoric of Temporality."

12  Abrams's term. See *Mirror*, pp. 272–285.

13  This reference in Schlegel's history of philosophy (the Cologne Lectures) is a specific criticism of the Cartesian model.

14  Walter Benjamin, *Gesammelte Schriften* I:1, ed. Rolf Tiedemann and Hermann Schweppenhauser (Frankfurt: Suhrkamp Verlag, 1974), p. 56. Schlegel describes this other term as a *Gegen-Ich* or a *Du*, rejecting Fichte's use of a *Nicht-Ich* (*KA* XII:337).

15  Benjamin, p. 55.

16  As Abrams contends it is, in *Natural Supernaturalism*, p. 181. Schlegel is clear on this: "Thinking and mental representation take the place for us of being: all being becomes thinking for us, we are nothing except what we think" (*KA* XII:389). As Benjamin (p. 18) cogently expands, "The relationship of thinking to itself present in reflection is regarded as that above all closest at hand for thinking, out of it are all others developed."

17 Novalis, *Schriften. Die Werke Friedrich von Hardenbergs*, ed. Paul Kluckhohn, Richard Samuel, et al. (Stuttgart: W. Kohlhammer Verlag, 1960). Quotations from Novalis hereafter abbreviated as *N*, followed by volume number, page number, and where applicable, fragment number, and cited in text. Here, II:247, frag. 454.
18 Benjamin, p. 60.
19 Both the discussion of Benjamin on pp. 30–31 and that of Jochen Hörisch on p. 136 are useful in delimiting the possibility of such regression.
20 David Simpson's study comes much closer to capturing this aspect of Romantic irony than most other works that deal more exhaustively with the topic. But rather than adopting his characterization of such irony as performative, I would suggest the alternative formulation "ethical," for without the possibility of engagement with a partner who can serve as a perpetual possibility of otherness, the question of authority becomes, as he well points out, virtually insoluble except as indeterminacy.
21 Benjamin on pp. 73–78 formulates this gap in aesthetic terms as that between *Kunst* and the *Werke* which make it up, without, however, exhausting it.
22 The problem with such polarities is that they tend to become laden with fixed evaluative characteristics, as occurs in Mellor's book (among others), where an ordering subject is confronted with a chaotic universe. The juxtaposition is tempting, but finally incomplete, for this is no more true than that the universe is a perfect order, which the subject creatively disorders.
23 "The intellectual intuition is nothing but the consciousness of a prestabilized harmony, of a necessary, eternal dualism" (*KA* XVIII:280, frag. 1026).
24 Schlegel depicts exactly this difficulty at the opening of *Lucinde*: "Every thought and whatever else is formed in us seems in itself completed, particular and indivisible like a person; one thing represses the other, and what just now was completely near and present, sinks soon back into darkness" (*KA* V:11).
25 De Man's article on irony and allegory explores this solution, as does Manfred Frank much more exhaustively in his study.
26 Hörisch's summary of this on p. 96 is excellent.
27 Negative irony is perhaps the fundamental variety, for negation lies at the basis of all interactive duality. Yet negative irony often fails to make the interdependence of the terms in every duality explicit and leaves the impression that its negation is definitive. Dialogic irony stresses the mutual presence of contradictory alternatives, without necessarily doing more than juxtaposing them. Both systemic and ethical irony move toward some resolution of such paradoxes, the difference between them lying in the omniscient status of the former ironist (who enacts the transcendental ego), whereas the ethical ironist seeks to subject his own stance to that glance of countervailing authority most completely performed by an other subject.
28 This is a term borrowed from Albert Cook and Charles Altieri, although my use of it is not identical with theirs. See Altieri, "The Qualities of Action: A Theory of Middles in Literature," *Boundary 2* 5 (1977):323–350 and 899–918, as well as Cook's books on enactment and his "Stendhal and the Discovery of Ironic Interplay," *Novel* 9 (1975):40–54. The latter article, though not directly dealing with enactment, is especially useful in its recognition that each ironic alternative somehow comprises the other. This study of the interplay of alternatives goes beyond the usual reading of irony such as Stendhal's as what I

have termed "dialogic," and points the way toward the intersubjective resolution characteristic of ethical irony.

29  A total interpenetration carried by Schlegel to its logical sources in his repudiation of the logical premises on which difference and identity are based. See,
for instance, *KA* XII:318–319. Novalis traces interpenetration back to a similar
role-exchange of feeling and thought. See Hörisch, pp. 110–111. Yet to make
the conjunction of contraries seem effortless, as does Hirsch, for instance, in
his comparison of Schelling and Wordsworth, is to neglect the difficult process
by which one comes to attain paradox. E. D. Hirsch, Jr., *Wordsworth and Schelling* (New Haven: Yale Unversity Press, 1960).

30  Its movement might be described as a regressive dualism in contrast to the
progressive Hegelian dualism.

31  This state is both rather more than the indeterminacy Simpson often equates
with irony, as on p. 190, and rather less than the shared understanding Booth
evokes to tie down dangerously unstable ironies. It is both infinite and finite at
the same time.

32  An alternative approach might, as Simpson's does, focus on the text itself as an
enactment for the reader. But that perspective emphasizes an interpretive indeterminacy that somewhat overstresses the uncertainty of the communicative
act, at least from the viewpoint of ethical irony.

33  Recent scholarship has begun to remedy this inattention. Hans Eichner's introduction to the novel in *KA* V provides useful comments on its overall
structure and themes. Gisela Dischner's edition, *Friedrich Schlegels Lucinde und
Materialen zu einer Theorie des Müßiggangs* (Hildesheim: Gerstenberg Verlag,
1980), collects useful supplementary materials on the novel's reception and her
own preferred theme, indolence. Hörisch's book remains the most useful
treatment, however, because it focuses on the key element of role-exchange,
which it treats in terms of the broader perspective of early Romantic philosophy.

34  Novalis's use of the term *Blütenstaub* (pollen) as title for a collection of fragments shows that the Romantics conceived this act of fertilization at the levels
of comunication and of reflection as well. This sense for the full implication of
the organic metaphor, and even its inevitable association with death, is absent
from many scholarly treatments of it, where only wholeness and growth are
emphasized.

35  Schlegel often reiterates the idea that we are only a piece of ourselves (*KA*
XII:337 and 392, *KA* XVIII:506, frag. 9, and here at *KA* V:71), a problem replicated in language: "These particular words give always again only one side, a
piece of the connection, of the whole, that I would like to intimate in its full
harmony" (*KA* V:77).

36  See Strohschneider-Kohrs, p. 98.

37  Kierkegaard, pp. 302–315.

38  Schlegel made a similar critique of unlimited subjectivity even earlier, in his
1796 characteristic of Jacobi's *Woldemar* (*KA* II:65 and 74).

39  Hörisch's summary of role-exchange brings out the passage from self-sufficient egoism to a more adequate, because dualistic, self-image: "In that subjectivity, which experienced the disintegration of the self-referential logic of
reflection as narcissistic sickness, relates itself to itself over its Other, is it
present to itself" (p. 109). The attained self-presence of which Hörisch speaks,

the *Universalitätsanspruch der Poesie* seems to me, however, exactly what is in question here—whether it remains a claim or passes into an experienced condition, and if so, for how long.

40  It is further ironic that Julius does not realize even here the extent to which he has been guilty of exactly the same distortion in his earlier lyric elevation.

41  Frank, p. 131, points out that this paradox is impossible to get behind, for the subject must always assume its own existence before it proceeds through reflection to attempt to confirm it. It must already know what it is if it is to be able to recognize itself when it is reflected back to itself. In a similar way, as Hörisch indicates, the subject must always already assume the subjectivity of the other, which can only be evidenced through interaction with it. "But rather, reflective subjectivity would also rest on a *petitio principii*, because it must already, before the summons emanating from it to self-definition, know its correlate, another summoning intelligible selfhood, as analogous to itself" (p. 133).

42  In the more abstract terms of Schlegel's Cologne Lectures, "On the first level no genuine unity occurs, it is simple likeness, an indeterminate unity, simply as absence of fullness, of duality: only on the third level does unity in its genuine form occur, as opposite to the second level, which is that of duality and separation" (*KA* XII:435). This echoes my earlier discussion of the third level of consciousness where intersubjectivity emerges from the subject-object split.

43  Johannes Mahr, *Übergang zum Endlichen* (Munich: Fink Verlag, 1970). Mahr's book is the best extended treatment of this novel, notable for its interpretation of the novel within the context of Novalis's thought as a whole.

44  Bruce Haywood contends that it is the constant tendency of Heinrich's mind to think in images that makes him a poet. If so, one should add that it is the propensity of the text to open these images to interpretation, to demand such interaction from Heinrich and the reader, that makes it an ironic text (*Novalis: The Veil of Imagery* [Cambridge, Mass: Harvard University Press, 1959]).

45  This quote, as the one above, comes from a letter of Feb. 27, 1799, to Caroline Schlegel and reports his first reaction to the just-received manuscript of *Lucinde*.

46  Novalis thus recaptures a process found by Levi-Strauss to be characteristic of mythic thought in general. Claude Levi-Strauss, "History and Dialectic," in *The Structuralists from Marx to Levi-Strauss*, ed. Richard and Fernande DeGeorge (Garden City: Anchor Books, 1972), pp. 209–237, especially p. 229. Schlegel's comment on analogy reinforces its connection with irony and conscience. "Analogy is a thoroughly moral way of proof" (*KA* XVIII:285, frag. 1061).

47  Mahr, p. 25. Hans-Joachim Mähl, *Die Idee des goldenen Zeitalters im Werk des Novalis* (Heidelberg: Carl Winter Universitätsverlag, 1965), makes the same point, for instance in reference to the apparent pure idealism of the essay, "Die Christenheit oder Europa," p. 333.

48  Mahr, pp. 77–78, develops the parallel between this role for the subject and the similar status of the reader, whose (ideal) interpretive activity duplicates that of Heinrich within the novel.

49  As Mähl puts it, "The reaching of the Absolute is no final condition of this progress worth striving for, because it would abolish the existence of the person, annihilate his individual consciousness" (p. 290).

50  Though the four experiences are in some measure similar, it is important to

recognize the divergence in operation between the two dreams, the "Märchen" and the vision of Mathilde. As Mahr, p. 31, notes, they become progressively more communal. Heinrich's role also becomes more active and passes finally to the waking vision, where self-possession can be maintained.

51  Minor divergences include the fact that the father has, perhaps needs, a guide, where Heinrich does not, and the old man whose beard has grown into the table. Mahr's interpretation of Heinrich's subsequent journey as a realization of his father's dream demonstrates another level of coherence between real and ideal that defines Novalis's text (Mahr, pp. 59–62).

52  For useful treatments of the "Märchen" in detail, see Paul Kluckhohn's introduction to Novalis's collected works (N I:41–47), Mahr, pp. 210–249, and Haywood, pp. 113–133.

53  The death of Novalis's own fiancé produced a similar result in his own life, which serves as a model for the experiences of Heinrich. "Her death tore Hardenberg from the immediacy of his youthful amorousness and took him over into larger connections encompassing the individual existence" (Mahr, p. 248). That this experience caused a fundamental shift in Novalis's development is unlikely, for as Mähl well argues, Novalis was already predisposed to the implications of just such an event as his experience at Sophie's grave of their immortality (Mähl, pp. 297–300).

54  Mahr, p. 205.

55  The particularity of Novalis's Romanticism can perhaps be seen when one considers alternate versions of visionary experience, which tend to be unmediated. The transfiguration of Hyperion in Hölderlin's novel, for instance, occurs as an isolated confrontation with and merging into nature, which may indeed have consequences for the social sphere, but is not grounded on interpretation in the way Heinrich's visions are.

56  Since Schlegel knew this novel long before his Cologne Lectures, it seems inevitable that its positioning of conscience at the center of the subject should have influenced him in marking a similar role for it in those lectures, through which irony comes to be displaced into a new term.

57  The argument that a choice is necessary and that is the human alternative that will have to be sacrificed is made by David Ferry, The Limits of Mortality (Middletown: Wesleyan University Press, 1959). Ferry contends further that this forced choice produces resentment in the poet against those traces of mortality he cannot abolish. Geoffrey Hartman, on the other hand, finds that for Wordsworth, "the self is not this or that, but between" (Wordsworth's Poetry: 1787–1814 [New Haven: Yale University Press, 1964], p. 198). Hartman's terms are displaced from those of Ferry, however, for Hartman sees the imagination as an infinite power confronting the singularity not of humanity but of natural objects. Though the refusal to choose between the two is seen as the source of Wordsworth's power, these two terms display a similar tendency to collapse into each other, to evade in some way any primary dualism.

58  Hartman, p. 137.

59  Ferry's development of the consequences of this process on pp. 3–15, is a useful one, though he rather polemically emphasizes Wordworth's resentful response and underestimates his sincere effort to maintain the dualism.

60  This idea is skillfully developed by Hartman, for instance, in his analyses of the Boy of Winander and "Strange fits of passion," pp. 19–25.

61 A notable exception to this, perhaps, is "Tintern Abbey." There, after the usual ascent to a transcendent perspective, Wordsworth descends in an unusual apostrophe to a particular person, Dorothy, whom he here manages to perceive in just that aspect of being able to replace him that Matthew refused to recognize. The only possible resolution of time is such an other person, whose life after the subject's death is a form of immortality. Yet even this goes over into the wish that this particular scene and his particular presence might live on in her mind. One then sees that replacement, even here, remains a kind of duplication of an integral self. "But she is no more than a version of himself at an earlier stage" (Ferry, p. 110).

62 Frederick Garber, *Wordsworth and the Poetry of Encounter* (Chicago: University of Illinois Press, 1971), pp. 25–27.

63 Brooks's article on irony and Paul de Man's "The Rhetoric of Temporality" develop the connection most explicitly, though de Man refrains from integrating Wordsworth wholly into the ironic model he has developed, speaking instead of his "wisdom."

64 Thus, while these moments involve "the momentary presence, before the poet's attention, of Nature, or the concrete world *as a whole*," it is nonetheless the temporal continuity of the subject with itself rather than an external wholeness that defines them (Newton P. Stallknecht, *Strange Seas of Thought* [Durham: Duke University Press, 1945], p. 9).

65 Geoffrey Hartman, *The Unmediated Vision* (New Haven: Yale University Press, 1954). See especially pp. 5, 38–39, and 44, where Hartman defines the vision as an absence or obliteration of the normal situation of relatedness.

66 Hartman follows this process with his usual acumen in the Alps scene of book 6 of *The Prelude* (*Wordsworth's Poetry*, pp. 42–48). This experience of unsolicited revelation is very much like Schlegel's analysis of wit.

67 One can contrast this with Schlegel's or Novalis's emphasis on understanding as an essentially progressive act. "Sense understands something only in that it takes it up into itself as germ, nourishes it and lets it grow to blossom and fruit" (*KA* II:256, frag. 5).

68 Ferry puts the issue with his usual sharpness on p. 100. "Both intelligence and the temporal scene must be obliterated, or their obtrusiveness ameliorated, before the metaphysical contact can be made." This stands in contrast to the totality of childhood, which could find the particular wholly satisfying, a state Hirsch terms "enthusiasm" (pp. 15–25).

69 For Hartman's Wordsworth, the imagination is necessarily apocalyptic, a truth it is the task of Wordsworth's poetry to conceal. Relevant passages are in *Wordsworth's Poetry*, pp. 63, 88, 147, and 225.

70 John Jones, *The Egotistical Sublime* (London: Chatto & Windus, 1954), pp. 25–34.

71 Abrams puts a more positive light on this disharmony, but still sees the mind as moving from one extreme to another. Whether extremes are fundamental or merely "occasional" is crucial to how one reads Wordsworth. "The overall tenor of *The Prelude* indicates that Wordsworth means to represent such absolute dominion of the mind over outward sense not as the ideal of perceptual experience, but as an occasional extreme that helps to rescue him from the disastrous opposite extreme" (*Natural Supernaturalism*, p. 370). Garber, p. 84, sees the inequality of the two forces without conceding that communion is thereby made impossible.

72 A problem Wordsworth shares with the Arab of book V. "Both desire to save the Imagination from the abyss of desert and ocean, man's solitary isolation from and utter absorption into Nature" (Harold Bloom, *The Visionary Company* [Garden City, N.Y.: Doubleday & Co., 1961], p. 147).

73 Thus the earth's swallowing of Lucy in "A slumber" and Hartman's apocalyptic imagination are two versions of the same process of a collapse of dualism. Relation of any kind is conceived by Wordsworth as absorption, however harmoniously two voices may sing one tune. The cutting of a dialectical relation leaves both terms effectively empty.

74 *Don Quixote* was also, of course, one of Schlegel's models of the ironic novel, brought to attention in Germany by Tieck's translation of it in 1799 (*KA* II:281–283).

75 It is interesting that a double displacement has occurred in book V. In the 1805 *Prelude*, the dream of the Arab was a friend's (Coleridge's), but has now been appropriated by the narrator, whereas the first versions of the Boy of Winander, now distanced as a separate character, made him the poet himself.

76 Where the comic involves separation from and eventual return to a stable social order, irony seeks out those mechanisms that might serve to reestablish a waning or absent social order and questions the worth of all given social truths. Irony lacks the self-assurance, but also the hubris, of comedy.

77 The relevant possible definitions of the novel are thoroughly considered by Gerry Brookes, *The Rhetorical Form of Sartor Resartus* (Berkeley: University of California Press, 1972), pp. 1–15, who argues that it is a persuasive essay.

78 Charles Frederick Harrold, *Carlyle and German Thought: 1819–1834* (London: Hamden Books, 1963), p. 79.

79 All quotations of this text are from Thomas Carlyle, *Sartor Resartus*, ed. Charles Frederick Harrold (Indianapolis: Odyssey Press, 1977) and will hereafter be cited in the text by pagination; here, p. 219. References to the preeminence of silence abound in Carlyle's writing, as in *The French Revolution* (London: Chapman & Hall, 1896), p. 27, where he concludes that even history, or any such change, is "disruption," "loss," "disease." He applauds the phrase, "Happy the people whose annals are vacant."

80 Thomas Carlyle, *On Heroes, Hero-Worship and the Heroic in History* (London: Chapman & Hall, 1897), p. 156.

81 Ibid., p. 65.

82 Thomas Carlyle, "Characteristics," in *Critical and Miscellaneous Essays*, vol. 3 (London: Chapman & Hall, 1899), p. 27.

83 In *Heroes*, p. 30. All we can know of this universe of spirit is that it is other. "That it is a Force, and a thousandfold complexity of Forces; a Force which is not *we*. That is all; it is not we, it is altogether different from *us*" (*Heroes*, p. 8).

84 Ibid., p. 45.

85 Ibid., p. 55.

86 Harrold (pp. 87–95) points out how Carlyle radically alters Kant's analysis of the subjectivity of human knowledge by using it to deny the existence of the nontranscendental world of reality. G. B. Tennyson, *Sartor Called Resartus* (Princeton: Princeton University Press, 1965), usefully compares this technique with Jean Paul's humor, pp. 275–283, but in conflating humor, irony, and wit he obscures the very distinctions that were fundamental to Romantic irony. Tennyson also analyzes how this negative irony works at the stylistic level, pp. 107–110.

87 Harrold's discussion of the nature of *Entsagen* and its relation to Goethe demonstrates once again Carlyle's editorial absolutism in his treatment of the ideas of others (Harrold, pp. 214–230).
88 Ibid., p. 109.
89 Tennyson, p. 327.
90 Both Albert J. LaValley, *Carlyle and the Idea of the Modern* (New Haven: Yale University Press, 1968), pp. 91–103, and Mellor, pp. 126–127, argue that a dialectical interchange is in fact taking place between the editor's ordering and Teufelsdröckh's chaos. Yet Carlyle's locating of these traits in separate characters, separate poles that never do come into personal contact in any significant way in the course of the novel, reveals a commitment to a profoundly nondialectical dualism, one that cannot permit the full involvement where actual reversal of roles becomes possible. Though the editor does indeed move into Teufelsdröckh's orbit, he does not succeed in retailoring him in any fundamental way. Even his editorial adjustments of the life and opinions are imposed on him by Teufelsdröckh, who seems to sit laughing above the process he has initiated, confidently guiding its outcome. The retailoring of the Clothes Philosophy is a concession to the editor's still unripe insight, not a concession to an independent perspective or a comment on the intrinsic validity of the Clothes Philosophy. Not Teufelsdröckh, but his garment, is retailored, and then only so that the truth of the original pattern might be realized.
91 This absorption and lack of dramatic or ironic difference is the reason for the sensible comments by Brookes on the editor's status (pp. 48–49). "Our interest is in coming to know the Clothes Philosophy, not the fate of the editor. Any incipient interest in his fate or character is carefully controlled in order to maintain our interest in the Clothes Philosophy and is never allowed to usurp interest from that set of ideas."
92 Tennyson provides numerous useful comments on Carlyle's use of metaphor, though he sees as expansive and energizing the analogical tendency I would term reductive. See pp. 166–167 and pp. 252–254, which treat Carlyle's use of opposition in a similar fashion.
93 Harrold, p. 236.
94 Both the merging of editor and Teufelsdröckh and the critical tendency to treat *Sartor Resartus* and Carlyle's life as interchangeable display the risk involved in an incomplete discrimination of the partialness of and difference between subjects, the tendency to draw them all into a single pattern.

*Chapter 3*

1 The biographical element is most justifiably stressed by Lionel Stevenson's readings of the novels in *The Ordeal of George Meredith* (New York: Charles Scribner's Sons, 1953). What is unfortunate is that the all-too-tempting parallels of Meredith's life and his favorite themes should be determinative of so much critical consideration of his texts, to the detriment of other critical approaches. V. S. Pritchett, *George Meredith and English Comedy* (New York: Random House, 1969), is especially prone to loose psychoanalyzing of some trait of Meredith's life to explain what he feels to be the unevenness of many novels. See especially pp. 71–72. Pritchett's anecdotal assessment makes a fine introduction to Meredith, but as serious criticism falls noticeably short of the

standard of his predecessor, E. M. Forster, *Aspects of the Novel* (London: E. Arnold, 1974), pp. 134–138.

2 Both Norman Kelvin, *A Troubled Eden* (London: Oliver & Boyd, 1961), and Donald David Stone, *Novelists in a Changing World* (Cambridge, Mass.: Harvard University Press, 1972), provide a rather schematic view of Meredith's juxtaposition of reason and the Comic Spirit as the defender of common sense as the core of a somewhat blindly optimistic didactic position in Meredith. A richer treatment is that of Joseph Moses, *The Novelist as Comedian* (New York: Schocken Books, 1983), which provides a welcome alternative to views that diminish Meredith to the stature of a last Victorian, a literary dinosaur notable for some few stylistic or narrative anticipations of more modern fiction. Moses opens up the complexity of Meredith's works by treating them in terms of an ironic attitude (if not quite in the sense I mean to establish), thus clarifying the dialectical relation between the comic and reason in Meredith. Comedy is "reason, that is, consciousness in search of a design" (p. 25). "Like irony, the Comic Spirit is a finer, more persistent awareness, and like irony, too, it is a critical self-consciousness emphasizing the discrepancy between subjective vision and objective appearance" (p. 31). This is a much more broadly applicable sort of didactic intent that moves well out from traditional Victorian values.

3 Pritchett, p. 38. Yet it is precisely this kind of reading of types that Meredith castigates, as in Sir Austin's sermon to Richard (*ORF*, XXI:183). All quotes from Meredith's works are from the Memorial Edition (New York: Charles Scribner's Sons, 1909–1912), and will be cited hereafter in the text by title, chapter number, and page number, according to the following abbreviations:

| | |
|---|---|
| *The Shaving of Shagpat(SS)* | *General Ople & Lady Camper(GO)* |
| *The Ordeal of Richard Feverel(ORF)* | *An Essay on Comedy(EC)* |
| *Evan Harrington(EH)* | *The Egoist(E)* |
| *Sandra Belloni(SB)* | *The Tragic Comedians(TC)* |
| *Rhoda Fleming(RF)* | *Diana of the Crossways(DC)* |
| *Vittoria(V)* | *One of Our Conquerors(OOC)* |
| *The Adventures of Harry Richmond(HR)* | *Lord Ormont & His Aminta(LO)* |
| *Beauchamp's Career(BC)* | *The Amazing Marriage(AM)* |

4 Especially good on this point is Gillian Beer, *Meredith: A Change of Masks* (London: Athlone Press, 1970). "[Meredith] was able to experiment far more radically than his contemporaries with the language of the novel and with the *flux*, as distinct from the *development*, of character" (p. 189).

5 This shifting of relationship is well traced in the "Modern Love" sequence by John Lucas, "Meredith as Poet," in *Meredith Now*, ed. Ian Fletcher (London: Routledge & Kegan Paul, 1971), pp. 14–33.

6 David Howard's "*Rhoda Fleming*: Meredith in the Margin," in Fletcher, pp. 130–143, first developed the idea of Meredith's "subversive fiction" in a fine article on that generally neglected novel. Moses, of course, has extended the operation of irony through many aspects of Meredith's works. Meredith himself seems generally to have used the term *irony* only for verbal irony, as something close to satire, and not as a stance like that of the Comic perspective, as in the *Essay on Comedy*, pp. 133–136.

7 Judith Wilt, *The Readable People of George Meredith* (Princeton: Princeton University Press, 1975). Wilt's reliance on Sartrean theory, however, leads her at

times to overestimate the effective ability of an individual to combat its existential isolation by enacting contrary or complementary roles.

8  Here I would diverge from Moses, whose view of irony persists in seeing it as an attribute of an individual ego, able self-reflectively to change itself. I hope to show that Meredith's novels demonstrate the barriers to and dangers in seeking to become one's own "opposing self" (Moses, p. 13). Thus Moses elsewhere separates irony from the fixity he, wrongly in my view, believes characteristic of the common sense of the Comic Spirit. "In all these statements, Meredith's requirement of common sense and consensus is superfluous—except insofar as he requires a wisdom unassailable by the Comic Spirit and therefore final" (Moses, pp. 37–38). There is no real reason why consensus cannot itself be ironic, even the expression of irony, as in the Platonic dialogues.

9  Schlegel's term for this attained consensus is *das allgemeine Individuelle*, the general or universal individual/individualness. See the Cologne Lectures, specifically *KA*, XII:397.

10  Joseph E. Kruppa, "Meredith's Late Novels," *Nineteenth Century Fiction* 19 (1964):274. This is strikingly similar to Schlegel's phrase from *Lucinde*: "Only in the answer of its You can every I wholly feel its infinite unity" (*KA* V:61).

11  Beer, p. 147. Similar arguments are made by Kelvin, pp. 194–197, and Kruppa, p. 276, who concludes, "[Society] is ultimately not a ground of values and cannot replace an interpersonal relationship." The transition between them may indeed be vague, but it is of the utmost concern to Meredith to determine if and how it can be achieved.

12  Dorothy van Ghent, *The English Novel* (New York: Harper & Row, 1967), pp. 229–230.

13  Laetitia says only, "He worships himself" (*E*, XLIX: 325), which is not a full definition of an egoist. It is important to note, however, that comedy is not to be seen as social corrective in Meredith, for true reason exceeds both social conventions and what is taken for common sense, whose actual evidence in society is so indiscernible that one must simply have faith that it is there (*EC*, p. 47).

14  John Goode, "*The Egoist*: Anatomy or Striptease?" in Fletcher, pp. 205–230, sees in this split between illusory and full self-awareness Meredith's revision of the positivist view of egoism.

15  This process occurs repeatedly throughout Meredith's fiction, from *Richard Feverel* on, as in this description of Sir Austin: "His was an order of mind that would accept the most burdensome charges, and by some species of moral usury make a profit out of them" (*ORF*, XL: 473).

16  A similar blindness governs the structure of the text as well, since we are limited, as usual in Meredith, to those perceptions and memories accessible to the characters.

17  Richard Stevenson, "Laetitia Dale and the Comic Spirit in *The Egoist*," *Nineteenth Century Fiction* 26 (1972):406–418, summarizes the various arguments made by critics in favor of Clara or Vernon, but overstates his case for Laetitia as a self-enlightened character. Particularly startling is his claim that Willoughby's and Laetitia's union is to be a "healthy marital relationship" (p. 414). More balanced and convincing is Robert Baker's consideration of the Comic

Spirit as satyr, not identifiable with any one character ("Faun and Satyr: Meredith's Theory of Comedy in *The Egoist*," *Mosaic* 9 [1976]:173–193).

18 Just this does result from Harry Richmond's sense of unique insight—a smug self-satisfaction and sense of superiority, although the origin of that vision is not made clear there (*HR*, IX:112).

19 Daniel Smirlock, "Rough Truth: Synecdoche and Interpretation in *The Egoist*," *Nineteenth Century Fiction* 31 (1976):313–328, reads the entire novel as a probing of the powers of any kind of representative discourse, always in doubt because always partial and reductive.

20 Examples abound in Meredith's fiction and can be made up of the slightest of words, as in Georgiana Powy's dismissal of Sandra Belloni: "What a storm it was, and what conflict, agitated the girl and stupefied her, she cared not to guess, now that she had the suitable designation, 'savage,' confirmed in all her acts, to apply to her" (*SB* XLVII:206). Classification ends reflection.

21 Wilt not only identifies that intellectual detachment with characters in the text but extends it to include the stance often attributed to Meredith of the "civilized reader." "Meredith invites the reader to join his narrative in lofty survey of the follies of our fellows, and then implicates both himself and us in those same follies" (Wilt, p. 141).

22 The penalty for failure to do so is assessed on Everard Romfrey in his stubborn refusal of understanding of Nevil Beauchamp. "Gentlemen of an unpractised imaginative capacity cannot vision for themselves exactly what they would, being unable to exercise authority over the proportions and the hues of the objects they conceive, which are very much at the mercy of their sportive caprices" (*BC*, XXXIII:52).

23 Beer (pp. 155–156) provides an excellent analysis of such half-conscious evasiveness via images in Diana's recollection of Lugano.

24 Moses (p. 81) provides the necessary and welcome transition to irony when he notes, "Irony is not a rejection, however, but a refocusing to permit examination of *how* a statement is truth." One of the most encouraging aspects of recent work on irony is the increasing recognition that irony is not so much a matter of negation as one of gradations, of shades of validity.

25 This relation is made explicit in *Diana*, where Meredith brings to our attention how "the clear reading of others distracted the view of herself" (*DC*, XL:449), attributed here, as we shall see in Clara's case as well, to an evasion of her sexuality. Meredith elsewhere sees the cause of such blindness in obsession with any single idea (*BC*, XXXVIII:110). Carinthia uncannily reiterates Clara's very situation. "One idea is a bullet, good for the day of battle to beat the foe, father tells us. . . . With one idea, we see nothing—nothing but itself" (*AM*, XXX:317).

26 As examples, Baker, p. 179, and Beer, pp. 132–133.

27 Smirlock's treatment of this passage is an excellent one, although his sense of the cause of linguistic inaccuracy seems to move away from the central point of the passage by attributing it to situational flux (p. 324), whereas it is the irremediable bias of the speaker, his involvement in a human interaction, that slants his view. It is on the basis of the latter perspective that one can evaluate the efficacy of irony as a positive, intersubjective response to the interpretive relativism that Smirlock's article suggests to be the limit of discourse.

28 Here I would differ from such critics as Stone (p. 168), Gillian Beer, "*One of*

*Our Conquerors*: Language and Music," in Fletcher, pp. 265–280 (especially pp. 268–269 and 275), and Thomas L. Jeffers, "Meredith's Concept of Nature: Beyond the Ironies of *Richard Feverel*," *ELH* 47 (1980):121–148 (especially p. 135), who agree that Meredith would at some point accept the necessity of the inexpressible. Meredith's works seem rather to demonstrate the contrary implication that a reliance on or submission to such constraints can only be destructive, and his own practice seems an equally strong assertion of the need to press continually against the limits of the linguistically possible. Words may not outstrip experience for Meredith, but neither should they be allowed to fall too far behind it.

29 The most thorough treatment of this scene is by Baker on pp. 182–185, whose analysis of the unconscious motives at work here and in the later brandy glass scene is exceptionally useful.

30 A striking instance is Carinthia in *The Amazing Marriage*, who shifts back and forth among identification with her father, her brother, and her husband, but who is never really independent for any lengthy period. Similarly, Rhoda Fleming says of herself and her sister, "You can only mean that we are to be separated and thought of as two people; and we are one, and will be till we die" (*RF*, XIV:128).

31 Though even this is oddly indirect, as Laetitia makes her assessment of Willoughby's self-love not to him directly but to his aunts in his presence (*E*, XLIX:325).

32 Michael Sprinker, " 'The Intricate Evasions of As': Meredith's Theory of Figure," *Victorian Newsletter* 53 (1978):9–12, usefully points to the possible origin of such truth about one's nature and feelings in extralinguistic interaction, but underestimates the degree to which this must be brought into language to be made effective.

33 Meredith's last completed novel, *The Amazing Marriage*, is most acutely aware of how vision of self and of others is necessarily mediated. Gower Woodseer succeeds in seeing Carinthia by merging his vision with that of her maid, Madge. Fleetwood's acquisition of knowledge is a precise statement of the conditions of what I have termed ironic intersubjectivity. "For the young man embracing a character loses grasp of his own, is plucked out of himself and passes into it, to see the creature he is with the other's eyes, and feel for the other as a very self" (*AM* XLI:426). This is exactly the dialectic of vision and blindness enacted by *The Egoist*.

34 Kelvin on pp. 114–120 and 143 overreads the extent to which this involves an obliteration of the individual, whose preservation is of crucial concern for Meredith in all his novels. Relationship requires the association of individuals, not replaceable units or counters.

35 There is, interestingly, a Letitia in the novel—Ripton's sister—who almost anticipates her successor as she surreptitiously reads, but without interpreting, Richard's letter to Ripton about the outcome of the hay-rick incident (*ORF*, XI:82–87).

36 It may therefore be a sign of some hope that Richard's and Lucy's child, who resembles Richard in all else, has his mother's eyes.

37 Stevenson's biography of Meredith is marked in its preference for the lyric effusions in the novels, as is Pritchett's study (see p. 51), and this perspective is raised into a theory of natural transcendence by Jeffers.

38 David Foster, "Rhetorical Strategy in *Richard Feverel,*" *Nineteenth Century Fiction* 26 (1971):185–195, treats this aspect in terms of foreshadowing, arguing that Meredith thus prepares adequately for the tragic outcome. But foreshadowing alone does not seem fully adequate to justify logically for the reader the turn from lyricism implicit in the empty conclusion.

39 As, for instance, Richard's pursuit of knight-errantry, explored by Phyllis Bartlett, "Richard Feverel, Knight-Errant," *Bulletin of the New York Public Library,* July 1959, pp. 329–340.

40 This self-mediated experience of reality is similar to a frequent process of linguistic anticipation of reality, which usually, however, takes place through a third person's eyes. Thus Aminta first sees Lord Ormont through Weyburn's vision of him, and Woodseer's phrases are Fleetwood's first introduction to Carinthia in *The Amazing Marriage.*

41 Kelvin's claims for the interpenetration of the two seem excessive in light of the always problematic role of "natural" character in Meredith's novels. "Meredith . . . saw nature as an active and benevolent principle that reveals to man his kinship with the rest of creation and that teaches him how to order his private, public, and political life" (p. 3).

42 Jeffers, p. 143.

43 This pattern is frequent in Meredith's novels, as in the case of Edward Blancove, who delays his reconciliation with Dahlia Fleming because he associates her with Robert. "He detested brute force, with a finely witted man's full loathing; and Dahlia's obnoxious champion had grown to be associated in his mind with Dahlia" (*RF,* XXI:213).

44 Richard Stevenson, "Comedy, Tragedy, and the Spirit of Critical Intelligence in *Richard Feverel,*" in *The Worlds of Victorian Fiction,* ed. Jerome Buckley (Cambridge, Mass: Harvard University Press, 1975), pp. 205–222, has effectively pointed out the limits on Richard in this scene. His claim that Lucy is an emerging critical intelligence, however, is not really plausible, as my analysis of her indicates. The real problem here is not so much Richard's lack of self-reliance at all (p. 220), but rather the fact that his revelation is not really intersubjectively grounded.

45 This inability to discriminate adequately between public and private matters is something with which Meredith as well as his characters seems to struggle. Shaping public affairs to personal needs works against both Nevil Beauchamp and Richmond Roy, whose larger schemes seem complete failures. Arnold Kettle, "*Beauchamp's Career,*" in Fletcher, pp. 188–204, however, feels that the fusion made by Meredith does satisfactorily explain each sphere in terms of the other (p. 194). This again, however, seems an instance of analogization, tricky at best in Meredith's terms.

46 Beer's assessment is again very sensitive to the realities of Meredith's production. "He attempted to establish a level of reality which would avoid equally the rose pink and the drab, but he frequently found that he could create reality only through alternation, not fusion, of extremes" (pp. 46–47). This fusion of perspectives, I would argue, can only be, and was gradually perceived by Meredith to be, an intersubjective act.

47 Beer, p. 91.

48 Howard's insightful treatment of *Rhoda Fleming* puts it thus: "It seems almost as if the notion of an individual moral ordeal and progression were itself too egotistical" (p. 139).

49 Sir Austin, in one example, almost succeeds in getting through to Richard for a full confession of the latter's love, when he goes over to the moral terms of the "Foolish Young Man" and the "Woman" and loses Richard completely (ORF, XXI:180).

50 "For it is the shameless deception, not the marriage, that has wounded you" (ORF, XXXIII:333). Richard's earlier reaction to his separation from Lucy was similarly couched in terms of plot and conspiracy (ORF, XXVI:247). As in the case of Lord Fleetwood, life seems to be an irony only for one who is not himself ironic (AM, XXVIII:291).

51 Like R. Stevenson's argument, Sprinker's reading of Lucy ("The Hoax that Joke Bilked," Mosaic 10 (1976):133–145) as a figure of pure positivity and health (which he sees Meredith as subconsciously intent on destroying) underestimates Meredith's ironic judgment of any mode of vision.

52 This metaphor of disease in One of Our Conquerors is well treated by Robert Baker, who also provides useful comments on the "Judith" motif in the novel ("Victorian Conventions and Imagery in George Meredith's One of Our Conquerors," Criticism 18 [1976]:317–333).

53 Falls are frequent in Meredith's work, from Richard Feverel onward. "Then truly the System triumphed, just ere it was to fall" (ORF, XV:119). Yet Meredith never works out the pattern to anything like the elaborate mythic system of Joyce's Finnegans Wake, preferring to remain closer to the resonances in the minds of his characters. It seems markedly unfair, however, to assert that Meredith's novels are flawed by a lack of such aesthetic discipline, as does Donald Fanger, "George Meredith as Novelist," Nineteenth Century Fiction 16 (1962):317–328. More recent criticism, such as Margaret Harris, " 'The Fraternity of Old Lamps': Some Observations on George Meredith's Prose Style," Style 7 (1973):271–293, has done much to illustrate just how precise and functional Meredith's use of imagery is, if one only devotes to him the same care readers routinely bring to Joyce.

54 Although Meredith occasionally gives the impression that sentimentalism and egoism are special attributes of unformed youth, his works deal increasingly with persistence of those traits at later stages of life as well. "Egoism is not peculiar to any period of life; it is only especially curious in a young man beginning to match himself against his elders, for in him it suffuses the imagination; he is not merely selfishly sentient, or selfishly scheming: his very conceptions are selfish." Continuing with the same image bestowed on Victor Radnor, Harry concludes, "The central I resembled the sun of this universe, with the difference that it shrieked for nourishment, instead of dispensing it" (HR, XLV:184).

55 Beer assumes that it is and that that is why Victor evaded it: "Victor cannot recall it because he cannot accept its lack of originality" ("One of Our Conquerors: Language and Music," p. 272). This explanation is plausible, but equally plausible is the idea that the Idea is so threatening, so revelatory of self, that even when mad Victor cannot confront it and only thinks that he has it. Its vagueness is at the very least a critical joy, since it can be twisted into virtually any shape the critic might please. Wilt's construing of it (p. 184), for instance, is a persuasive restatement of her own theory of comedy as social connection.

56 Meredith explains this effect at some length in describing Juliana, the invalid heiress of Evan Harrington. "It is false to imagine that schemers and workers in

the dark are destitute of the saving gift of conscience. They have it, and it is perhaps made livelier in them than with easy people; and therefore, they are imperatively spurred to hoodwink it. Hence, their self-delusion is deep and endures" (*EH*, XLII:520).

57 See also XLI:494.

58 It is underestimating this function of Nesta in the novel, her awareness of the need for interpretive interaction as well as her instinctive judgments, to claim that the novel as a whole displays Meredith's own despair at the possibilities of language and belief that music would be a "liberating alternative." See Beer, p. 185, and her essay in Fletcher, pp. 275–280.

59 The idea of secular confession becomes even more prominent in *The Amazing Marriage*, where it is played off against the negatively evasive Catholic version, one-sided because monologic (*AM* XLIII:454–455 and XLVI:495).

60 This is also Evan's major crime. "He longed for the sugar-plum; he knew it was naughty to take it: he dared not for fear of the devil, and he shut his eyes while somebody else popped it into his mouth, and assumed his responsibility" (*EH*, XVIII:242; also see XXXIII:435, where he recognized his complicity).

*Chapter 4*

1 Jacques Lacan, *Le Séminaire III: Les Psychoses* (Paris: Éditions du Seuil, 1981), p. 29. All quotes from Lacan will be cited hereafter in the text, according to the following abbreviations:

   E—*Écrits* (Paris: Éditions du Seuil, 1966)
   I—*Le Séminaire: Livre 1 (1953–1954): Les Écrits techniques de Freud* (Paris: Éditions du Seuil, 1975)
   II—*Le Séminaire: Livre II (1954–1955): Le Moi dans la théorie de Freud et dans la technique de l'analyse* (Paris: Éditions du Seuil, 1978)
   III—*Le Séminaire: Livre III (1955–1956): Les Psychoses* (Paris: Éditions du Seuil, 1981)
   XI—*Le Séminaire: Livre XI (1964): Les Quatres concepts fondamentaux de la psychanalyse* (Paris: Éditions du Seuil, 1973)
   XX—*Le Séminaire: Livre XX (1972–1973): Encore* (Paris: Éditions du Seuil, 1975)

2 As it is, for instance, in the book by Anika Lemaire, *Jacques Lacan*, trans. David Macey (Boston: Routledge & Kegan Paul, 1977), pp. 1–5.

3 This point is well put by Jean-Luc Nancy and Philippe Lacoue-Labarthe, *Le Titre de la lettre* (Paris: Éditions Galilée, 1973). "The place of the Lacanian subject is nonetheless the subject. Fundamentally . . . it is in a *theory of the subject* that the logic of the signifier here disposes itself" (p. 67). This indication is especially significant in that their text is a reading of one of the most linguistically centered of the *Écrits*, "L'Instance de la lettre."

4 The *other* refers in Lacan both to the imaginary other and to the symbolic Other, and in that sense it is never really an individual subject. Yet at the same time, the other remains another person who can enact one or the other of those roles, and who is therefore always potentially a subject like the first subject, somewhere between the two extremes.

5 The summary by Anthony Wilden in his commentary on Lacan points out the various forms of the Other in Lacan's discourse and stresses the final resort to intersubjectivity as its core. "In this sense the unconscious is the Other for the

subject, since it is the unconscious subject who tells the truth, and the test of truth in human relations is not the reality or perception it represents, but intersubjectivity. The unconscious, in its necessary dialectical relationship to the unconscious of others, is the test of the truth of the message" (Jacques Lacan, *The Language of the Self*, trans. and comm. Anthony Wilden [Baltimore: Johns Hopkins Press, 1968], p. 264). One might also point out that the truth of the message will involve defining those very structures of human relationship in and through which language operates.

6 See also XI:27. There is a clear parallel with Schlegel's conception of *Witz*, which likewise stressed its revelatory character and its synthetic operation.

7 Again one hears an echo of Schlegel, in his comments on dreams and everyday language. See *KA* XVIII:150, frag. 323.

8 Lacan traces this imperative back to the origins of analytic discourse in the correspondence of Freud with Wilhelm Fliess, which enacts the very process of unconscious communication that Freud was seeking to discover. "The conversation of Freud with Fliess, the fundamental *parole*, which is then unconscious, is the essential dynamic element. Why is it unconscious at that moment? Because it exceeds infinitely what both, insofar as individuals, can then apprehend of it consciously" (II:150).

9 Lacan goes on to explain his exemplary instances of this, the locutions such as "Tu es ma femme" or "Tu es mon maître" that can only be repeated by the other by reversal of the *je-tu* structure, which carries along with it the related necessity of likewise reversing the terms of identity that occur in the phrases. This literal inversion represents metaphorically the interpretive inversions present in all discourse, its echoing transformations.

10 The particular character of the Lacanian subject can perhaps be seen more clearly in a contrast to the Hegelian dialectical subject, where the dissymmetry of terms permits one of them to escape from and transcend a limited relation. In the master-slave dialectic, for instance, the slave alone will continue the process toward absolute spirit, by attaining a consciousness of the relationship within which he is apparently frozen. Yet his real and inescapable servitude means that freedom depends upon a hypostasization of reason, which can permit an immanence of the absolute spirit beyond any individual. "The cunning of reason means that the subject, from the origin and up to the end, knows what he wants" (*E*, p. 802). This equation of knowledge and desire is the point at which Lacan breaks with Hegel, establishing with the unconscious basis of desire its necessary intersubjectivity and submission to the mediation of linguistic encounters. There can be no possibility of an absolute knowledge, for that would imply the existence of language apart from parole, apart from its enactment. "Absolute knowledge is that moment when the totality of discourse closes itself on itself in a perfect non-contradiction, up to and including therein that it posits, explains and justifies itself" (I:290). It is the impossibility of such knowledge, of any absolute knowledge whatsoever, that necessitates and guarantees the permanence of intersubjectivity in the Lacanian system. To the total recall of the Hegelian model, Lacan opposes the forgetting characteristic of the unconscious, and to his Absolute Spirit, a spirit relative to every particular human dialogue.

11 Lacan's definition of structure is interesting in this regard, for it mentions just this process of enactment as the solution to the inadequacy of either descrip-

tion of experience or theoretical reduction of experience. "[Structure] operates not like a theoretical model, but like the original machine that puts the subject there on stage" (*E*, p. 649).

12  One might, for instance, contrast it with metaphor, where the judgments of the subject, its status as subject, are not so crucial to the resolution of the trope. Neither the one who makes nor the one who interprets a metaphor is so directly implicated and located by the choice of a particular image.

13  Just as Lacan indicates that all use of language implicates and touches on the nature of language. "Thought only founds being by knotting itself into *parole*, where every operation touches on the essence of language" (*E*, p. 865).

14  Lacan's reading of Freud's analysis of Dora can be found in *E*, pp. 218–222.

15  All three terms are Lacan's, but the second is somewhat shifted in meaning. Lacan uses the term *je social* (*E*, p. 98), although he maintains there that it evolves with termination of the mirror stage, rather than being an aspect of it. This question brings out the difficulty of treating Lacan's mythic scenes, such as the mirror stage or the fort-da game, as real events. Each scene collapses several aspects of the subject into a single moment, the precedence of which is impossible to determine in any genetic sense. Yet their separation can help clarify the powerful explanatory function these scenes provide by oscillating among various functions of the subject or the ego. Further complicating the explication of such scenes is the fact that each really contains all the others, that their separation is necessarily artificial. The mirror scene contains in embryo all the subsequent developments of the subject, while one can also say that it is only in the fort-da game, for instance, that the mirror stage acquires significance.

16  This transition means that the concepts of mastery, even self-mastery, and death, as absence from oneself, will be similarly intertwined. "This image of the master, which is what he sees beneath the form of the specular image, is confused in him with the image of death" (I:172).

17  This process is an ominous one, for its description by Lacan suggests the lack of real intersubjectivity at the base of it. "The subjective half before the mirror experience is the paralytic, who cannot move himself alone except in an uncoordinated and maladroit fashion. What masters him is the image of the *moi*, which is blind, and which carries him" (II:66). The mother at whom the infant gazes answers only with an absent regard, unaware of the significance of the moment and blind to the ravages of the Imaginary in her own life, which her ignorance will force her child to repeat.

18  In one sense, it is the most responsive gaze that is also the blindest, the fullest answer that proves the most destructive of the child's identity, as an article by Serge Leclaire on an obsessional makes clear: "Philo, or the Obsessional and His Desire," in *Returning to Freud*, ed. Stuart Schneiderman (New Haven: Yale University Press, 1980), pp. 114–129; see especially p. 125.

19  Wilden, p. 160.

20  The absent desire of the mother is made concrete in the gaps of her own discourse articulating the child's desire, the inadequacy of which reveals her attention and desire as being only partially focused on the child. "The desire of the Other is apprehended by the subject in what does not fit, in the lacks of the discourse of the Other; and all the *whys* of the child testify less to an avidity for

the reason of things, than they constitute a putting to the test of the adult, a *why do you tell me that?* always resuscitated from its depth, which is the enigma of the desire of the adult"(XI:194).

21 It should, of course, be noted that the postulate of such a purely imaginary stage, where desire would exist independently of language, can only be a myth designed to clarify certain aspects of the Imaginary as it really exists—always already intermingled with the Symbolic and the Real. It is itself dependent on the prior, equally imaginary stage of self-identification. "But it is clear that the structural effect of identification with the rival is not self-evident, except on the plane of fable, and is only conceivable if it is prepared for by a primary identification that structures the subject as rivalling himself" (*E*, p. 117).

22 This fact need not be evident to the desiring subject, who may well remain tied to a particular object of desire, a state Lacan calls "fantasy" or "fantasm." See Jacques Lacan, "Desire and the Interpretation of Desire in *Hamlet*," *Yale French Studies* 55/56 (1977):11–52. See especially p. 28 for the discussion of the object in demand and desire.

23 Fredric Jameson quotes Edmond Ortigues's explanation of the possibility for both Imaginary and Symbolic use of language: "The same term may be considered imaginary if taken absolutely and symbolic if taken as a differential value correlative of other terms which limit it reciprocally" (Jameson, "Imaginary and Symbolic in Lacan: Marxism, Psychoanalytic Criticism, and the Problem of the Subject," *Yale French Studies* 55/56 [1977]:338–395; here p. 377). Jameson's article is one of the best pieces on Lacan, for it is neither hermetically Lacanian nor unsympathetically critical of Lacan's work. It tests his terms rather than simply echoing them. Jameson also gets to the core of the questions posed by Lacanian analysis, above all the problem of the level at which one should begin to define the subject.

24 Wilden, p. 268.

25 Catherine Clément, *Vies et légendes de Jacques Lacan* (Paris: Éditions Grasset & Fasquelle, 1981), p. 185. Clément's book is one of the most clearly written and entertaining books on Lacan, a mixture of reminiscence, anecdote, and explication that at times strikes closer to the core of a Lacanian formulation than other more roundabout and ponderously cautious treatments of Lacan's theory.

26 Shoshana Felman, "To Open the Question," *Yale French Studies* 55/56 (1977):5–10; here, p. 8. One might, however, wish to take issue with Felman's assertion that irony is absent from psychoanalytic discourse and even to cite Lacan as proof of the contrary possibility. Any fully intersubjective discourse, whether literary or not, contains the possibility of the ironic posing of the question of identity that brings authority and knowledge into question.

27 Fredric Jameson's assessment of authority in the Lacanian system therefore seems to me closer to the spirit of irony. "We may further document the archaic or atavistic tendencies of ethical or moralizing thought by observing that it has no place in the Symbolic Order, or in the structure of language itself, whose shifters are positional and structurally incapable of supporting this kind of situational complicity with the subject momentarily occupying them" (p. 357). In this sense, ironic dialogue is a political act in which the human relations at the basis of the city are to be refounded and reconstituted.

28 The further jump from interrogation to irony is made in a formulation of Lacan contained in Lemaire (p. 113). "His intellectual approach, which he himself qualifies as 'ironic'—having, that is, an interrogative import."

29 The conception of language as a pact covers language both in its descriptive and interrogative aspects. "Naming constitutes a pact, by which two subjects at the same time agree to recognize the same object" (II:202). "Every interrogation is essentially an attempt at agreement of the two *paroles*, which implies that there is first agreement of the languages" (I:275).

30 Jameson on pp. 383–384 argues that the Real serves as the third term in Lacan's theory, as the irreducible entity that holds Imaginary and Symbolic apart. This solution seems plausible, however, only if one recognizes that it is the Symbolic system that makes possible any third term whatsoever.

31 Jameson contrasts this incapacity within language to the frequently idealizing tendencies of other structuralists and poststructuralists. "In Lacan, however, an analogous sense of the alienating function of language is arrested in Utopian mid-course by the palpable impossibility of returning to an archaic, preverbal stage of the psyche itself" (p. 359). Behind the Symbolic, of course, lies the prior alienation of the imaginary gap within the developing subject.

32 This slippage is brought to a halt by the *point de capiton* whose multiple meanings convey the way Lacan's own language enacts the multivalency of language on which he insists. The *point de capiton* is in one sense the end of a sentence, the moment when its meaning is totalized (E, p. 805), in another the focus of significative rays from throughout the sentence, a key word (III:303). Derrida insists that it establishes the replicability and identity of signification, but Nancy and Lacoue-Labarthe (p. 57) more accurately refer to its provisional or "mythic" status. See Jacques Derrida, "Le facteur de la vérité," *Poétique* 21 (1975):96–147; here, p. 132. Derrida's analysis of Lacan's "Purloined Letter" seminar is marred somewhat by its refusal to recognize the positional nature of roles and its insistence on only their essential, ontological basis.

33 Nancy and Lacoue-Labarthe bring out the correlation between slippage of the signifier and that of the subject. "No more than signification can be finished, can arrest itself, no more than the signified cannot be subtracted from its perpetual slippage—no more can the subject be that, or this, which would give a meaning to meaning, which would make or would constitute the meaning" (p. 67).

34 All these relations, to be sure, remain governed by the pursuit of an illusory particular object, so that desire combines the specificity of need and the universality of demand. The object becomes a focal point, representative of the entire network of desire. "There is therefore a necessity to the effect that the particularity thus abolished should reappear *beyond* demand. It reappears there, in effect, but conserving the structure that is concealed in the unconditioned of the demand for love" (E, p. 691).

35 This is the basis of Lacan's objection to Sartre's analysis of the *regard*, and his insistence that the interdependence of these *regards*, as mediated by desire, is an essential element in the explication of their destabilizing effects (XI:83).

36 This father has a role clearly more metaphoric and less easily traceable to actual development than that of the mother. It is not the actual father who is in question here so much as the entire Law which an actual person can, but need not, represent.

37 In psychoanalytic terms, this produces an obsessional. See Serge Leclaire, especially pp. 119 and 124. Clément makes the further point that this failure will also inhibit a complete entry into the symbolic world: "Without paternal law, without effacement of the desire of the mother, no signifying enchainment, no normal language" (p. 201).

38 Elsewhere, Lacan stresses even more strongly the symbolic operation of the Oedipal complex. "This fundamental law is simply a law of symbolization. That is what the Oedipal complex means" (III:96).

39 Jameson, p. 373. Nor is the Law a wholly homogeneous force, for it preserves all the aspects of accidental and personal self-locution. "His history is unified by the law, by his symbolic universe, which is not the same for all" (I:222).

40 Thus, Lacan's statement that "il n'y a pas d'Autre de l'Autre" highlights a definition of the subject as that which confronts an Other that is radically unlike and unassimilable to it. Only a subject can have an Other; if the Other had an Other, it would itself be a subject. The Other takes on a different character depending on the perspective from which one views it, as Wilden remarks: "It is not possible, for instance, to define the Other in any definite way, since for Lacan it has a functional value, representing both the 'significant other' to whom the neurotic's demands are addressed . . . as well as the internalization of this Other (we desire what the Other desires) and the unconscious subject itself or himself" (pp. 263–264).

41 It is this dialectical dependence of the Other and the Law on the irreducibly particular instances of parole that preserves Lacan's theory from the theoretical sameness that Derrida or Nancy and Lacoue-Labarthe find there: "It is indeed in consequence the homoiosis 'itself,' the homoitic aletheia, if one can put it thus, that will have governed 'L'Instance de la lettre' from one end to the other" (p. 148). The Other is not so much any articulable rules of language or social organization one might disengage (Nancy and Lacoue-Labarthe, p. 34), as instead a virtual unity implicit behind all interlocution and relationship, rendering them possible without exhausting their significance.

42 Derrida notices the dependence of the adequacy of language on intersubjectivity, but persists in substantializing the Word, as though it had some power in itself and apart from either the dialogue in which it is inserted or the whole system of language within which it is embedded. "The *true parole* is the *parole* authenticated by the other in sworn or given oath. The other renders it adequate to itself—and no longer to the object—in sending back the message in inverted form, in rendering it true, in identifying henceforth the subject to himself, in announcing *that he is the same*. The adequation—as authentification—passes via intersubjectivity" (Derrida, p. 142). Lacan does not try to render the word adequate to itself nor to identify the subject with itself, but to explode just the sort of integral and isolated subject such categories entail. Self-identity exists only via immixtion with others. Wilden comes much closer to Lacan's meaning when he points out that the role of symbols is to vanish before the dramatic interaction they formalize. "Thus they cease to be symbols in any important sense; it is the *act* of exchange, with its attendant mana or *han*, which symbolizes the unconscious requirement of exchange through displaced reciprocity . . . as a means of establishing and maintaining relationships between the members of that society" (p. 231). The *effect* of symbols, not their nature nor even their relations among themselves within a system, is their

most salient characteristic. They constitute and define an intersubjective and ethical world.

43 The capacity to do this defines for Lacan the end point of an analysis. "It is the last relation of the subject to a genuine Other, to an Other who gives the response that one does not expect, which defines the terminal point of the analysis" (II:287–288).

44 Shoshana Felman, "The Originality of Jacques Lacan," *Poetics Today* 2, no. 16 (Winter 1980–1981):45–57; here, p. 51.

45 Shoshana Felman, "Psychoanalysis and Education: Teaching Terminable and Interminable," *Yale French Studies* 63 (1982):21–44; here, p. 33. She adds in "Originality of Jacques Lacan" that this knowledge therefore exceeds even the combined knowledge of the participants in a dialogue. "The dialogue is analytical in that it is not equal to the sum of its parts: the knowledge for which the analytic dialogue is a vehicle is not reducible to the sum total of the knowledge of each of its two subjects" (p. 47).

46 This ethic is given excellent formulation in Stuart Schneiderman's discussion of the mechanisms of the "pass," by which candidates for analyst status in Lacan's school were accorded the right to begin their practice (*The Death of an Intellectual Hero* [Cambridge, Mass: Harvard University Press, 1983], pp. 65–70 and 80).

*Chapter 5*

1 The way in which irony operates is effectively illustrated in Plato's *Republic*, where the abstract discussion of justice becomes a format in which the personal identities of Adeimantus and Glaucon come to be revealed, examined, perhaps even modified. Plato's dialogues are superb examples of this ironic displacement of interest in which the ethical implications of philosophical principles are repeatedly demonstrated by the course of the dialogue itself.

2 Whether one should more appropriately use *communities* here, and how one would be able to do so, are questions that inevitably arise at the point where the analyses of this text reach their limit.

3 The question of Beckett's affinities with the doctrines of the Romantic movement has yet to be explicitly dealt with at any length in the critical literature. Hugh Kenner does, however, provide a useful starting point for such an inquiry in a brief comparison of Beckett and Wordsworth (*Samuel Beckett: A Critical Study* [Berkeley: University of California Press, 1968], pp. 178–180).

4 Martin Esslin, ed., *Samuel Beckett: A Collection of Critical Essays* (Englewood Cliffs, N.J.: Prentice-Hall, 1965). His discussion of how one can read Beckett is on pp. 10–15.

5 One example among many, notable for the clarity with which it expresses a common presupposition of Beckett criticism, comes from Howard Harper's essay on *How It Is*. "The longer the process [Beckett's writing] goes on, the more apparent becomes its fidelity to certain laws: Each work must be a truly new thing, but must emerge naturally out of everything which has gone before. The new work must go beyond everything in the canon, and at the same time subsume that canon" (Edouard Morot-Sir, Howard Harper, and Dougald McMillan III, eds., *Samuel Beckett: The Art of Rhetoric* [Chapel Hill: North Carolina Studies in the Romance Languages and Literatures, 1976], pp. 249–270;

here, p. 250). Harper's tendency toward neat identifications hampers an otherwise interesting essay on this novel, where much emerges from his recognition that "Beckett forces us to learn to read all over again" (p. 254).

6  The universalizing tendencies are particularly evident in existential readings of Beckett, with their stress on *the* human condition, as in the otherwise sensitive reading of Michael Robinson, *The Long Sonata of the Dead: A Study of Samuel Beckett* (London: Rupert Hart-Davis, 1969). See especially pp. 19ff.

7  Esslin, p. 12.

8  Ibid., p. 14.

9  H. Porter Abbott, *The Fiction of Samuel Beckett: Form and Effect* (Berkeley: University of California Press, 1973), p. 7. See pp. 5–9 and also p. 134 for a more complete elaboration of the term as Abbott uses it.

10  The discussion of the "mess" comes, of course, from Tom Driver's talk with Beckett, reprinted in Lawrence Graver and Raymond Federman, eds., *Samuel Beckett: The Critical Heritage* (Boston: Routledge & Kegan Paul, 1979), pp. 217–223.

11  The most detailed, considered, and attentive reading of Beckett's criticism as a body of work and not simply a collection of aphorisms is that of John Pilling in his study of Beckett's later prose (James Knowlson and John Pilling, *Frescoes of the Skull: The Later Prose and Drama of Samuel Beckett* [New York: Grove Press, 1980], pp. 214–256). Pilling is especially good at noting the shifts implied by various restatements of Beckett over the course of the years.

12  Israel Shenker's article was from the *New York Times* of May 5, 1956, and is reprinted in Graver and Federman, pp. 146–149. This polarity is frequently evoked in Beckett criticism, as in Abbot's statement, "For Joyce's aims were positive where Beckett's are negative" (p. 28). Judith Dearlove finds the polarity, put in terms of the Apollonian and Dionysian, especially attractive, even though she concedes in a note that "it is problematic whether the idea and phrasing in this interview are Beckett's or Shenker's" (*Accommodating the Chaos: Samuel Beckett's Nonrelational Art* [Durham: Duke University Press, 1982], p. 153). This polarity may finally be more unfair to Joyce than to Beckett, by locating him as just another of a long tradition of artists performing similar versions of the same literary shortsightedness. Beckett's own polemical intent in abetting such polarization, thus to distance himself from Joyce, can hardly be underestimated here.

13  Two extended studies of this work are worthy of note: John Pilling, "Beckett's Proust," *Journal of Beckett Studies* 1 (1976):8–29, and Steven J. Rosen, *Samuel Beckett and the Pessimistic Tradition* (New Brunswick: Rutgers University Press, 1976), pp. 123–220. The former stresses Beckett's continuity with Proust, the latter the way in which Beckett's misreading of Proust served him in defining his own, very different aesthetic. Both, however, see this brief text as revelatory of the later Beckett's own doctrine and practice.

14  See Rosen's discussion (pp. 153–172) of relativism and pessimism as Beckett's response to the radical nature of this split.

15  Rosen recognizes this trait and explains it as a function of a philosophical presupposition. "Correlative with his philosophical rejection of the continuum, each of his critical judgments must be an all-or-nothing matter" (p. 133). "As usual, Beckett allows no blurring of harsh and logical realities; there is no middle ground between the temporal and the extratemporal; we must have

one or the other" (p. 203). This is certainly true at one level of Beckett's text, but as I hope to show, such philosophical neatness is upset by Beckett's own analysis.

16  Samuel Beckett, *Proust* (New York: Grove Press, 1970), p. 56; page numbers hereafter cited in text.

17  The measure of Beckett's difference here can be measured by the moment in *Company* where discouragement fosters not memory and self-revelation, but a desire to avoid just such things. "But if on occasion so disheartened it is seldom for long. For little by little as he lies the craving for company revives. In which to escape from his own" (Samuel Beckett, *Company* [New York: Grove Press, 1980], p. 55; page numbers hereafter cited in text).

18  The reader might notice here that my procedure involves something of a reversal of Beckett's study, a reversion from its conclusion-resolution back to prior stages and perspectives I argue remain unresolved. Surely Beckett, if any author should impress on us the need to read backward as well as forward, to resist the seductive rhythms of the linear.

19  The use of *soul*, an infrequent word in Beckett's vocabulary, perhaps indicates the groping for a higher assurance that occurs when one's model of consolation breaks down. *Fictitious* is similarly charged for any reader of Beckett (*Proust*, p. 27).

20  Rosen also points out that involuntary memories are further undermined by the momentary nature Beckett ascribes to them. They, too, are in time and subject to degradation and hence leave no discernible impact on everyday life. Rosen argues effectively that Beckett's interpretation unduly minimizes the restorative power of the experience in Proust's eyes (p. 203).

21  One could effectively argue that Beckett's own literary work presents us with the reverse, a rhetoric of damnation into which a (readerly) reality of salvation is subtly reimported. But the identification is perhaps too neat to be wholly true.

22  A connection Beckett himself emphasizes within the chronology of Proust's work (*Proust*, p. 35).

23  This point is well treated by Olga Bernal, who sees Beckett's subjects permanently trapped in the Proustian moment of awakening (*Langage et fiction dans le roman de Beckett* [Paris: Éditions Gallimard, 1969], p. 63).

24  The phrase *agony and enchantment* is Abbott's, with whom I am forced to part when he sees behind the experience of reading Beckett an encounter with a "true" reality: "If Beckett is successful, he generates in us the kinds of agony and enchantment that attend any true perception of things as they are" (p. 4). As I will argue, successful is just what Beckett is not. The operation of memory, whether involuntary or voluntary for that matter, is so radically different in Beckett's own work that the more appropriate statement comes from *Company*: "As then there was no then so there is none now" (p. 22). Without a coherent past, the subject in any traditional sense can hardly be said to exist.

25  Here again Abbott is exemplary in his attention to the eddying back and forth rather than the flow of Beckett's texts. He stresses Beckett's penchant for reversing the direction of his work, for writing the unpredictable. See, for instance, pp. 38 (on *Murphy*), 76 (on *Mercier and Camier*), and 110–111 (on the *Trilogy*).

26  Samuel Beckett, "Three Dialogues," reprinted in Esslin, pp. 16–22; here, pp. 17

and 21. These dialogues are highly interesting and worth more scrutiny than I can pause for here, in part because they display a kind of dialogic interaction so infrequent in Beckett's fiction. Beckett's final speeches in the three dialogues (silence, weeping, expression of gratitude) are masterly.

27 Dearlove should be noted as an exception, for she deals subtly with the dialectical turns in play here (pp. 6–7). If failure is involved in any imposition of a merely human order on a chosen subject or occasion, then the writer must inevitably fail, for even to speak is to import illicit certainties and relations into discourse. Real failure, like ironic ignorance, is impossible to sustain. "It is not enough to assert that there may be no relation between the artist and his occasion. The intelligibility of the words belies their proposition; language cannot be nonrelational; the artist must inevitably fail" (p. 7). Fail to fail, that is. "Because total prohibition of associations is impossible, Beckett's terminology becomes caught on the horns of artificial dilemmas as his dichotomies . . . suggest a neatness and order which are alien to a world whose 'key word . . . is "perhaps" ' " (p. 9).

28 It is the lack of such insistence that separates the narrator of *How It Is* most sharply from his predecessors. Bernal stresses the negative force of such an attitude: "Le vrai Je est ici lutte contre toute nostalgie d'être" (p. 57).

29 In the talk with Driver, Beckett praised the cathedral at Chartres in these terms: "There is the unexplainable, and there art raises questions that it does not attempt to answer" (p. 220). To some degree this is a retreat from his earlier position, insofar as the statement of any problem already contains the germ of its solution, as Beckett himself noted in regard to Proust.

30 For the former, see Robinson, p. 32, for the latter, Rosen, pp. 19, 54–55, and 66.

31 For this, see Abbott, pp. 73–74, and in more detail, Ludovic Janvier, *Pour Samuel Beckett* (Paris: Éditions de Minuit, 1966), pp. 175–215, or Ruby Cohn, *Samuel Beckett: The Comic Gamut* (New Brunswick: Rutgers University Press, 1962).

32 Here, Rosen, p. 49, Dearlove, p. 125, Raymond Federman, *Journey to Chaos: Samuel Beckett's Early Fiction* (Berkeley: University of California Press, 1965), p. 83, or Ruby Cohn's celebration of the lyric element in Beckett, *Back to Beckett* (Princeton: Princeton University Press, 1973). Especially interesting is the frequent recourse to the self-justifying power of religious terminology to assure Beckett's triumph. Federman's "paradise of creativity" (p. 83) is matched by Dearlove's "heavenly power of the imagination" (p. 125), to mention just two instances. Pilling also has recourse to the implicit Romantic basis of Beckett's salvation. "Imagining has become, for Beckett, less and less a matter of exercising the will, and more and more a matter of waiting for the mercies vouchsafed by inspiration" (p. 147). And later, "Beckett is well on the way here to constructing a paradise that need not necessarily be lost, the paradise of the imagination" (p. 156). Paradise, however, is what Beckett seems not to regain for us, however great our patience in the pastures of hell or purgatory.

33 See Dearlove, p. 108, and also David B. Hesla, "Being, Thinking, Telling, Loving: The Couple in Beckett's Fiction," in Morot-Sir et al., pp. 11–23, where Beckett is rather startlingly rehumanized.

34 One thinks, inevitably, of the fort-da game, discussed in my chapter on Lacan in his terms as not a mode of mastering imaginatively a recalcitrant reality by reenacting it but as an entrance into the Symbolic Order where a fragmentation of the subject can lead to its reconstitution as a social being.

35 Dieter Wellershoff, "Failure of an Attempt at De-Mythologization: Samuel Beckett's Novels," trans. Martin Esslin, in Esslin, pp. 92–107; here, p. 107.

36 Samuel Beckett, *Three Novels* (New York: Grove Press, 1965), p. 148; page numbers hereafter cited in text. The speaker here, of course, is Moran, with whom the critic, despite his greater affection for Molloy, may finally be more intimately associated.

37 Bernal's excellent study is the only extended treatment of the convergence of Beckett's work with current theories of language and subjectivity, an area of investigation that clearly deserves far more attention. An equally fine consideration of Beckett in terms of linguistic theory is Allen Thiher, "Wittgenstein, Heidegger, the Unnamable, and Some Thoughts on the Status of Voice in Fiction," in *Samuel Beckett: Humanistic Perspectives*, ed. Morris Beja, S. E. Gontarski, and Pierre Astier (Columbus: Ohio State University Press, 1983), pp. 80–90. Thiher's discussion of the "equivocation" and the "critical irony" in Beckett (pp. 88–89) comes close to the kind of uncertainty and fragmentation that seem to me at the core of Beckett's work. Also interesting is an essay by Iain Wright, " ' What matter who's speaking?': Beckett, the Authorial Subject and Contemporary Critical Theory," *Comparative Criticism* 5 (1983):59–86, which provides interesting comments on the polarization of current critical debate on the issues with which Beckett grapples, but which is less convincing in its treatment of Beckett's own work.

38 "The more deeply one penetrates it, the more complex Molloy's story becomes. It cannot be pinned down to a single meaning, it does not objectify its significances, but transforms and mixes the images and speaks, like the imagination of myth-makers, in open and approximate analogies" (Wellershoff, in Esslin, p. 96). The same is true of all of Beckett's works and in one sense is something of a critical commonplace. Yet insofar as we do not recognize that Beckett's texts resist not only single significations but any coherence of attitude or response or patterning, we have not gone far enough in trying to read Beckett.

39 Samuel Beckett, *Waiting for Godot* (New York: Grove Press, 1954), p. 11.

40 Pilling (p. 169) puts the difference well in regard to *Ping*: "It is Beckett's *Finnegans Wake*, perhaps, with the important difference that it encourages not polyvalence but absolute monovalence." The same remark could be extended to much of Beckett's later work.

41 A good instance of this is *Krapp's Last Tape*, where the seemingly secure difference between past and present voices is continually swallowed up by the Krapp of the present. "We're of one mind, all of one mind, always were, deep down" (Beckett, *Stories and Texts for Nothing* [New York: Grove Press, 1967], p. 77).

42 Wellershoff (p. 106) mentions the connection of Beckett with German Romantic irony, which is extensively discussed in Wolfgang Schröder, *Reflektierter Roman* (Frankfurt: Verlag Peter D. Lang, 1981). The problem with Schröder's analysis is that by largely confining himself to the aesthetic aspect of Romantic irony, its self-reflexiveness and parabatic quality, he is unable to do much more than pick out traits already on the surface of Beckett's texts, gathering various elements under a general rubric that does not really extend our understanding of Beckett.

43 It could, of course, be argued that this is the case with much literature (or even

much nonliterature). The difference is that the absence of a hierarchically marked significative order in Beckett's works forces us continually to confront this potentiality.

44 Prior instances of this would include Moran's and Malone's catalogs of questions ranging across a variety of disjunct categories (*Three Novels*, pp. 167 and 272).

45 Samuel Beckett, *How It Is* (New York: Grove Press, 1970), p. 7.

46 The notion of a beginning served an analogous function in *The Unnamable*. "For I am obliged to assign a beginning to my residence here, if only for the sake of clarity" (*Three Novels*, p. 295). And Malone had his three projects, embedded within which were three separate stories. One could, of course, easily continue the list, but three examples seem sufficient.

47 A similar device is discussed by Enoch Brater, "The *Company* Beckett Keeps: The Shape of Memory and One Fablist's Decay of Lying," in Beja et al., pp. 157–171. Despite the wealth of external literary allusions in Beckett's work, their force is frequently more like a kind of self-quotation. One needs to go back not primarily to the source but to Beckett's own prior uses of it. "External allusions in this work are primarily there to remind us of the same literary patterns Beckett has urged us to consider before as he weaves the web of his own private mythology" (p. 162). Thus Beckett confirms the continuity of his literary identity—in a purely verbal way, of course.

48 Dearlove (p. 105) does just this, stressing its temporal facet. It seems to me, however, that this ability to collect and unify the various instances is precisely that of which Beckett would deprive us.

49 The convenience of this exclusion of the one position where he would suffer as tormented should not be underestimated here. Or perhaps all we have is itself part 4, the record of the narrator's life with Bom, the tale he contrives to amuse or appease his tormentor: "he would oblige me to have had a life" (p. 60). Any interaction with Bom would then have been repressed, or displaced into fantasy elements.

50 Bernal, pp. 222–223; Janvier, p. 134.

51 Kenner, p. 190.

52 Esslin, p. 107.

# Index

Abbott, H. Porter, 175, 223*nn*9, 12, 224*nn*24, 25
Abrams, M. H., 46, 47, 48, 200*n*21, 201*n*3, 202*nn*6, 7, 16, 207*n*71
Absolute, the, 200*n*11, 201*n*2; as creation of subject, 28–30; imagination and, 79, 81; internalization of, 25–28; irony and, 24–25, 31–43, 51–53; love and, 55; mediation of, 63–65; nature and, 46, 71, 73–74, 75, 77–78; the Other and, 160, 165, 167; revelation and, 84–86; unattainability of, 19–22, 50–51, 54, 57, 66, 82, 87–88, 90, 205*n*49; as Universe, 23–25
allegory, 10–13, 23, 24, 30, 63, 65, 67, 69
Allemann, Beda, 199*n*4, 201*n*27
Altieri, Charles, 197*n*16, 199*n*30, 200*n*19, 203*n*28

Baker, Robert, 211–12*n*17, 215*n*52
*béance, la* (imaginary gap), 139–40, 141, 145, 152, 158, 170
Beckett, Samuel, viii, 17, 197*n*17; irony and, 172–74, 193–94
   *Company*, 193, 194, 224*n*17
   *How It Is*, 186, 187–94, 225*n*28
   *Krapp's Last Tape*, 226*n*41
   *The Lost Ones*, 193, 194
   *Malone Dies*, 227*nn*44, 46
   *Molloy*, 184–85, 186–87, 226*n*36, 227*n*44
   *Proust*, 176–82, 188
   *Stories and Texts for Nothing*, 226*n*41
   "Three Dialogues," 182–84, 224–25*n*26
   *The Unnamable*, 183, 188, 227*n*46
   *Waiting for Godot*, 186
Beer, Gillian, 93–94, 113, 210*n*4, 212*n*23, 212–13*n*28, 214*n*46, 215*n*55, 216*n*58

Behler, Ernst, 195*n*3, 196*n*12
Benjamin, Walter, 48–50, 202*n*16, 203*nn*19, 21
Bernal, Olga, 224*n*23, 225*n*28, 226*n*37
Booth, Wayne, 6–8, 10, 195*n*2, 197*nn*14–19, 204*n*31
Brookes, Gerry, 208*n*77, 209*n*91
Brooks, Cleanth, 1, 74, 207*n*63

Carlyle, Thomas
   "Characteristics," 84
   *The French Revolution*, 208*n*79
   *On Heroes*, 82, 83, 84, 85, 86, 208*n*83
   *Sartor Resartus*, 54, 82–90, 208*nn*77, 86, 209*nn*90–92, 94
Clément, Cathérine, 219*n*25, 221*n*37
Comic Spirit, the, 94, 95–96, 210*n*2, 211*n*8, 211–12*n*17
conscience (*das Gewissen*), 6, 40–43, 53–54, 58, 67, 69–70, 85, 206*n*56
Cook, Albert, 203–04*n*28

Dearlove, Judith, 223*n*12, 225*nn*27, 32, 227*n*48
death, 66–71, 72–81, 123, 139–40, 158, 218*n*16
de Man, Paul, 10–15, 17, 197*nn*22, 24–27, 202*n*11, 203*n*25, 207*n*63
demand, 142, 144, 145, 159, 160, 161, 164, 220*n*34
Derrida, Jacques, 220*n*32, 221*nn*41, 42
desire, 58–60, 68; Imaginary Order and, 142, 143, 144–46, 149, 152, 220*nn*21, 22, 34; as lack, 129, 141, 218–19*n*20; Symbolic Order and, 154, 158–62, 164, 170
dreams, 33, 65–66, 186, 217*n*7

**229**